DATE DUE

2008

Studies in Major Literary Authors

Edited by

William E. Cain
Professor of English
Wellesley College

A Routledge Series

Studies in Major Literary Authors

William E. Cain, *General Editor*

WALLACE STEVENS AND THE
REALITIES OF POETIC LANGUAGE

Stefan Holander

Routledge
Taylor & Francis Group
New York   London

First published 2008
by Routledge
270 Madison Ave, New York, NY 10016

Simultaneously published in the UK
by Routledge
2 Park Square, Milton Park, Abingdon, Oxon OX14 4RN

Routledge is an imprint of the Taylor & Francis Group, an informa business

© 2008 Taylor & Francis

Typeset in Adobe Garamond by IBT Global.
Printed and bound in the United States of America on acid-free paper by IBT Global.

Library of Congress Cataloging in Publication Data
Holander, Stefan, 1971–
    Wallace Stevens and the realities of poetic language / by Stefan Holander.
        p. cm. — (Studies in major literary authors)
    Includes bibliographical references and index.
    ISBN 978-0-415-95596-6 — ISBN 978-0-203-92786-1 (e-book)
    1. Stevens, Wallace, 1879–1955—Criticism and interpretation.   I. Title.
    PS3537.T4753Z664 2008
    811'.52—dc22   2007044404

ISBN10: 0-415-95596-3 (hbk)
ISBN10: 0-203-92786-9 (ebk)

ISBN13: 978-0-415-95596-6 (hbk)
ISBN13: 978-0-203-92786-1 (ebk)

For Guro

Contents

Abbreviations

WORKS BY WALLACE STEVENS

CP   *The Collected Poems of Wallace Stevens.* New York: Alfred A. Knopf, 1954.

CPP   *Collected Poetry and Prose.* Ed. Kermode, Frank and Joan Richardson. New York: The Library of America, 1997.

NA   *The Necessary Angel: Essays on Reality and the Imagination.* London: Faber & Faber, 1984.

L   *The Collected Letters of Wallace Stevens.* Ed. Holly Stevens. Berkeley: University of California Press, 1996.

OP   *Opus Posthumous.* Revised, Enlarged and Corrected Edition. Ed. Milton J. Bates. New York: Vintage Books, 1990.

Permissions

Acknowledgments

This book has been a part of my life for a long time, and I would like to thank everybody involved in or affected by it, whether directly or indirectly.

First of all, it was only thanks to the knowledge, patience and grace of my supervisor Lars-Håkan Svensson that I was able to finish this project at all, and if I had not been introduced to the doctoral studies at the English Department in Lund by Sven Bäckman, none of this would have happened. Thanks to a grant from STINT (Statens institut för främjandet av forskarutbildningen) I was able to spend an invaluable Fall term at the English Department of New York University in 1999. Toward the end of this long process, Hjalmar Gullbergs och Greta Thotts Stipendiefond awarded me a grant to help me finish my project, and Finnmark University College gave me financial support to obtain copyright permissions.

I am deeply grateful to Christopher Collins for accommodating for me academically in New York, for your invaluable teaching and friendship, and your and Emily's hospitality. Heartfelt thanks to Robert Archambeau for your encouragement, your poetry and the hospitality with which you and Valery took care of me in Chicago. My fellow doctoral students at Lund—Sara, Petra, the Lenas, Berndt and Annelie above all—provided a stimulating intellectual milieu which, for good or bad, has shaped the way I approach literature and the corridors of academe. My historian friends Stefan Nordqvist and Martin Wiklund have always brought lively conversation, intellectual challenges and friendship around philosophical matters. At the very root of my love of poetry are Juan Antonio López García, Victor Irún Vozmediano and Mats Adrian who introduced me to the world of Lorca, Cernuda, Guillén and Salinas, and a truly poetic lifestyle. Damian Finnegan, Philip Clover and Matthew Gifford taught me everything I know about aestheticism, English public schools and medieval eschatology. Thanks also to Frank Kjørup for your personal and academic companionship in New York and Copenhagen, and for having sharpened my senses to the miracles of language.

I am deeply indebted to my parents and my sister for all their help and support, to Joakim Sjöbeck and Marianne Røst for helping me out in a time of need. Dankert and Kirsten Røst provided me with the most beautiful writing location in the world. I am also grateful to my students, employers and librarians at Finnmark University College for giving me the necessary leeway to complete this. Thanks to Bart Eeckhout and Edward Ragg for advice on the publication process, and to John Serio and Deborah Garrison for helping me at a crucial point in my efforts to obtain permission to reprint Stevens' poetry. Beverly Maeder's help and encouragement at the final stages of my work on this book have been very important for me: a million thanks to you.

On a more personal level, I am indebted to María del Carmen López García, who shared the first years of this project with me. I am very happy to have finished this book in the company of Guro Røst and our son Ola, both of whom have had to adjust their lives to enable me to do this.

Introduction

There it was, word for word,
The poem that took the place of a mountain.

He breathed its oxygen,
Even when the book lay turned in the dust of his table.

"The Poem That Took the Place of a Mountain" (*CP* 512)

STEVENS' TRIALS OF DEVICE: POETRY AS A STRUGGLE WITH LANGUAGE

This is a study of Wallace Stevens' poetic language. Announcing this may immediately evoke a hotly contested area of critical debate in which Stevens has played a major, if often unbecoming, part: the relationship between modern poetry and what is often summed up in a simplifying way as modern reality. It also raises a question that is not less vital just because it is difficult, perhaps even insoluble: what is, and is not, indicated in the concept of poetic language? The fact is that most of us, as Stevens proposed "are never," or at least rarely, "at a loss to recognize poetry." But this does not, as he added, appear to make it "easy for us to propose a center of poetry, a *vis* or *noeud vital*, to which, in the absence of a definition, all the variations of definition are peripheral" (*NA* 44–5). To the contrary, students of poetry have often attempted to find ways of defining—which has often meant defending—the peculiar meaningfulness of poetic art, often assuming that it may depend on the existence of precisely such an essence or *noeud vital*. In spite of the apparent self-confidence of Stevens' remark, at a high point of his career, and despite the glories of his poetry, his poetic project can also be seen, both in its theory and its practice, as a defense of poetry.

In the lecture quoted here, delivered at Harvard in 1946, Stevens' image of the poet's role attained almost megalomaniac proportions—"if the poet discovered and had the power thereafter at will and by intelligence to reconstruct us by his transformations" he "would also have the power to destroy us" (*NA* 45). This idea, however, was at odds with the acute realization that *his* language, his *poetic* language, was also the language of everybody else, of people who were not only, as Harold Bloom reminds us,[1] his poetic forefathers, but the people around him, those which Ortega y Gasset had frightfully summarized as "The Mass Man." This sense of exteriority and collectivity in language suggests that, in several senses, poetry's language is a 'material' language, and that the imagination—Stevens' Romantic synonym for poetic creativity—could not simply be imagined as an "act of the mind," a matter of workings of consciousness, but needed to deal directly with this 'material.' 'Material' may suggest several, mutually implicated, meanings: the physical body of the letter as ink on the printed, mass-produced page; the phonetic sound the letters refer to as realized physically in the human body and captured by the senses; the phonemic, linguistic entity referred to by this sound, and the meanings created by their differential combinations within a language system; the sense in which this language system itself is shaped by its function within a social, cultural and political order and, not least, the way this order is built on a 'material' economic structure in which a book of poems, for example, can function as a commodity for consumption. In this taxonomy, 'material' is in each case (except possibly in the case of the ink) a metaphor for, indicating, something else.

When Beverly Maeder, whose innovative study of Stevens' poetry attempts to avoid his own dualistic and consciousness-based idea of poetic language, proposes to study the "surface texture" or "material body" of his poems, she implies more or less all of these meanings, and their interconnections.[2] Her focus on Stevens' concrete work of linguistic renovation in terms of the most fundamental "non- or extra-ontological" patterns of the English language—graphic, prosodic, figurative, grammatical, lexical, syntactic, but also ideologically operative—brings out its liberating, future-oriented possibilities. This study aims to continue along similar lines, assuming that the material of poetry is to a significant extent language itself. It will do so, however, by taking a step 'back' into Stevens' dualistic universe to consider a more problematic sense of 'materiality.' If poetic language is understood as an expressive means or instrument, a 'device' itself problematically autonomous—prior and exterior—it may not only suggest new possibilities for creativity, but is likely to insinuate a conflict with a conception of poetry as mental act or subjective expression. To explore this predicament, I will not primarily direct the reader's attention to Stevens' most apparent moments of artistic mastery, in the sense that we may experience that it transcends historical, ideological and linguistic constraints. The primary focus will instead be on a number of poems from the period of aesthetic and ideological unease when Stevens returned to publishing in the early 30s, adding a few poems to his first collection, *Harmonium,* and writing the poems included in *Ideas of Order,* a collection which Stanley Burnshaw suggested, in a famous critical intervention in 1935, was "screeching with confusion."[3]

In this period, more visibly than in any other, Stevens' art was under a keenly felt pressure to represent and ideally intervene in reality as conceived from a social and political rather than ontological viewpoint. This was a very difficult task indeed since 'the real'—a term of both epistemological and ethical import, and a great deal more severe than the merely 'realistic'—was often understood as *opposed to* the aesthetically valuable. In this sense, my discussion responds to a tendency, in evidence from the very beginning of Stevens' career, either to praise his poetry for artistic self-sufficiency or criticize it for its reluctance or incapacity to represent and communicate with reality in its social and political aspects, reproaching him for 'escapism,' 'dandyism,' 'hedonism'[4] and later 'monologue.'[5] While any response to such extreme positions itself risks becoming a 'defense,' bringing simplistic results and rehearsing old arguments, such statements are not only frequent and powerful enough to command attention but also indicate a quality which is essential to Stevens' modernism: a fear of exclusion and of expressive and cultural impotence which accompanies his search for exclusiveness and informs some of his poetry's constitutive metaphors.

In this sense, my study tries to capture one of the fundamental, creative, paradoxes of Stevens' poetry. At the same time as it claims enormous expressive powers, taking "the place of mountains," or mounts a poetics of resistance against hegemonic political and religious discourses, his poetry is both pervaded by and motivated by a sense of ominous futility. Thus, even when considered as a means to expressive freedom, idiosyncrasy and self-determination, poetry is in this way always threatened by its own possible enclosure, both because of its deviant particularity which risks a separation from the world, and its unfortunate, unwilling, belonging to it. This generates a sense of failure to be indispensably unique, as it appears to be merely repeating that which already exists.

In my approach as well as my choice of poetry, my study relates to Helen Vendler's notion that Stevens' later poetry has overcome a long, arduous process of 'trials of device.'[6] This phrase, from the line "A blank underlies the trials of device," (CPP 477) of the late poem "An Ordinary Evening in New Haven"

(*CP* 465–89), was used by Vendler to indicate the struggles with a resilient poetic language set off in the thirties by powerful 'realist' demands for social and political relevancy. Such 'trials of device,' then, were also 'trials of reality,' since one way of meeting the new demands on poetic language would be to move it closer to modern material, cultural and linguistic reality, possibly (as Stevens feared) by renouncing poetic difference and privilege altogether. This study assumes that neither the 'devices' nor the 'trials,' the sense of poetry as a continuous struggle with language, ceased to be central sources of creativity in Stevens' later poetry. A close look at a period in which they appear at their most intense—and in which their materiality is both heavily emphasized and amply defined—may be useful for what it enables us to see of vital elements in Stevens' poetry, both earlier and later.

I begin by investigating Stevens' conception of poetic language as an exclusive interior reality, a private space, and how this idea comes to shape Stevens' ambiguous view of abstraction as both a means of capturing the eidetic or cognitive essentials of reality and a means of fateful and falsifying closure to the actual world. Both implications, I argue, are closely tied to his sense of the material aspects of poetic language and the complex figurative and kinesthetic use of inherited poetic device, including his ambivalent and ironic use of diction, metaphor and prosodic form. Starting in Stevens' end-of-century experiences at Harvard and continuing through his subsequent encounter with urban modernity in New York, the argument makes its way to Stevens' troubled thirties and, finally, to a few examples his later poetics, on which most positive critical accounts are based, and where the idea of abstraction plays a central role. One particularly powerful image will play a central part in this argument: the idea that poetry is not only written within the confines of a room, but that it implies, even composes, a room. This is not just a metaphor for the poet's mind rooted in the concrete writing situation but also related to the fact that Stevens' sense of enclosure, in both these senses, was tightly intertwined with his fear of an inadequate language.

Chapter II studies a number of poems grappling with an impasse described in two central metaphors of poetic transcendence; motion, closely linked to the desire for aesthetic change, and voice, describing the capacity for authentic or idiosyncratic speech. The sense of impasse conveyed in these poems, I will argue, is intensely ambiguous, as Stevens' very mobile metaphorics represents poetry's expressive and kinetic failure as very close indeed to indicating a renovation of language. This argument is developed in Chapter III, which studies how Stevens' poetry both uses and (re)presents mutually implicated 'devices'—images, diction and rhythmic patterning—that are perceived as hostile to fresh perception and expressive singularity.

Here too, the study deals with significant ambiguities, since his acknowledgment of linguistic and cultural decay, vulgarity and repetitiousness is also understood as a way to accomplish renovation and idiosyncrasy. Chapter IV deals closely with Stevens' imaginative enactment of poetry's necessary movement toward 'reality' in a programmatic and linguistically fascinating poem, "Farewell to Florida," whose ambivalent but obsessive exploitation of the mutually implicated "devices" of rhythmic and metaphoric movement is discussed in terms of the notions of poetic transcendence and failure suggested in the preceding chapters.

My study is a result of a sense of wonder at two different but closely related phenomena: on the one hand, the capacity of Stevens' poetry to generate widely different, often contradictory, critical response[7] and, on the other, the comparative scarcity of studies of his poetry 'as poetry,' in terms of its peculiar forms of linguistic expression. My argument is indebted to the articles of the special 1991 issue of *The Wallace Stevens Journal* named "Stevens and Structures of Sound," and in books by critics such as Marie Borroff,[8] Anca Rosu,[9] Andrew Lakritz[10] and Maeder, who, along with rhetorically oriented critics like Charles Altieri,[11] Jacqueline Brogan[12] and Angus Cleghorn,[13] have explicitly or implicitly intended to formulate a value in Stevens' poetic language within a modernist context whose dominant notions of formal change have often appeared either indifferent or hostile to it. Such critics have also aimed to remedy the tendency in Stevens criticism to relegate the discussion of poetic construction into marginal, shorthand observations, rather than a vital part of textual research—a tendency which Marjorie Perloff in 1985 (I believe wrongly) blamed on a similar uninterest in Stevens himself.[14]

The formalist trend in Stevens studies bears an interesting relation to another development: the biographical and historicist research of the late eighties and nineties, when critics like James Longenbach,[15] Frank Lentricchia,[16] Alan Filreis,[17] Joan Richardson,[18] Milton Bates[19] and George Lensing[20] drew attention to relatively unexplored, even disregarded, periods in Stevens' career, most importantly to moments when his art was under pressure or in crisis. These critics offered new diachronic perspectives on his poetry, exposing significant differences not only between different periods in his career, but also between different poems. Together, I would argue, historicist and formalist studies of Stevens do not only enable an understanding of his poems as a response to complex historical moments but also, in the sense of Stevens' contemporary Kenneth Burke, as *strategic* utterances, pervaded by a historicity defined partly in their own, often intentionally deviant, language.[21]

To an extent, I read Stevens's poetry with a sense of historical context. The period under scrutiny below has not only been central to historicist readings, but is also one in which his poems are highly attentive of their own contemporaneity and, in a sense, theorize their own historicity—which in Stevens' case can mean both a lack or excess thereof. It is crucial to this study, however, that their way of doing this is in *poetry*, in the peculiar language of singular poems, which includes their rhythm, meter and sound-patterning. Even when the original historical context of the poem recedes from attention, my analysis will thus move closer to the way such moments are represented in the scripted 'realities' of a poem, understood in terms of a response, even when such a response appears deviant, distorting and dismissive.

STEVENS AS FORMALIST

In this study, Stevens will be approached as a 'formalist' poet, concerned with refashioning and expanding the possibilities of poetic diction and prosody. In a study of the formal impulses shaping both the writing and reception of modern American poetry, Stephen Cushman has helpfully distinguished two common ways of understanding the term 'formalist.' On the one hand, it has been used to indicate poets who are content to write in traditional metric form—like the present-day "New Formalists." While Stevens has often been defined in this way, Cushman places him mid-ways between such "formalists" and their clear-cut opposites: poets for whom 'form,' as a pre-existing, conventional constraint on expression, carries a strictly negative sense. A next-to perfect formulation of the latter can be found in T.S. Eliot's retrospective account, in a lecture at Glasgow University in 1942 called "The Music of Poetry," where he described the formal revolution of modern poetry as consisting of

> . . . a revolt against dead form, and a preparation for new form or for
> the renewal of the old; it was an insistence upon the inner unity which
> is unique to every poem, against the outer unity which is typical.[22]

Clearly, the anti-traditional impulse implicit in this statement should be weighed against other declarations in which Eliot argues that traditional patterns can, and should, play a vital part in modern poetry, whose very modernity may depend on the poet's immersion in literary tradition, suggesting that a formal renewal is most likely "a renewal of the old," and thus, in line with his first metaphor, a kind of spectral revival of the dead. What is more, Eliot's practical criticism continuously stressed that "new form" needs to be more rigorously shaped than the poetry that precedes it.[23] It is precisely in this sense, Cushman argues, that *any* strong American poet is essentially formalist: "The canonical poets [in America] have not been content with simply saying what they have to say; they have also been deeply concerned with the way they say it. They are not only, or even primarily, poets of statement but also of style and form."[24] In this sense, the most passionate 'anti-formalists' *in particular* are often primary purveyors of what Cushman calls "fictions of form." Such 'fictions'—like the 'spontaneous overflow of emotion,' the 'verbal icon,' 'defamiliarization,' 'open' vs. 'closed' form—range more or less explicitly from writerly, i.e. mimetic and expressive assumptions to notions of reader reception, often combining the two by implication. Crucially, they often imply a two-term relationship ('form' itself being one member of an ancient form-matter binary): very often between poetry and modernity, or—in those cases where modernity is identified as the Democratic promise of the New World—poetry and America: a "fiction of form is a fiction about *modern life* (parts of it are inaccessible to certain literary forms), a fiction about *literary forms* (certain forms can do things other forms cannot), and a fiction about *the relationship between them* (the poet ought to find the right form for modern life)."[25]

The term 'fiction,' however, should not simply be taken to indicate a lack in truth value. 'Fictions of form,' Cushman explains, serve as powerful cognitive frameworks that operate "alongside" poems, developing or extending "the original, appearing to analyze or explain but instead compounding precisely that which needs to be analyzed or explained."[26] Consequently, they not only shape critical terminologies and evaluative paradigms but may already be inherent in terminologies derived from other disciplines, such as cognitive theory. By telling readers what to look for and what to experience—in short, what poetic writing and reading is ideally about—we may well suppose that they even have the power to influence the interpretive and experiential outcome of concrete acts of reading, telling readers what to expect, what to read for, and how to formulate the value and experience of poetry.

Stevens' poetry has often been viewed with suspicion from the point of view of mimetic or epistemological 'fictions'[27] that are more or less explicitly based on the idea that the relationship between poetry and reality is, or should be, one of correlation, appropriateness or embodiment. Significantly, these ideas have often been linked to Stevens' unclear position in terms of the practice and conceptuality of modernist poetic language.[28] The very ambiguity of his position, however, makes Stevens of great interest in a discussion like Cushman's: he is a formalist both as a poet who relies on inherited forms *and* as one for whom the form of poetic utterance is never neutral or 'natural,' but plays an essential part in its creation of meaning. Ideas about his poetry's closure to historical reality, largely based on the idea (and ideal) of 'open' form, have often merged with views of his poetry guided by the normative vocabularies of Imagism's ideals of clarity, objectivity and precision. In both views, his poetic language has been criticized in more or less explicitly moralistic terms, as as too exclusive, elitist and aestheticist, and as too casual, conventional and hedonistic.[29] Accordingly, Stevens' role within the discourses of modernism has also to some extent been defined by his vague position in relation to the idea of modernism's 'free verse revolution.'

While Eliot and Pound furnished formal vocabularies for their poetry to an extent at which it may be wise to be wary of their tendency to prescribe response, Stevens' statements on form appear half-dismissive, vague and contradictory enough both to demand further explication and to be rather unhelpful in relation to his poetry. But while his changing attitudes toward modernist formal change at times appear studiedly polemical, suggesting a sense of rivalry with other strands of modern poetry, they often relate in interesting ways to his sense that formal elements are of the utmost importance. In a Journal entry of July 4, 1900, he exclaimed "Perish all sonnets!," adding that while sonnets "have their place . . . they can also be found tremendously out of place: in real life where things are quick, unaccountable, responsive" (*L* 42). In 1909, in the process of fashioning his new poetic idiom, Stevens described his early use of rhyme as obsolete and inadequate:

> In the "June Book" I made "breeze" rhyme with "trees," and have never forgiven myself. It is a correct rhyme, of course—but unpardonably "expected." Indeed, none of my rhymes are (most likely) true "instruments of music." The words to be rhymed should not only sound alike, but they should enrich and deepen and enlarge each other, like two harmonious notes. (*L* 157)[30]

Donald Wesling takes this statement to suggest that when "the correct device is also the expected one and by definition outworn, the act of composition will bristle with difficulties, with unforgivable wrong choices."[31] This means, Wesling argues, that the device itself must be "parodied, distorted or avoided in such a way as to make its absence very remarkable."[32] In this view, Stevens' discourse of the true and unprecedented, of "making it new," is not against rhyme as such, but against its conventionalized, expected and uneventful uses.

In 1921, Stevens declared that he was "for" free verse as a conscious attempt at invigorating poetic language,[33] and that he saw poetry uninformed by aesthetic theory as incapable of gauging its needs, and possibilities, for relevance. His attitude toward free verse, however, was to become more skeptical. In the mid-thirties, when free verse had established itself as the dominant mode of serious poetic writing he objected, much like Eliot and Pound had, to an overly 'democratic' interpretation of free verse as an opening to perfect expressive liberty. In "The Irrational Element in Poetry" (*OP* 224–33), a lecture delivered at Harvard in 1936, the feeling that "You can compose poetry in whatever form you like" indicates a frighteningly momentous sense of choice:

> It is not that nobody cares. It matters immensely. The slightest sound matters. The most momentary rhythm matters. You can do as you please, yet everything matters. You are free, but your freedom must be consonant with the freedom of others. (*OP* 230)

This fearful sense of the drama of formal choice, in the vocabulary of Hobbesian ethics, contrasts with how Stevens, in a poetic credo formulated in 1938 for *The Oxford Anthology of American Literature,* addresses the idea of formal freedom in a deceptively dismissive and flippant way:

> There is such a complete freedom now-a-days in respect to technique that I am rather inclined to disregard form so long as I am free and can express myself freely. I don't know of anything, respecting form, that makes much difference. The essential thing in form is to be free in whatever form is used. A free form does not assure freedom. As a form, it is just one more form. So that it comes to this, I suppose, that I believe in freedom regardless of form. (*OP* 240)

Even though Stevens here claims that there is "nothing, respecting form, that makes much difference," and that one therefore can "disregard form," suggesting a casual, even ungrateful, attitude toward modernism's profound investment in formal change, he clearly agrees with Eliot's view that "only a bad poet could welcome free verse as a liberation from form."[34] Thus, if we take him to mean that there is nothing in any *particular* form that guarantees freedom, that there *is* no 'free form,' Stevens' idea of "freedom regardless of form" will mean 'freedom regardless of what forms you are, inevitably, bound by.' This idea could not only be a comment on his own eclectic, dynamic and apparently 'free' use of repetitive, metric and graphic form, but also a slur against the free verse 'fictions' of 'open form' which, as Cushman argues, all too often lead "to platitudes about poets who use traditional forms to insulate themselves from historical experience and those who use experimental forms to plunge themselves" in its midst.[35] 'Meaning' in Stevens' formulation is not entirely the poet's own, as a pre-formal "attempt of somebody to say something" would be. This notion, and the deliberately blurred distinction between the attempt at saying something and the means of doing it, the 'device,' indicate an anguished but creatively dynamic concern at the center of Stevens' poetics, and the difficulty of a great deal of modernist theory to grasp his kind of poetic modernity.

In response to an enquiry in the *Partisan Review* in 1948, Stevens stated his opposition to "a usage with respect to form as if form in poetry was a derivative of plastic shape." Modern poetry, he argued, was not a "privilege of heteroclites" (*OP* 314). Here, Stevens denounces certain forms of automatized response to poetry which, as a matter of course, make readers understand the prestigiously modern as the most conspicuously experimental and formally deviant modes of poetry, a habit which implies that the events and premises of a liberating historical moment have petrified into a conveniently repeatable formula. In "Two or Three Ideas" (1952) Stevens would identify himself with the poets who "have something to say" and "are content to say it" rather than with those who have "little or nothing to say" and are primarily "concerned with the way in which they say it." There is a final 'formalist' concession, however, when Stevens agrees that "the style of a poem and the poem itself are one," and acknowledges that the poets with "nothing to say" actually "are, or will be, the poets that matter" (*OP* 258). More than simply a matter of confusion or deviousness, this statement is emblematic of Stevens' way of acknowledging the importance of formal renovation while avoiding fixed positions or alliances.

In the *Partisan Review,* Stevens had answered the question of whether the forties, "unlike the twenties," was "not a period of experiment in language and form" by criticizing the question itself, arguing that poetry is "nothing if not experiment" and that "experiment in form is one of the constants of the spirit" (*OP* 313). What an experiment in form is "in its proper sense," he proposes, is "a question of what appears within the poem itself," meaning the "things created and existing there" (*OP* 314). Thus, he appears to argue, it is neither a poem's pure content (the "poem" that in Eliot's formulation above comes "before the form") nor its final materialized form (its "objective correlate") but its realization in concrete historical interpretation, whose enabling contexts and assumptions, if the poem is successful, may be partly altered in interpretation itself. 'Form,' in such a view, will come about, become relevant, only in a close, interpretive, temporal, involvement with all of a poem, semantics, graphic form and rhythm together, rather than by a glance at its visual shape.

Stevens declined to supply any concrete idea of what modern poetry would look or sound like, but his Princeton lecture of 1941, "The Noble Rider and the Sound of Words," contains a discussion of historical tendencies of language transformation closely bound up with modernist formal change. Stevens refers to F.W. Bateson's idea that artistic languages, "considered semantically," develop "through a series of conflicts between the denotative and the connotative forces in words; between an ascetism tending to kill language by stripping words of all association and a hedonism tending to kill language by dissipating their sense in a multiplicity of associations" (*NA* 13). In other words, art fluctuates between a preference for the 'realist' capacity of language to refer accurately, valued by science and philosophy, and an inclination for suggestive, polysemic modes of expression. Stevens, supposing that the present is always "an illogical complication" (*NA* 13), supports the idea that the art of his day (he mentions the interest in semantics and the work of Joyce) is moved by a connotative tendency, even though the weight of contemporary events should make artists more interested in moving toward the real. The preference for connotation, however, is itself understandable as a move "toward the imagination in other directions" (*NA* 14), suggesting the presence of a realist, epistemological impulse in art even at its most polysemous, imaginative and hedonist.

The pronouncement in "The Noble Rider," that "above all else, poetry is words; and . . . words, above everything else, are, in poetry, sounds," is a knowing anomaly in the face of longstanding realist pressure on poetry, and strikingly deviant in relation to modern poetics as defined by Imagism. Stevens argues against the notion that music, related to the expressive instrumentation of metric poetry, is an invalid metaphor for poetry: "I do not know of anything that *will appear to have suffered more* from the passage of time than the music of poetry *and that has suffered less*" (662 my italics). In "Effects of Analogy," an essay first published in 1948, Stevens quotes Eliot's early *Rhapsody of a Windy Night*, whose free verse is full of rhythmic patterning—delayed rhymes, assonance, alliteration—to argue against the idea of music as an obsolete metaphor for poetry. "It is simply," he argues, "that there has been a change in the nature of what we mean by music," which is "like the change from Haydn to a voice intoning." This voice, he explains

> is like the voice of an actor reciting or declaiming or of some other figure concealed, so that we cannot identify him, who speaks with a *measured voice* which is often disturbed by the feeling for what he says. There is no accompaniment. If the poet occasionally touches the triangle or the cymbals, he does it only because he feels like it. Instead of a musician we have an orator *whose speech sometimes resembles music.* We have an eloquence and it is that eloquence that we call music every day, without having much cause to think about it. (*NA* 125–6 my italics.)

The combination of speech and song in Stevens' image gives primacy to rhythm: the 'speech' of poetry is like the voice of an actor/orator declaiming in controlled measures, while variation is provided by an occasional disruption caused by a tremor of expressive sincerity destabilizing the musical flow of words. The "accompaniment" of poetic devices such as rhyme and meter, is no longer required but remains as an option, to be used when the modern poet finds it appropriate, simply "because he feels like it." As much as it is meant to describe Eliot's poem, this definition surely gives a sense of Stevens' own late poetry, where long sentences, full of qualifications and rhetorical reversals, are played out against an abstract, frequently pentametrical, but flexible prosodic pattern.

Stevens' image is not far from Robert Frost's idea of metric 'counterpoint,' or from Eliot's view that free verse, defined "only in negatives: (1) absence of pattern, (2) absence of rhyme, (3) absence of metre" should always be accompanied by "the ghost of some simple metre," which "should lurk behind the arras in even the 'freest' verse; to advance menacingly as we doze, and withdraw as we rouse."[36] An understanding of Stevens' late poetry on this model has been founded on the sense that 'device' and subjective intent have finally become identical. Reading Stevens' "The House Was Quiet and the World Was Calm," J.V. Cunningham has argued that while its meter is recognizably a "a loosened iambic pentameter," it is "loosened firmly and as a matter of course, almost as if it were *speech becoming meter* rather than meter violated. It has in fact the stability of a new metrical form attained out of the inveterate violation of the old. It is both modern and traditional."[37] But such an achievement, apparent or not, was hard-won and, in view of the despair infusing much of Stevens' late poetry, quite inconclusive. Also, the conquest of rhythmic fluency may also, as this study will suggest, be related to the poem's scene: the house had not always been quiet and the world calm. In this study, it is Stevens' sense of struggle with poetic language—his 'trials of device'—that are of interest, if only as a way of understanding the eventual greatness of his late work, as it arguably ceases, in Cunningham's words, to be "parasitical on what it rejects."[38]

In order to study Stevens' somewhat disembodied concept of poetic creativity it will be complemented by a sense given to it almost a century ago—and a continent away from Stevens—by a group of theorists working in times of great social and aesthetic change: the Russian Formalists. Their legacy, developed in Czech Structuralism and vital to much of today's rhythmic theory, is valuable not only because of their main objective, to look at poetry *as* poetry, in its possible differentiation from other forms of expression, but also because of their pragmatic, and finally inconclusive, take on the meaning and character—the very status—of this distinctiveness. Crucially, they located the uniqueness of poetic language precisely in its tendency to draw attention to the word 'itself,' the physical or material aspects of language, rather than its intended object, whether subjective or objective. Victor Shklovsky's initial, polemical, reversal of artistic motivation, arguing that the thematic content of literary art was only a pretext for flaunting its 'device,' was eventually reformulated in terms of structural linguistics as a formally accomplished displacement of perceptual prominence from the 'signified' to the 'signifier,' which Roman Jakobson formulated as "the projection of the principle of equivalence from the axis of selection to the axis of combination."[39] Jakobson's suggestion was that poetic language is a result of the distribution of equivalent elements—sounds, words, syntactic patterns—pertaining to the same paradigmatic axis onto the syntactical sequence, where such resemblances would normally be downplayed in favor of clarity of meaning. In this way, the 'art' of poetry can be seen an act of force intentionally exerted on ordinary language: Jurij Tynianov argued that "poetic construction" by "pushing forward . . . one group of factors at the expense of another . . . deforms the subordinate ones"[40] i.e. actively disrupts our perception of the language functions that are common to 'natural' communication.

As Vendler's remark on 'trials of device' suggests, American fictions of form may have been averse to the idea of aesthetic 'deformation.' While Stevens (like his Romantic and Symbolist predecessors) frequently suggested that the opacity introduced by the material linguistic sign is essential to poetry, many of his poems make obtrusive poetic "device" play the part of a limiting, claustrophobic, even nauseous presence; 'deforming' precisely in the sense of hampering or obstructing true and accurate speech. The positive sense of Stevens' poetic language, as an experiment in creative freedom, or a celebration of the physicality of sound, can thus be seen to vie with another sense, that poetic language is an oppressive *a priori,* a reified and institutionalized cultural formula.

One of the greatest strengths of the Slavic Formalists was that the textual/linguistic idea of poetic language was qualified by the weight given to readerly and contextual factors. Jakobson's late formulation of the "poetic function" as the foregrounding of "the message," the material—sonic, graphic, rhythmic—properties of the linguistic sign, should be understood as a textually based, but ultimately *perceptual* foregrounding over and against the "set (Einstellung) toward the referent, an orientation towards the context—briefly the so-called REFERENTIAL," "denotative," "cognitive" language functions which "is the leading task of numerous messages."[41] Thus, Jakobson's idea is not that other language functions cease to operate, or are cleanly disrupted or 'undermined,' but that they are forced to recede from perceptual dominance. Consequently, the Slavic Formalists suggested that poetic language is most profitably studied when assuming that it is inseparable from, and participates actively in, the ever-developing historical world of propositional, i.e. referential and representational languages. As Jan Mukarovský explains:

> There is a constant struggle and a constant tension between self-orientation and communication so that poetic language, though it stands in opposition to other functional languages in its self-orientation, is not cut off from them by insurmountable boundaries.[42]

Indeed, Mukarovský argues, it is only when it is conceived of as relatively autonomous (*relatively* autonomous as well as relatively *autonomous*) that poetry can be of "practical" use outside the aesthetic sphere: "Precisely because of its aesthetic 'self-orientation' poetic language is more suited than other functional languages for constantly reviving man's attitude toward language and the internal composition of the linguistic sign and for showing new possibilities of its use."[43]

The linkage between the intrinsic, structural and textual aspects of poetry and the *ex*trinsic, readerly and contextual ones, was also crucial to the politically potent notion—prominent in the first phase of Russian Formalism—that poetic language is able to rouse readers from stale and conformist habits of thought and perception. Poetry may, as Shklovsky put it, renew the "perceptibility" of both language and the world by "defamiliarizing" or, as Mukarovský later put it, "de-automatizing" the reader's sense of their connection.[44] This idea, Todorov has suggested, replaced mimesis as the task of poetic language with one of "revelation" of the world.[45] Similar 'fictions of form' have been applied to Stevens by Schaum, Brogan and Cleghorn, who have valued his poetry for its 'resistance' to hegemonic languages, and by earlier 'deconstrutive' and Heideggerian critics—Riddel, Hillis Miller, Michael Beehler, Paul Bové—whose work was instrumental in bringing out the disruptive potential of Stevens' language. As I have argued elsewhere, however, their efforts at harnessing Stevens into a radical cultural force often implied downplaying the nostalgic and politically conservative aspects of his poetics. [46] Also, their almost exclusive focus on rhetoric and metaphor entailed an inattention to the way Stevens' poems move and unfold temporally in concrete 'constructive' reading acts. To an important extent, this meant downplaying the idea—central to deconstruction 'in theory'—of the critic's medial role as a culturally predisposed reader and co-creator.[47]

In comparison, Maeder's research represents a kind of formalism that allows for constructive dialogue both with historicist research and the most important critical possibilities of poststructuralist 'anti-realism.' Her study of how Stevens' poetry wrestles with the grammar, syntactical patterns and central metaphors of English, understood as a shared, historical language, is also sensitive to the relatively controlled temporality of the poetic reading act, assuming that poems are realized chiefly in the dynamic relationship between the text and a reader disposed to follow its course from beginning to end. Marie Borroff has likewise argued that to understand "how diversity of diction in Stevens is dramatically motivated, we need to think of it in terms not of static patterns of contrast but of temporal unfolding."[48] In this sense, her argument is open to the idea of the historical contingencies of both reading and writing, and to the fact that, as Henri Meschonnic has argued, the rhythmicity of poetic language, produced in a concrete reading event, is a historical activity: even though, or perhaps because, such a historical experience differs from, and obscures, the original context in which the poem was produced.[49]

Even if Russian Formalism saw a possibility to break with complacent social and political attitudes in poetic language, poetry's power to do this resides in a *simultaneity* of construction and deconstruction as mutually implicated aspects of the poetic production and reception. While Shklovsky's definition of poetry as "difficult, roughened, impeded language"[50] can be understood as a consequence of his early association with the avant-garde aesthetics of Russian Futurism, it is also congruent with poetry's capacity for euphony and rhythmic patterning, and its transformation of word perception through semantically energizing juxtaposition and repetition. The artistically imposed awareness of the word's 'wordness' may thus be an effect of structural integrity. While begging for constructive interpretation as a unitary sequence of words, lines and stanzas, a poem is able to make its 'decoding' full of tensions and obstacles that are themselves inseparable from its movement toward closure, as well as the pleasure of experiencing it. The event of "defamiliarization" could thus be described as relying on a process of (de)construction, suggesting an interdependence of construction and deconstruction—formation and deformation—in poetic reading.

For the Slavic Formalists, the graphic condition of poetry's "*versified* language"[51] was essential. This does justice to the fact that poetry's dominant cognitive condition, especially after the advent of modernist practices, is as a written or printed form of expression. Not only will most readers of poetry (certainly of Stevens' kind) experience the rhythm of poems through mental enactment, and not through reading, or having them read, out loud, but modern poetry is often *written* in ways that makes it difficult to enjoy all of its facets in a vocal performance. The rhythm of poetry, as the Slavic Formalists defined it, is thus not a purely acoustic phenomenon, but to some extent *inscribed* in the poem's verbal structure; even if (or because) such an inscription admits to different interpretations.[52] The temporal duration of poems is thus realized as an effect of the goal-directed intent to recover semantic meaning, prompting the eye to move from one verse line to the other, until the poetic sequence is completed. Such a journey can be fraught with tensions, stops and starts, expectations and revisions. In this way, the recognizable spatial forms of old and modern poetry, such as lines and stanzas, are potent cognitive markers, encouraging readers to commit to, and expect, a certain form of temporal realization of a written sequence. Thus, a poem can be seen as a verbal-musical score or a mental script, whose unfolding in reading, line by line and word by word, resides in is its fulfillment of semantic and syntactic structures as a sequential pattern in time.

Hence, it could well be argued that while modernist writing often proclaimed a break with the forms of metrical poetry, it actually turned the verse line and the stanza into more potent semantic factors, amplifying the expressive range of elements like enjambment and punctuation. While orderly, proportionally grouped lines and stanzas often still function as icons of poeticity and visual indications of beginning and closure, they have increasingly become instruments for linguistic trickery, polysemy, cognitive interruption, and surprise. As Frank Kjørup has argued, the fact that such formally provoked frustrations of the reader's desire for meaning are now to some extent expected,[53] and thus conventional, does not necessarily undermine their aesthetic potency. Kjørup's achievement is to show that a close engagement with poetic language has the potential to be uniquely exciting and vitalizing, perhaps because a poem's formal appearance of construction—and its corresponding imperative to readerly 'formation'—stages its capacity to put aesthetically significant obstacles in the way of the reader's will to comprehend.

Free verse can, on the one hand, be understood as a way to achieve a greater closeness to colloquial speech, giving line breaks and stanzaic structure similar roles to punctuation in prose, or to express the disorder of modern reality or consciousness. On the other, it has also enabled poets to 'denaturalize' expressive and representative language, by foregrounding its morphological, phonological and syntactic composition as it is altered by its collisions with lines, stanzas and rhythms. These two aspects of modern poetry's graphic condition can nevertheless be seen as complementary, as both shape individual poetic styles which we are likely to define in terms of expressive idiosyncrasy, even 'tone' or 'voice.' Even if poetry's stylized, patterned or 'denatured' language distinguishes it from what Barbara Herrnstein Smith calls a "natural utterance"[54] we are likely to read any kind of poem, be it a poem of non-sense letters or a blank page, as informed by communicative intention. As Paul de Man observed, to approach a poem as an "intentional object" is crucial, both since this is what calls forth a reading in the first place, and because it is what opens a poem to a 'unique plurality' of signification, and thus, to a simultaneous sense of integrity and radical otherness.[55] It is only, one could argue, if one assumes the presence of authorial intention that its opposites, the unfree, aleatory or ideologically determined aspects of artistic creation, and the poem's ontological separation from its historical author, become interesting, or even troublesome. A formulation such as that of J. Hillis Miller, who has defined Stevens' "authentic voice" as "a principle of discontinuity," illustrates this by framing Stevens' deconstructive disruptiveness in the vocal metaphor informing traditional ideas of lyrical poetry.[56] As Donald Wesling has put it, even if the notion of the "organic" may only be an "illusion," it is an illusion central to modern poetry, as the "primary myth of post-Romantic poetics" and its views on the "impropriate" or "appropriate" role of the poetic device.[57] In this sense, poetry's peculiar combination of difficulty and simplicity, mediation and immediacy, withdrawal and materiality, depth and superficiality, carries strongly ethical implications, which have been formulated prominently by the prosodic theorist Derek Attridge, influenced by the ethical philosophy of Emmanuel Levinas and the later Jacques Derrida. In line with other theorists like Amittai Aviram,[58] Meschonnic, Julia Kristeva,[59] Christopher Collins[60] and Susan Sontag,[61] Attridge has emphasized poetry's 'unreadability,' its active resistance to theory and paraphrase, as an important aesthetic and ethical intuition in poetic modernism which has been developed in 'postmodern' theory.[62]

In terms of a very basic aesthetics of reception, any attempt to 'make sense of' printed letters on a page taken to be a poem can thus be understood as an attempt to 'humanize' an initially foreign, unrealized material entity. In reading Stevens, I will argue, the ability to maintain the "humanizing" idea of the poetic text as "voice" may be as important as a sensitivity to its "dehumanizing" investments in poetic device. Only then are we able to experience the crucial creative tensions shaping his particular employment of poetic language, as "A Man Whose Pharynx Was Bad," whose voice is challenged by, working both with and against his own vocal cords, the material possibilities and constraints of poetic language. In this sense, the act of reading and analyzing poetry could also be seen as a trial—indeed, to borrow Vendler's expression, a 'trial of device'—of the capacity to handle that which we may finally, getting closer to the poem's full meaning, remain unable to understand.

In several of the poems that are central to my argument below, the ethical concern for others is subordinated or repressed in favor of individual truth and artistic harmony. This turn away from others, which has been criticized throughout Stevens' reception history, acquires a different meaning when it is kept in mind that the actual world that his poetry escapes from, or which he escapes from *in poetry*, is one in which communication is experienced as distorted, superficial and inauthentic, where the individual is at the mercy of languages that are radically hostile to himself. In this sense, the self-orientation or self-enclosure of Stevens' poetic language (undeniably also a measure of an actual cultural elitism and social ex-clusivity) can be understood as a response to the need to assume a distance, and create a sense of otherness, in relation to the languages of the social and public sphere. Significantly, Levinasian arguments on Stevens have resulted in opposed evaluations, depending on whether the idea is that other beings should be represented in poetry, or whether poetry, refraining from, even preventing, finalizing representation, should be about or enact the ethical difficulties of representation.[63]

The difficulty or opacity of Stevens' language was evaluated already in 1932, when R.P. Blackmur argued that whereas T.S. Eliot and Ezra Pound tried to condense sensual impressions and beliefs in their poetry, Stevens' use of words was not less precise, but instead makes "you aware of how much is already condensed in any word."[64] Stevens' aesthetic manipulation of English, Blackmur suggested, was capable of opening up the full semantic richness of words from its occlusion in common use; a perception elaborated in Bart Eeckhout's recent work.[65] Lakritz, with a base in American philosophical pragmatism, has more recently proposed "density" as the proper adjective to describe Stevens' language, distinguishing it (again) from the poetry of Eliot and Pound, which "often requires the knowledge of other languages, historical referents, myth, and so on."[66] Although this appears, as I believe wrongly, to suggest that that is all there is to the 'condensations' of Pound and Eliot and that the Stevens reader can dispense with that kind of erudition required by their texts, it is simply, Lakritz argues, that the 'density' of Stevens' allusions makes it differ in character from those of Pound and Eliot. Accordingly, research into Stevens' literary intertexts has been quite different. While Bloom has analyzed Stevens' influence-represssions—how influences have been agonistically repressed, or almost repressed, out of view—Eleanor Cook's research has paid close attention to Stevens' labyrinthine and perverse manipulations of allusion and cunning uses of etymology.[67] The 'density' of Stevens' poetry may also explain both the proliferation and difficulty of attempts to tie his poetry to philosophical inter-texts:[68] it appears to contain both a maximum of intellectual intention, and a maximum of that which may undermine its functioning as philosophical language. In this sense, it may appear as fragmentary and integrative at once: even when it offers difficulty, puzzlement or frustration this is an effect of the very elements which offer the 'hedonistic' physical and mental satisfactions of rhythmic and figurative 'closure.'

Finally, I would like to suggest another important affinity between Stevens and the Slavic Formalists, who eventually recognized that poetry's capacity for deviation and creating vitalizing linguistic and cultural disorder is due precisely to its special status in such a cultural order. The Formalists arrived at such an "anti-Romantic conclusion," Todorov argues, "precisely because of their Romantic presuppositions."[69] Despite their resentment of impressionist subjectivity, identified with Romanticism and its Symbolist aftermath, their ideas of artistic autonomy were clearly indebted to Romantic aesthetics. Thus, it was "the careful analysis of the 'works themselves'" allowed by Romantic thought which finally engendered what he has called their "third," most radical conception of poetic language, that "a specificity [of poetic language] does not exist . . . in a universal or eternal sense," only "in a historical and culturally circumscribed" one.[70] But even so, the idea of poetry's "relative autonomy" formulated by Tynianov[71] and Mukarovský,[72] contained not only an evident relativist notion, threatening to subvert the idea of a poetic language altogether, but also a potentially conservative one, that poetic functionality will keep on reformulating itself in new historical moments; as though it had a purely differential center or *noeud vital.*[73]

Thus, the formalists were not only pioneers in the kind of research that this study undertakes, the analysis of poetry's creative employment of graphic and rhythmic patterns, but also serve as a model for how a heavy investment in the specificity of their founding concept led them to a keen sense of its possible disruption or dissolution. This parallels modernist, not least Stevens' own, efforts to find a definite social purpose for poetry, as well as to define its peculiar capacities more closely, while exposing it to the perils of an encounter with its own relativity and its implications in other forms of discourse. Such anguish over poetry's uniqueness is also an anguish over its possibilities of cultural relevance, as well as its cognitive and expressive capacities. The elements of Stevens' language analyzed here are in this sense not only empirically palpable but, at the same time, both culturally and semantically unstable.

RHYTHM, METER AND RELIABILITY: DESCRIBING POETIC LANGUAGE

The rhythmic and metric aspects of Stevens' language will frequently play a central role in this study. As such, it will bring an element to the discussion that is relatively marginalized in contemporary literary study. This may not only be due to a lack of competence in metric analysis, but to related factors such as its difficulty to conform to the kinds of knowledge sought for in literary academe, and the fact that its methods and terminologies after the advent of free verse are in a state of constant revision. In 1965, Helen Vendler explained her inattention to the role played by "cadence, rhythms, and sounds" in Stevens' poetry, by suggesting that literary criticism has "yet to find a way of making notes" on these phenomena "both reliable and readable."[74] Forty years later, theories of meter and rhythm form a diverse and conflict-ridden field with multiple interdisciplinary binds: to evaluative literary criticism, linguistics, rhetoric, musical theory, anthropology and philosophy. The conflictive character of the discipline (or disciplines) is partly due to the fact that it has inherited the basic theoretical quandaries of literary scholarship as a whole, and partly because it is in the process of coming to terms with the most important challenges to its methods and terminologies brought by modernist poetics. These methodological complications, however, themselves reflect important aspects of Stevens' poetic language, which can be meaningfully studied as central to his poetry.

Metric 'scansion,' the most longstanding way of describing the prosodic organization of the verse line may, as Annie Finch has suggested, be experienced both as "lusciously, reassuringly objective" and "exhilaratingly, infuriatingly subjective."[75] Attridge has cautioned that being "certain that you 'hear' a particular pattern in a poem is no guarantee that it exists beyond your idiosyncratically nurtured perceptual facilities."[76] This may be due to a combination of factors: the democratizing consequences of free verse poetics and the changes it caused to the linguistic and rhythmic sensitivity of poetry readers, the insistently theorized need for cultural relativism in today's postmodern world, and, not least, sheer personal idiosyncracy. Together, these factors not only make it difficult to make predictions of rhythmic response that are accurate and valid, but are likely to throw suspicion on such attempts. The 'subjectivity'—Vendler's 'unreliability'—of rhythmic analysis, however, is not only that there could be disagreements on the prosodic organization of single lines, stanzas or poems, but also that any attempt at determining the 'function,' 'meaning' or 'significance' of patterns of rhythm in a poem— Vendler's 'readability'—will be fraught with subtlety and difficulty. Clearly, the 'material' medium of poetic rhythm, verbal language, is not just any kind of sonic or physical material, but is always already imbued with conventionally accepted (and therefore eminently disputable) meaning. The difficulty of an approach such as mine is that I attempt to understand the function of rhythm and meter in individual poems, rather than simply to enrich a metrical vocabulary or classify Stevens' different meters. This demands that I am able to make meaningful connections between prosodic patterning—

rhythm, meter and sound-patterning—and the semantic structures of his poems; making interpretations that will, in turn, affect my argument on the general tendencies of his poetics which I attempt to describe. Since there are few apparent models for this kind of research, my method needs to be inventive, argumentative and remain open to falsification.

In the process of abandoning, or complementing, traditional metrics and foot-prosody theories of poetic prosody have increasingly distinguished meter from the larger (and more complex) concept of rhythm, a process which is closely related to modern poetic art's 'liberation' of poetic language from its metrical straitjacket. In the view of the Slavic Formalists, Victor Erlich has explained, "verse can dispense with meter, but not with rhythm."[77] This study will apply Attridge's definition of meter as "an organizing principle which turns the general tendency toward regularity in rhythm into a strictly-patterned regularity, that can be *counted* and *named*."[78] While Attridge defines rhythm in general terms as "a patterning of energy simultaneously produced and perceived; a series of alternations of build-up and release, movement and counter-movement, tending toward regularity but complicated by constant variation and local inflections,"[79] it is crucial to his idea that it implies an experience of temporal movement: "Although strictly speaking the idea of 'movement' implies travel in *space,* rhythm is what makes a physical medium (the body, the sounds of speech or music) seem to move with deliberateness through *time,* recalling what has happened (by repetition) and projecting itself into the future (by setting up expectations), rather than just letting time pass by." Thus, "[r]hythm is *felt* as much as it is *heard* or *seen.*" [80]

The rhythms of written poetry are, however, significantly different from rhythms experienced in other contexts and by way of other material media.[81] The discussions of poetic rhythm below will presuppose that a poem is realized "word for word," which means that it is a temporal event closely regulated by spatial, syntactic and verbal structure. Although some aspects of a poem as a unit of meaning—the length of its lines and the meters we associate with it, its duration as a temporal utterance, for example—can and will be perceived immediately or predicted, as a visual sign, a painting or a photograph, this study is based on the notion that a full response to a poem should be guided by an experience of its 'way' of expression. This is an attempt to do justice to Shklovsky's idea that one of the main purposes of poetic language may actually be "to increase the difficulty and length of perception," since "the process of perception is an aesthetic end in itself."[82]

On a basic level, our interpretive performance of poetic "scripts" depends on our degree of familiarity with the most basic conventions and constraints of a given language, such as reading, in the case of most Western languages, from left to right, the rules of English grammar and pronunciation, its distribution of syllables and stresses, but also with our skills in the 'supra-segmental' aspects of language such as, in Attridge's words, its "patterns of . . . intonation, its pauses, its control of speed, and its modes of emphasis."[83] Further, we need a certain familiarity with poetic patterns, and a performative capacity to (re)produce them, which includes a sensitivity to various kinds of repetition and variation, such as the distribution, or avoidance, of rhyme patterning, anaphora, parallelisms, forms of euphonic sound patterning such as assonance and alliteration.[84] Frank Kjørup, referring to Manfred Bierwisch's idea of "poetic competence"[85] has extended this into an idea of "versificatory competence," suggesting that poetry's graphic deformation of language is one of its most central artistic possibilities.[86]

With recourse to the psychological notion of 'set,' Attridge distinguishes between a 'rhythmic set' and a 'metrical set.' While the former, he argues, is "the widespread disposition to perceive rhythmic structures in sound stimuli" manifested in "the perception of alternating patterns in objectively undifferentiated sounds like the tick of a clock," the role of the metrical set increases when rhythm "grows more complex, its embodiment in language less direct, and the element of convention more significant." Then, "[t]hrough experience, the reader grows familiar with this or that metrical form in his language, until he responds readily to the rhythms it creates." This means that the reader "can . . . be said to have acquired a set for that metre; if one were using a linguistic analogy, one would say he had internalized its rules."[87] Metric competence is thus to a greater (or at least more evident) extent a cultural competence: pertaining to those which distinguish one cultural group—national, ethnic or social—from another, or bring members in one group, or distinct groups, together. Below, I will assume a level of linguistic and metric competence, such as the capacity to recognize a basic pentameter or tetrameter structure, but I will take care to explain thoroughly when rhythmic analysis becomes, as often in Stevens, subtle or uncertain.

Several of my discussions will draw on Attridge's theory that any given "metrical pattern" in English poetry, composed of "an alternation of beats and offbeats," realizes one of two possible "underlying rhythms," the *four-beat rhythm,* the most fundamental and immediately accessible of rhythmic patterns, or the *five-beat rhythm,* whose expressive and cultural value, Attridge argues, is due to the fact that "it is the only simple metrical form of manageable length which escapes the elementary four-beat rhythm, with its insistence, its hierarchical structures, and its close relationship with the world of ballad and song."[88] Thus, as both Attridge and Anthony Easthope[89] suggest, the five-beat rhythm is able to allow "the rhythm of language [to] speak louder, and the elementary rhythmic form more softly."[90] The 'elementary' quality of the four-beat rhythm is to some extent reflected in its independence of the amount of syllables per line for its realization. While four-beat meters may be what metrists have called accentual-syllabic, the product of the interaction of stress-patterns and regular syllabic grouping,[91] its force is such that it will impose itself even on lines with more or fewer syllables, largely through what 'temporalist' metrics has called *isochrony*, but which Attridge prefers to call *stress-timing*, in order to underline that the time—*chronos*—of a poem is not measurable in terms of exact chronometrical intervals. A four-beat structure may consist only of three realized beats, demanding that the last beat of the line, what Attridge calls a "virtual beat"[92] be 'felt.' The five-beat line, however, which is controlled by a more 'abstract' and 'artificial' rhythm, often a variety of *iambic pentameter*, features no such possibility.

The most important, and most instructive, 'scanning' problems in this study will occur when these two rhythmic principles appear to converge, or become undecidable, in the same poem: when, for example, a syllabically regular pentameter frame is shot through with strong, integral four-beat phrases, when a five-beat rhythm is an effect of stress-timing rather than syllabic regularity and when an established four-beat rhythm is syllabically expanded and accommodates for pentameter phrasing. This will, in turn, require a sensitivity to the presence of two different, conflictive and paradigmatic, possibilities of rhythmic reading; a quandary which Donald Wesling understands as central in modern discussions of prosody, as "the traditional and open-field prosodies coexist without shared assumptions," attempting "to describe different kinds of texts."[93] Whereas "open field" prosody, apt to perceive the cumulative creation and cognition of rhythm, may partly explain the 'naturalness' of the rhythmic set and the readiness to perceive and produce strong-stress four-beat patterns,[94] traditional 'metric' prosody may often be useful for understanding syllabically regular poems like Stevens' "Sunday Morning" and, not least, the creative principle behind them.[95] The readings below do not pretend to be conclusive and normative, telling readers how a poem needs to be read, but simply aim to open the dimension of rhythm and meter to readers of Stevens' poetry. For this purpose, moments of metric variation and analytic uncertainty can be very important, as they may by themselves suggest both the power and the intricacy of Stevens' rhythmics.

Listening to Stevens' own recorded recitals is certainly very interesting, but does not make analytical (and performative) choices easier. Most available readings, mainly recorded in very old age, are performed with pausated slowness, spacing out the words in a way that is likely to put the listener on the verge of losing the rhythm altogether. Stevens often declines to give line breaks any aesthetic weight by underlining them in pronunciation,[96] and his intonation may at times appear as very unexpected, even perplexingly odd.[97] Clearly, Stevens' own performative choices do not necessarily set up a norm that we will want to follow. Also, the fact that the elderly Stevens, whose pentameter had 'loosened' considerably from the time of poems like "To the One of Fictive Music," preferred not to accentuate prosodically weaker, meter-making, syllables, does not make pentameter disappear as an important clue to the rhythm of such poems. Rather, it indicates the cognitive and performative volatility of his rhythmic patterning as a highly expressive and versatile device, capable of producing euphonically and rhythmically pleasing patterns as well as frustrating, monotonous or rhythmically disappointing ones, deriving rhythmic and semantic energy from the possibilities of moving between traditional and 'free' verse.

Here, the idea of 'substitution' that was central to traditional accentual-syllabic theory—the way an 'iamb' may be replaced by a 'troché,' a 'spondee,' a 'pyrrhic' or a trisyllabic 'foot'[98]—will as a rule be replaced by Attridge's method of measuring metric tension and regularity in terms of the way metrical beats may coincide, or not, with a stressed syllable, making for either a *demotion* of a stressed syllable or a *promotion* of an unstressed one. Attridge's terminology does not discard the creative/cognitive relevance of the 'abstract' principle of meter when it appears to be verifiable, nor that some poets may indeed have been thinking in 'feet' when writing. It implies, however, that a concrete, vocalized or silent, rhythmic perfomance does not consist of a realization of two simultaneous patterns at once—the abstract meter and the natural voice—but of one unified, if tense and multifaceted, temporal experience. In this respect, the foot is not necessarily a rhythmic unit of its own, even though it may well come to structure or even prescribe rhythmic response. Attridge's concept of "beats" as central to rhythmic cognition also helps make sense of syllabically excessive lines (of fifteen, even sixteen syllables) which, in a pentameter context, are cognizable as five-beat lines, even when they are anything but iambic. Following his method in *Poetic Rhythm: An Introduction,* primary stresses will be indicated by /, secondary stress as \, an unstressed syllable as x, and a metric beat as _. An unstressed syllable promoted into taking a beat, for example, will thus be represented as x̲, describing a tension between rhythmic patterning and ordinary stress-patterning. In places where a fourth *virtual beat* makes itself rhytmically experienced as part of a four-beat sequence outside even though it is not actually present in the words, it will be indicated by a stress sign within square brackets [/].

Another notion central to this study, exploited by theorists like East-hope, John Hollander,[99] and Annie Finch,[100] is that metrical patterns or fig-ures may carry conventionally recognizable connotations and lend various degrees of expressive authority or irony to poetic diction. Meter may thus be useful not only because of its exploitation of the 'poetic function,' moving us toward, as Aviram suggests, a "zero-point of meaning,"[101] but precisely by virtue of its semantic and stylistic connotations, which on occasion make it analyzable on a similar semantic level as 'diction' or 'allusion.' This is a functional potential which Attridge calls "associative" and which may help us relate to what he defines, with great caution, as the "iconic" and "affective" possibilities of poetic rhythm.[102] Even if such analysis of poetic language as idiolect, which Bart Eeckhout has recently defined under the term "tone," may appear as highly subjective and intimidatingly falsifiable, it may be a very important task, especially in view of the reluctance of critics to account for aspects of poetry such as sincerity vs. irony, solemnity vs. bathos, emo-tional restraint vs. sentiment.[103]

The cultural and semantic connotations of meter may, of course, be more or less consciously perceived by readers more or less aware of metrical tradition: what for some may be a shocking metrical deviation, or an unmis-takable case of iambic pentameter, may go entirely unperceived by others who have no problem in relating to the poem's rhythm from principles unre-lated to metrical regularity. By drawing attention to patterning that may not be immediately apparent this study will thus frequently be prescriptive, but will be cautiously so. I will explore the allusive aspect of meter less in terms of complex, semantically energizing intertextual reference than in terms of allusion to 'tradition' (often Romantic tradition) as such: which, in Stevens' complex relation to it, is a question of oldness and decay as well as solemnity and cultural prestige, often ironically and simultaneously.

Meter, as Finch's work underlines, has both a writerly and a readerly/ analytical aspect, since both a compliance with and a rejection of metric patterns may be crucial dynamic possibilities for modern poetic creativ-ity.[104] In Stevens, as I will try to show, they form part of the same aesthet-ics.[105] His hugely variable meters are central to his poetry's creation and decreation of meaning, and some of the most challenging and ambiguous passages in his poetry may in fact, as Dennis Taylor has suggested, be the most scannable.[106] In this study, the idea of meter as an 'abstract' principle is interesting precisely because Stevens' poetry has often been understood, for the most part negatively, as 'abstract'—a notion frequently related to the relative scannability of his meters. This sense, as I will describe in the first chapter, is also intrinsic to his poetry itself, as very regular metrical figures frequently come to signify and enact poetry as closed, self-perpetuating and tautological—even 'monological'—in relation to an exterior reality or truth principle.

Chapter One
Stevens' Closures

The sun, that brave man,
Comes through boughs that lie in wait,
That brave man.

. . . .

Fears of my bed,
Fears of life and fears of death,
Run away.

That brave man comes up
From below and walks without meditation,
That brave man.

"The Brave Man"

WHITMAN, SANTAYANA, STEVENS: ANXIETIES OF INFLUENCE

In a retrospective lecture given in Glasgow in 1942, "The Music of Poetry,"
T.S. Eliot gave an account of the developments in poetic discourse at the
beginning of the 20th century which he and Ezra Pound protagonized. The
vision of poetic change in Eliot's speech appeared to agree with a statement
made by Stevens in "The Noble Rider and the Sound of Words," a talk delivered at Harvard the year before, that "the imagination is always at the end of
an era." For Eliot, however, the idea that such revolutions are *always* happening—that a successful poem is itself a miniature revolution—coexists with
the notion that revolutionary poetic changes, produced in reaction to the
aloof refinement and expressive decay of fins-de-siècle, are cyclic, collective,
and historically verifiable, spaced out at approximately a century's interval:

Every revolution in poetry is apt to be, and sometimes announce itself to be a return to common speech. That is the revolution which Wordsworth announced in his prefaces, and he was right: but the same revolution had been carried out a century before by Oldham, Waller, Denham and Dryden; and the same revolution was due again something over a century later. The followers of a revolution develop the new poetic idiom in one direction or another; they polish or perfect it; meanwhile the spoken language goes on changing, and the poetic idiom goes out of date.[1]

Very conspicuously, Eliot's Anglocentric history of poetry omits a voice which preceded Eliot's own revolution—"something over a century" after Wordsworth's preface to the *Lyrical Ballads*—with the uneven number of approximately seventy years, but with an equally powerful claim in the history of poetic transformation, and precisely in the name of a return to common speech: Walt Whitman. In this sense, the modernist agency of Eliot and Pound can be seen as fighting on two fronts. There is Whitman's notion of poetic modernity, intent on clearing the ground of all obstacles for untrammeled expression, regarding struggles to perfect poetic technique as something of a non-issue. On the other side, there is poetry like Stevens', which appears to flaunt its sound material and traditional metric form at the expense of the presentational powers of the poetic image. Interestingly, later Poundian objections to Stevens' poetics have had a strong Whitmanian component, which suggests an often unacknowledged affinity at the core of Eliot and Pound's versions of modernism and, not least, their normative legacies.

Although Stevens received his first poetic formation at a time when, as Robert Buttel explains, "the sweeping innovations of Whitman and the incisive wit and haunting suggestiveness of Emily Dickinson were largely ignored,"[2] he was, as Richardson points out, familiar with Dickinson and was to become well acquainted with Whitman.[3] Stevens's attitude towards Whitman was skeptical, like Eliot's, but instructively different. In a late statement on Whitman, one of very few, Stevens argued that Whitman's all-accepting poetic mind and utter lack of evasiveness appeared to have tied him all too closely to his own historical moment: "Whitman is disintegrating as the world, of which he made himself a part, disintegrates" (*L* 871).[4] The unflattering conclusion, that the main value of Whitman's poetry was as historical document, was bound up with the positive sense that Stevens was attempting to give to ideas of "escape," "resistance" or "evasion." As Bloom's intricate argument on Stevens' 'influence-repressions' suggests,[5] however, Whitman and his mentor Ralph Waldo Emerson were to leave traces in his poetry that may be most vital when not on the level of conscious allusion.

Even if Bloom's work does not often apply this intuition in terms of Stevens' rhythmic and metric form,[6] it is congenial with the argument I will make below. Like Bloom, I assume that Stevens' "poetic stance," which directly informs not only his diction and metaphors, but his prosody as well, is not just his own but to an important extent itself laid on him by tradition.

As opposed to the later moderns, whose poetics were shaped in periods of historical disenchantment and cultural pessimism, Whitman was at the outset intensely optimistic, anti-traditional and, in a strongly utopian sense, anti-historical. His pre-Civil War readjustment of poetic language did not only aim to connect (or, in Eliot's words, re-connect) with a new language, but with a radically new world and new forms of interpersonal and ecological relations. The initial decree of "Song of Myself" that the "you," the reader as well as a would-be poet, "shall no longer take things at second or third hand . . . / nor look through the eyes of the dead . . . / nor feed on the spectres in books"[7] suggests an epistemological desire that poetry should no longer be a thing of second or even, as Plato claimed it was, third hand experience. It defines the newly discovered possibility of original, Adamic naming as essentially American. While the poetic (un)dead inhabiting books were European, the intended, ideal "you" for which the poet "will be waiting"—a person inhabiting a wished-for future—is an American on his way to become fully so. "The United States themselves," Whitman writes in the preface to *Leaves of Grass*, "are essentially the greatest poem."[8] In "Song of Myself," however, Whitman's persona fears that he himself may—or has already—become such a bookish spectre: hence the paradoxical self-annulling imperative that "you shall not look through my eyes either, nor take things from me" but "look to all sides and filter them from your self,"[9] admonishing the reader and future poet fully to assume self-reliance in perception and expression.

This urge for independence and freedom is envisioned by way of an image that will be a frequent, if negative, presence in Stevens' poetry. To accomplish an original cognitive and expressive relationship to the world, the poet needs to leave the comfortable "perfumed" safety of "houses and rooms,"[10] a dramatic, difficult but heroically unconditional act of opening up—"Unscrew the locks from the doors, / unscrew the very doors from their jambs!"[11]—to an ambience called "the atmosphere," an "odourless," "undistilled,"[12] a-cultural space. This is not only an image of a new kind of 'nomadic' poetic freedom, but implies a theory of poetic language—in Cushman's words, a "fiction of form"—in which the too comforting and too limiting houses and rooms represent the domesticated, habituated, but all too safe modes of poetic expression. Remarkably, in roughly the same era as Whitman, Emily Dickinson, the other towering poetic figure of late 19th century America, wrote poetry in idiosyncratic, but recognizably traditional prosodic form, in which extreme domestic privacy, exclusivity and closure functioned as a 'via negativa' to epiphanic fulfillment. Dickinson's poetry of rural Puritan America was in many senses a poetry of rooms, in which the "soul," auto- and aristocratically "selects her own society / and then shuts the door."[13] Even if Stevens' poetry displays an affinity to Dickinson's in this respect[14] it is decisively more urban, and very problematically so. It is here, I argue, that its relation to Whitman's poetics becomes of great interest.

In "Song of Myself," the exterior world is at once more dangerous, more real, more true and more intoxicating than the domestic sphere, and is frequently imagined as Nature in intimate communion with the respiratory and sexual functions of man. This happens less by virtue of metaphorical resemblance, in which nature is perceived to be analogical to or reflective of the human subject, than by a vision of the metonymical implication of things, which refer synecdochically, as parts, to an integral whole through contiguity and participation. Characteristically, Whitman's long, often enumerative, lines appear designed to bring about a disorder in the synoptic, hierarchizing faculty of perception:

> The smoke of my own breath,
> Echoes, ripples, buzz'd whispers, love-root, silk-thread, crotch and vine,
> My respiration and inspiration, the beating of my heart, the passing of
>   blood and air through my lungs . . .[15]

More decisively, however, in an image that both radicalises and threatens to obliterate his poetry, the poetic doorways that have been opened lead out into chaotic city streets. Poetry's 'new world' is *urban:*

> The blab of the pave, tires of carts, sluff of boot-soles, talk of the prom-
>   enaders, . . .
> The heavy omnibus, the driver with his interrogating thumb, the clank
>   of the shod horses on the granite floor,
> The snow-sleighs, clinking, shouted jokes, pelts of snow balls,
> The hurrahs for popular favorites, the fury of rous'd mobs,
> The flap of the curtain'd litter, a sick man inside born to the hospital . . .[16]

The metropolis was hugely important to Whitman's poetry, as it was for contemporaries like Melville, Poe, Baudelaire and Pushkin.[17] In Whitman's case, the New York of mid-19th century immigration and rapid expansion not only shaped his world view, but also the prosodic and graphic form of his verse, which was required to function both as an outlet for unrestrained subjective expression and enable a sequential vision of the city's pristine and exhilarating scenery: Whitman's extreme subjectivism is, as is frequently the case in modernist poetics, an objectivism.

The city, however, provided Whitman's poetry with a larger and crucially different challenge. It could not be content with registering the city's outward appearance, the sonic and visual realities of its myriad of activities—or, like Wordsworth, regard the dormant potentiality of a city empty of people—but also assumed the far greater burden of giving expression to the city's turbulent, irrational and ethically challenging manifold of other selves and their irreconcilable realities:

> What groans of over-fed or half-starv'd who fall sunstruck or in fits,
> What exclamations of women taken suddenly who hurry home and give
>   birth to babes,
> What living and buried speech is always vibrating here, what howls
>   restrain'd by decorum,
> Arrests of criminals, slights, adulterous offers made, acceptances, rejec-
>   tions with convex lips,
> I mind them or the show or resonance of them—I come and I depart.[18]

Here, the indecisive syntax of the final sentence reveals a troublesome intuition, of immense value for a discussion of Stevens' urban poetry—does the speaker really "mind *them*," these others, or, finally, only their "*show* or *resonance* "? That is, are their voices just external material internalized by and enriching my poetry's sonic or graphic texture, or is any portion of their deeper spiritual reality able transcend in or through the words of my poem? Despite the widespread acceptance of modern theories of arbitrary signification, or because of a deep-seated, often undeclared discontent with them, this sense of linguistic impasse is still a problem for later poetic theory. We can, it appears, live with the gap between language and humanity (and thus both *between* and *in* humans) only as long as we conceive of it as being itself indicated or expressed in art, and thus on some level transcended.

The attempt announced in "Song of Myself" to enable poetry to let new, mutually incompatible experiences occur in poetry, is also figured as a critique of structured harmony and euphony. The act of 'unburying' the 'living' speech muted by poetic and cultural decorum, and thus to become the channel for 'long dumb,' because 'forbidden,' voices, is imagined as a transformation of poetic language from pleasingly controlled metrical measure into an artlessly spontaneous, thorny and disharmonious—both "untamed" and "untranslatable"—"barbaric yawp" sounded "over the roofs of the world."[19] Certainly, even if contemporaries may have understood Whitman's verse as barbaric, its peculiar combination of colloquial and quaintly old-fashioned language and its frequent reference to opera and oratorio,[20] may make it seem intensely musical to modern sensibilities. By virtue of the biblical and prophetic mode of anaphora, its principle of rhythmic coherence is located at the beginning of lines rather than at the end, enabling the reader/speaker to follow each phrase to its natural, speech-determined ending, enabling in prosody what Wordsworth called a "spontaneous over-flow of emotions."[21] But even if Whitman's ideas of what he was doing can be seen as partly contradicted by his practice (as many strong theories of poetic language) the figurative relation between the domestic imagery and traditional poetic modes is striking. Since the power of the uncreated yawp becomes accessible only when the doors of the house have been exploded or dismantled, the houses and rooms are also potentially a figure for the poet's consciousness and, which is more or less the same, his language.

Despite the historical events and cultural developments that obviously separate them, Stevens and Whitman were both influenced by Romantic poetry and thinking. But whereas Whitman's poetry can be understood to radicalize the most utopian aspects of Romantic naturalism, intensified by the promises of the New World, Stevens' fascination with Romanticism and the Victorian poets, visible in his early poetry, was defined by an elitist sense at fin-de-siècle Harvard of an expressive dead end, "that all the poetry had been written and all the paintings painted" (*OP* 218). In this atmosphere art was appreciated for mere enjoyment and alleviation of worldly pain.[22] Stevens' eventual "turn" to modernist poetic practices was of course not only the result of individual propensities and needs, but allowed for, among other things, by his reading of French Symbolist poets like Mallarmé, Valéry and Laforgue, important changes in intellectual sensibilities and other aesthetic fields such as music and painting, his probable attendance at the Armory Show in 1913, and his conviviality with the group of artists and intellectuals surrounding the *Others* magazine. The influence of contemporary painting on Stevens' early development, studied by Richardson,[23] Glen McLeod,[24] and Bonnie Costello,[25] and his inheritance from French Symbolism by Michel Benamou,[26] will not be developed further here. Instead, the focus of the following chapters will be established by comparing Stevens to Whitman in an area that will yield similarities as well as crucial differences: their ideas of the relation of poetic language with modern reality and its others.

As denizens of New York in different historical moments—Stevens moved there in 1900 to look for work as a journalist, the same profession that Whitman had for a long time—they share a crucially formative experience: both experienced the enormity of immigration into the New York area. But while Whitman experienced the First Wave, mainly from Northern and Western Europe, Stevens' turn-of-the century experience was of the ethnically and culturally more disparate Second Wave of immigration. Both experienced the city's uncompromising competitiveness, but whereas Whitman, coming from economically modest surroundings, led an itinerant life and, in a sense, had everything to gain, Stevens, who enjoyed considerable but not everlasting financial security, had, as Lentricchia has argued, everything to lose.[27] Whitman appears to have responded to the contemporary world, even in its violent and sordid aspects, with optimism, good faith, radical inclusiveness, and a magnanimous tolerance of human weakness, while Stevens' poetry frequently relates to the modern world and its others in images of closure, deviation and negation.

Before going to New York, Stevens left his upper-middle class home in Reading, Pennsylvania, to study at Harvard from Fall 1897 to Spring 1900 as a special student, following a practice common to his period, when young men often took courses as a preparation for Law School without intending to graduate. Through a circle of friends, Stevens came to know the Spanish-American philosopher George Santayana, with whom he spent time discussing literary and philosophical topics, often in Santayana's office. At the time, Santayana was writing an essay on Whitman and Browning, "The Poetry of Barbarism," that was to be included in the aesthetic treatise which Kermode has argued is "the key book to Stevens' thinking,"[28] the *Interpretations of Poetry and Religion,* first published in 1900. In the essay, Santayana censored Whitman for what, to his mind, was an all-accepting laziness and a lack of interest in plumbing the depths of human concerns. For Whitman, he argued, "the world has no inside; it is a phantasmagoria of continuous visions, vivid, impressive, but monotonous and hard to distinguish in memory, like the waves of the sea or the decorations of some barbarous temples sublime only by the infinite aggregation of parts."[29] This architectural metaphor for Whitman's negligence of the way structures shape the noumenal appearance of things, is also a critique of his poetry's alleged lack of the mnemonic, structuring and closural forces of meter[30]—or, as Eliot would formulate it in 1942, "the musical structure of the whole."[31] In 1952, Stevens would write a moving poem on Santayana's death, "To an Old Philosopher in Rome" (*CP* 508–11), in which he called his friend, perhaps in implicit comparison to himself, "an inquisitor of structures."

In his last year at Harvard, Stevens and Santayana had a brief poetic exchange that was strongly related to issues central to Santayana's essay: the relation between the culturalizing and structuring forces of the imagination and Nature. Stevens read a sonnet of his own to Santayana, beginning "Cathedrals are not built along the sea" (CPP 486), whose central image—a cathedral violently disturbed by the winds and spumes of the sea, turned into a savage echo-chamber of the a-cultural forces of Nature—provoked an appreciative but nonetheless corrective response. In Stevens' poem "the *precious* organ pipes" functioned as the vocal channel for a "low and constant murmur of the shore / That down these golden shafts would *rudely* pour / A mighty and a lasting melody" (*CPP* 486), suggesting an incompatibility between the instrument's preciosity and the rude, uncivil sounds played through it, which can also be understood in terms of a clash between religious forms and a violently irreligious natural world. In Santayana's sonnet response the forces of nature achieve a measured, musical articulation as "the wild winds through organ-pipes descended / To utter what they meant eternally";[32] structuring the noise of the sea, the pipes thus articulate an utterance already latent in it, but fulfilled only when converted into music. [33]

A Stevens poem like "The Idea of Order at Key West" is strikingly evocative of Stevens' and Santayana's sonnet dispute, thematizing a female singer-figure's attempt at articulating the impingements of the exterior world into poetic harmony or structure while insisting, as Stevens' poetry frequently does, on the radical incompatibility of human music and natural sound. In Stevens, Aristotelian images of mimesis are often challenged, if not cancelled out, when poetic language encounters a deceptively uncreated, chaotic "blank underlying"—motivating but also resisting—the poet's "trials of device." The difficulty to achieve critical consensus about the significance of this ethical and epistemological impasse can be understood in relation to a crucial aspect of the Stevens-Santayana sonnet debate, and largely in terms of what did *not* enter into it: the thorny issue of human alterity raised by Whitman's poetics. Whitman offered an extremely challenging model of poetic ambition to which Stevens both responded and tried to evade (he may, typically, have responded precisely by evading it): human others, and their ethical demands, cannot, at least not without an important ethical risk, be transformed into sonic or visual material. I would argue that Stevens' eventual answer—that they must be, since their poetic inclusion must simultaneously be an *ex*clusion or deformation—is, in its anxious complexity, very important for an understanding of his poetry. Both Stevens' response and his eventual evasion of

Whitman's commandments can be described more closely by examining a few crucially formative experiences in New York at the beginning of the 20th century.

A MAN WHO LIVED INDOORS: STEVENS AND THE CITY

After his period of cultural and poetic apprenticeship at Harvard—where he wrote articles and published poetry in the *Harvard Advocate*—the twenty-year old Stevens arrived in New York on June 14, 1900, searching employment as a journalist, with a mind to becoming a full-time literary man. Staying in a lice-infested room in a poor Manhattan neighborhood, Stevens was brought into close contact with aspects of social reality with which he had been quite unacquainted. The city's tumult of people and generous display of human misery entered the imagination of the young Stevens, who understood it partly in terms of his social and cultural sensibility, and partly in terms of the gravity of his own economic situation. When the city emerged in his poetry thirty years later, it would do so with complexity and ambivalence, in a strikingly non-Whitmanian way. Poetry, even as a thing of cities, would in no sense have become more compatible with its chaotic streets.

A record of Stevens' first experiences in New York is accessible in the journal he kept during those years, which, it should be noted, is a record of a young man who is not only writing *for* himself, but "writing himself," in the sense of forming an identity while looking at himself striking poses. In the Journal, the city is violently contrasted with the Romantic and Emersonian idealism that Stevens had imbibed in Reading, where he was raised by a hard-working but poetry-loving father, and at Harvard, where his studies had centered on Literature and Composition (apart from English, Stevens studied French Literature as well as Goethe and his German contemporaries).[34] A crucial facet of this clash, however, can be seen in his developing sense of poetry and poetic language, chiefly nurtured by readings of the English Romantics and Victorians, the poetry of Palgrave's *Golden Treasury,* and the American "Fireside" poets.[35] While his city experiences at times appeared radically unpoetic—or, as he was to call it, "anti-poetic"—poetry became one of his principal means of dealing with it.

Two imaginative patterns emerge in Stevens' early New York writings, both of which, especially in their productive combinations, would form part his later poetics. The first one defines the city as a protection against the threat of exterior nature, symbolizing mankind's creative ordering. In a Journal entry of 1904, on returning to New York from one of his habitual hikes in the countryside, Stevens ascribes pastoral qualities to the city:

> I thought, on the train, how utterly we have forsaken the Earth, in the
> sense of excluding it from our thoughts. There are but a few who con-
> sider its physical hugeness, its rough enormity. It is still a disparate mon-
> strosity, full of solitudes + barrens + wilds. It still dwarfs + terrifies +
> crushes. The rivers still roar, the mountains still crash, the winds still
> shatter. Man is an affair of cities. His *gardens + orchards + fields* are mere
> scrapings. Somehow, however, he has managed to *shut out the face of the
> giant from his windows*. But the giant is there, nevertheless. And it is a
> proper question, whether or not the Lilliputians have tied him down.
> There are his huge legs, Africa + South America, still, apparently, free;
> and the rest of him is pretty tough and unhandy. But, as I say, we do not
> think of this. (*L* 73 My italics.)[36]

Stevens' understanding of the city here is telling, as it appears to suggest an
ancient pastoral world rather than his own situation: he was not likely to
encounter many "gardens + orchards + fields" in the city he returned to. The
fact that his countryside excursions were often undertaken to get away from
it points instead directly to the second, contrary, intuition that the capitalist
metropolis was itself a manifestation of raw, merciless and a-moral nature,
a sense which, in turn, converted its rural and natural surroundings into an
idyllic repository of natural virtue and freshness.

A display of these sensibilities can be found in four short poems in
traditional form grouped together as the *Street Songs* (*CPP* 492–3). All four,
written while Stevens was still at Harvard, exploit contrasts between the city
and a pastoral idea of nature, as well as the images and idiom of Romantic
and Victorian poetry. In "Statuary," a statue of Dian and Apollo serves, like
Keats's Grecian Urn, as a silent symbol of ever-fresh youthful love, absolved
from the noises of the contemporary—"No clatter doth their gaiety disturb."
In "The Pigeons," the flight of birds "over the city and into the blue" (a possible precedent to the final image of "Sunday Morning") is as an imaginative projection of a desire to escape urban confinement. In a sonnet called
"The Beggar," urban poverty is denounced in the image of a poor woman,
"all rag and bone," who sits outside a cathedral making, as the poem quirk-
ily suggests, "mean" use of this holy place in order to obtain "a dreg / of the
world's riches." Whether the old lady (a possible forerunner of the bag-lady
in "The Old Woman and the Statue") *does* have a right to the place remains
ambiguous, and the poem enigmatically asks the reader to decide this. The
command that "If she doth abuse / The place," the reader should "pass on,"
is weighed against the idea, resting on a somewhat irreverent comparison
between begging and prayer, that the cathedral *is* indeed "a place to beg."

In the sequence's final common meter poem, "The Minstrel," city streets are valued merely as conduits to a pleasant, strikingly Wordsworthian, natural elsewhere:

> The streets lead out into a mist
>   Of daises and of daffodils—
> A world of green and amethyst,
>   Of seas and of uplifted hills.
>
> There bird-songs are not lost in eaves,
> Nor beaten down by cart and car,
> But drifting sweetly through the leaves,
>   They die upon the fields afar.
>
> Nor is the wind a broken thing
> That faints within hot prison cells,
> But rises on a silver wing
>   From out among the heather bells.

These images of urban dislocation of song and the interruption of the sound of the wind will return in Stevens' later poetry; the idea of mellifluous bird-song, understood as a fundamentally European inheritance, will be tested against ruder American voices, and the wind will be charged with representing entirely different aspects of reality.

The opposed image of the city as a civilized bulwark against the encroachments of merciless nature, is to be seen in an "Ode" (*CPP* 494–95) written in the same period, where a group of people, apparently all young men, are gathered into a room "To pack and bundle care away—And not to remember that over the dark / The sea doth call." The sea, an image of death, abides ominously in the background as "A patient workman by the city wall" which all the room dwellers will meet sooner or later: a disquieting echo of Wordsworth's image of nature's "inscrutable workmanship." In order temporarily to defy death, that will eventually have to be dealt with—only "not in May!"—"it is enough" for the young city-dwellers "to hear young robins sing / To new companions / In the morn," something which they appear to be particularly able to do from within the confines of their apartment. Clearly, the idea of city walls recalls the privileged spheres of old English cities (and the aspirations of American élite universities to emulate Oxbridge architecture and pastoral surroundings in the intimidating midst of urban jungles).

In the first Journal entry on his arrival in New York, in January, 1900, Stevens relied on similar images to represent the city to himself, and himself in relation to a place he was alternately to experience as both hostile to poetic creativity and as a "great place for thinking."[37] Stevens describes how "the steps of the street" in the working class area where he lived, "for squares were covered with boarders etc. leaning on railings and picking their teeth" and how "all around" him "were tall office buildings closed up for the night." The curtains of these buildings "were drawn and the faces of the buildings looked hard and cruel and lifeless" (*L* 38). Making a sudden change of tone, apparently due to his perception now being somewhat distanced, as from behind the closed doors of his room, Stevens writes that "This street of mine is a wonderful thing." The outside is now represented only as tenuous sound: "Just now the voices of children manage to come through my window from outside it, over the roofs and through the walls"(Ibid.). After reverting to denounce what he was later to call the "infernal money-getting" (*L* 42) of New York, as "a field of tireless and antagonistic interest—undoubtedly fascinating but horribly unreal" where "Everybody is looking at everybody else—a foolish crowd walking on mirrors" (*L* 38), he imagines his room as a paradisal space in which the unpleasant outside (both too lifeless and too full of life, full of an "unreality" which is nevertheless all too real) is transformed into a miniature Eden:

> The carpet on the floor of my room is gray set off with pink roses. In the bath room is a rug with a figure of a peacock woven in it—blue and scarlet, and black, and green, and gold. And on the paper on my wall are designs of fleur-de-lis and forget-me-not. Flowers and birds enough of rags and paper—but no more. In this Eden, made spicey with the smoke of my pipe which hangs heavy in the ceiling, in this Paradise ringing with the bells of streetcars and the bustle of fellow-borders heard through the thin partitions, in this Elysium of Elysiums I now shall lay me down. (*L* 38–39)

Stevens' playful transformation of worn-out rags and scraps of paper into Romantic images of flowers and birds (on July 4, 1900, Stevens will write that his flowers are now "in milliner's windows + in tin-cans on fifth-story fire-escapes" (*L* 42)) serves as Lentricchia's main example of what he calls "the social kitchen" of his poetics: "the aesthetic as a lyric process of moving toward the interior, from the real space of the streets of New York to the private space of his room, and then into the psychic space of consciousness (now perilously sealed to the outside)"[38] Lentricchia here alludes to the widespread notion of the 'perils' of lyric poetry as implying a transformation of real phenomenal or linguistic disparity into single vision. The trajectory indicated by his sequence of adjectives; real—private—psychic, corresponding to street—room—mind; explicitly locates 'reality' in the city's streets rather than in its private rooms or the minds of its inhabitants.

Significantly, the playful beautification of the city in Stevens' Journal was soon to be used as material for further imaginative, now strictly poetic, transformation. In another entry a week later, on June 22, 1900, Stevens has written a poem in common meter, "A Window in the Slums," to all appearances based on the (already heavily aestheticized) experience recorded in the Journal. Holly Stevens has persuasively argued that the poem was also inspired by the Victorian William Ernest Henley's poem "I.M. Margaritae Sororis,"[39] quoted in Robert Louis Stevenson's "Christmas Sermon," which Stevens had just read. To my mind, the poem's image of imprisoned children may also recall those locked up in the Tower of London in Shakespeare's *Richard III*, and, possibly, the unfortunate but sacred infants of William Blake's "Holy Thursday" poems:

> I think I hear beyond the walls
>   The sound of late birds singing.
> Ah! What a sadness those dim calls
> To city streets are bringing.
>
> But who will from my window lean
>   May hear, 'neath cloud belated,
> Voices far sadder intervene
>   Sweet songs with longing weighted—
>
> Gay children in their fancied towers
>   Of London, singing light
> Gainst heavier bars, more gay than their flowers
> The birds of the upclosing night
>
> And after stars their places fill
>   And no bird greets the skies;
> The voices of the children still
>   Up to my window rise. (*L* 40)

Unlike the walls, or "thin partitions" in the Journal, which signified a blunting filter against the urban world outside—whose very thinness, as Lentricchia suggests, adds to the exquisiteness of the interior[40]—these walls wistfully suggest a sense of ontological solitude. To the extent, however, that the image of cognitive isolation is what actually enables the poem's assertion of defiant hope, it can be seen as a kind of dramatic poetic pose and, as such, an image of a properly poetic power. The solitude of the imprisoned speaker is analogous to the solitude of the imprisoned children, dwellers of the same city sphere, but is also redeemed by their presence and the analogy it enables: they are innocent children singing gaily in spite of the city's forced partitions, defying their bereavement of natural rights. The prison walls are thus an essential part of their poesis: they both keep the infants from being exposed to the corrupting forces of urban modernity, and make their song feeble and indistinct enough to allow for imaginative interpretation.

In another poem from 1900, a "Sonnet" (*CPP* 497–8), an imagined adversary, akin to the powers casting the "shades of the prison house" in Wordsworth's "Intimations" ode, is boldly challenged to do the utmost to restrain him:

> Build up the walls about me; close each door;
> And fasten all the windows with your bars;
> Still shall I walk abroad on Heavens' floor
> And be companion to the singing stars.
> Whether your prison be of greatest height
> Or gloomier depth, it matters not. Though blind
> I still shall look upon the burning light,
> And see the flowers dancing in the wind.

The final tercets establish the speaker's empowerment even further, giving him complete—if imaginary—mastery of the situation:

> Your walls will disappear; your doors shall swing
> Even *as I command them,* I shall fare
> Either up hill or down, and I shall be
> Beside the happy lark when he takes wing,
> Striking sweet music from the empty air,
> And pass immortal mornings by the sea.

While the walls obstruct the speaker from partaking in that which may provide it with impetus and inspiration, they also free his imagination, granting privileged access to the beauties of Nature by closing out possibly unpleasant or inimical things and events. Hence, the 'still' or 'though' can be translated into 'because' or 'especially as.' In this way, Stevens' rebellion against 'houses and rooms' is conditioned on their primacy: the poem's predicament is its way to empowerment. These early poems actually continue in a mode tested in an earlier example of what Buttel has called the "house-prison imagery,"[41] a sonnet written at Harvard in 1898 called "Vita Mea" (*CPP* 481–2), whose speaker is imprisoned in "The House of Life,"[42] a "place of doom" where nature lies "sick and dead." Desperately "Hast'ning from door to door, from room to room," he finally perceives how the window-bars take on a bright, paradoxically beautiful sheen through the prism of his dejected tears. Such a notion of forced but fortunate isolation was to be central to Stevens' short play "Carlos Among the Candles," published in 1917, in which the protagonist's utter isolation in a room is a paradoxical precondition for his sense of identification with others. It is also implicit in the colorful artistic vision of "The Curtains in the House of the Metaphysician" (*CP* 62), where the wind ruffles the curtains of the speaker's mind-room in a suggestive way. It would also persist in poetic scenes like that of "Poem with Rhythms" (*CP* 245–6) and in the last of the *Collected Poems,* "Not Ideas about the Thing but the Thing Itself" (*CP* 534). "Effects of Analogy" illustrated its discussion of the possibility of an "intensification of reality," brought about by the poet's capacity for resemblance, by way of the following image:

> It is as if a man who lived indoors should go outdoors on a day of sympathetic weather. His realization of the weather would exceed that of a man who lives outdoors. It might, in fact, be intense enough to convert the real world about him into an imagined world. In short, a sense of reality keen enough to be in excess of the normal sense of reality creates a reality of its own. (*NA* 79)

There is, however, an aspect of the apartment which is 'material' in a more strictly economic sense. A crucial phase of Stevens' New York experience was the anguished realization of the frailty of his social position.[43] The reputed "split" in his later life—working full-time as an insurance officer while writing poetry on his spare time—can be seen as a consequence of Stevens' early, somewhat painful, resolve to make a steady living for himself before indulging in poetry.[44] In a Journal entry in 1903, Stevens described the passage from a parentally sponsored life of studies and poetic reverie into an adulthood of economic responsibility as a sort of "fall"; not just from innocence and freedom, but also from the illusion of stable social privilege.[45] Lentricchia suggests that Stevens' anguished new insight into economic realities was intensified by a sense of a chaos threatening not far beneath a very superficial order of things; an essential aspect of the American dream of upward mobility being "the dream of the middle-class in America," which, he argues, "is the nightmare of downward mobility."[46] The fearful loathing of being one of the socially and spiritually elect, but having to spend his most valuable gifts on "infernal money-making," was counterbalanced in Stevens by a sense of moral pathos implicit in the need to deal with responsibilities and a sense of community with the less fortunate others.[47] Thus, Lentricchia argues, "Stevens' version of the nightmare concluded with an effort to resist it, with what in his writing is an almost never expressed impulse, the utopian urge toward classless society."[48]

Naturally, Stevens' social and political ideas were bound to be shaped by liberalist American ideals that on some level assume classlessness as a fact of American life, making Americans regard success or failure, having or not having, in terms of individual capacity rather than social class. Even though Stevens "hoped" he was "headed left" in the thirties,[49] economic Liberalism was, as Joseph Harrington has argued[50], an essential aspect of the poetics Stevens was to develop from the mid-thirties onwards. From the end of the thirties onwards, Stevens would name the dismantling or disruption of collective fictions, the "decreative" discovery of "barenness" or "abstraction," by the socio-economically derived term "poverty"—a near-homonym for "poetry"—functioning both as a name for post-religious and, we could say, post-poetic deprivation and as a desired, imagined purity of imaginative perception. In *both* these senses, however, 'poverty' is bound up with a hierarchy intrinsic to poetic culture and poetic language, as a way to attain or rehabilitate what Stevens would call "nobility." The flexibility and elusiveness of these concepts in Stevens' later poetics can be deepened by a discussion of his Depression poetry, where they are exposed in more troublesome 'material' terms. In no other period, I contend, are the material conditions of writing, and along with it, the resilient 'materiality' of poetry as severely tested in its ideological, economic, and physical senses.

In the years of the Great Depression, the crisis in American economy, politics and identity beginning in 1929 and not ending until about ten years later, Stevens' employer, the Hartford Indemnity and Insurance Company was struggling to combine New Deal ideas of contingent *ad hoc* solutions to vitalize the American economy with a conservative image of reliability and stability that would inspire confidence among clients, an attitude which Filreis has pointedly called "a hegemonic approach to change."[51] Stevens' handling of insurance claims related to the Depression, providing comforting insurance solutions in frighteningly changing times to those who could afford it, did not only make demands on his skills as an insurance man. Just

as The Hartford's advertising agents "worked overtime to guarantee the contradictory tropes of stability and contingency"[52]—its own stability in the
face of the frightening unpredictability of current events—Stevens' thinking
about the relation between poetry, language and historical reality worked on
similar terms. A compelling textual instance of these concerns is "Insurance
and Social Change" (*OP* 233–7), an essay published in *The Hartford Agent*
in October 1937, which discusses the demands for national social security
raised by the socio-economic and political unrest of the thirties.

In Stevens' argument—which Filreis approvingly calls "an open-
minded affirmation of increased socialization in his industry"[53] and "a piece
downright progressive when put next to conventional insurance rhetoric of
the time"[54]—the idea of insurance is understood as a symptom of a desire for
protection against unpredictable contingency and irrevocable loss, of being at
the mercy of events beyond one's control. The central assumption, explaining both the need for social security and its disastrous effects, is that the most
basic human instinct is to strive for perfect safety, "to go on indefinitely like
the wax flowers on the mantelpiece" (*OP* 234). Stevens thus makes rhetorical use of a Darwinist notion of the drive for self-preservation, often used to
support a *de-regulation* (in Adam Smith's sense) of society, but at the same
time warns against the dangers of transferring this notion onto the collective
level. His caricature of a figure who is not content to "insure his dwelling
against fire" but who undertakes to "insure all people against all happen-
ings of everyday life, even the worm in the apple or the piano out of tune"
(*OP* 234), is made a great deal more sinister by his reference to the reifying and stereotyping mechanisms of totalitarian systems. But this is not, we
understand, because these systems really distort or deform humanity. Referring to H.G. Wells' futurist dystopia in *War of the Worlds,* Stevens argues that
"when Mr. Wells creates a world of machines, a matter-of-fact *truth* about
the world in which we live becomes clear for all the fiction" (*OP* 234 My italics). Considered as a piece of literature, then, the essay can be said to decon-
struct both the mechanical metaphor and its implied opposite, the organic.
While he acknowledges the vision of a mechanical universe as a "truth" of
human existence, Stevens characteristically suggests that such a truth neither
is nor should be considered as final. As political rhetoric, however, his argument demands that the reader assume both the desirability and possibility
of an organic and mobile social system, as an antithesis of the stereotyping mechanics of socialism and fascism. This anti-mechanical ideal may be
embodied, his Jeffersonian argument implies, in the vigor, spontaneity and
creative dynamism safeguarded by the best parts of the American cultural
and political heritage.[55]

Stevens concludes by arguing that the capacity of private insurance, as opposed to social security, must rely on a degree of *solvency,* whether of cash or of human capacity, the necessity "that each of us, in his own job, *has* to give" (*OP* 237 My italics). There is an obvious affinity between the idea that having (and perhaps taking) is a condition for giving, and Stevens' defence of poetry in the thirties. In this period, three decades after his first arrival in New York, having accumulated considerable wealth and life-long economic security, the economic metaphor for poetry becomes highly relevant to a consideration of his poetry and poetics. At a time when politics and economics were more obviously linked than ever before in American history, the material base for existence was more likely to be understood as a condition of possibility, ensuring (insuring) a durable capacity to perform. As one of the *Adagia*—his sprawlingly diverse and contradictory collection of proverbs written from 1934 to approximately 1940—formulates it: "Money is a kind of poetry" (*OP* 191); a poem or a poetic image is, in the words of *Ideas of Order*'s "Lions in Sweden," a "sovereign of the soul" (*CP* 124–5).

Accordingly, just as the activities of the insurance business should be "adapted to the changing needs of changing times (provided they are conducted at a profit)" in order to "endure on the existing basis" (*OP* 237), poetry needs both a sense of authority and stable credibility *and* to be constantly mobile, inclusive and attuned to rapidly shifting perspectives. Even if it has to be reliably *itself* before putting itself at risk, it can only insure itself by actively seeking out and confronting the "anti-poetic" aspects of reality. These difficult exigencies are essential to Stevens' trials of device as defined in this period, and reveal two different aspects of his poetics. On the one hand, it has a clear projective orientation, as in the intent declared in "Man and Bottle" (*CP* 238–9) to destroy "romantic tenements of rose and ice / In the land of war" and as in the famous formulation in "Of Modern Poetry" (*CP* 239–40):

> It has to be living, to learn the speech of the place.
> It has to face the men of the time and to meet
> The women of the time. It has to think about war
> And it has to find what will suffice. It has
> To construct a new stage.

This forward movement of modern poetry, however, simultaneously implies a 'defense of poesy.' The scene of many of Stevens' poems before the end of the thirties implies a world in which poetry is losing (or has already lost) its aura, its legitimacy and uniqueness of essence. Poetry is no longer the poet's *property,* guaranteed by the hierarchical foundations of poetic discourse, and the "ivory tower" is turned into a tower of Babel in which language is dysfunctional, out of expressive control, troublingly exterior. Poetry's loss of a proper language is, however, also imagined as a lack of a proper place for poetry and the poet, a sense that I will soon explore. In both senses, Stevens' poetry is acutely sensitive to the risk of being devoured by the disorderly (which may also mean *too* orderly, unchanging and unchangeable) exchange of discourses in modern culture. Stevens' thirties thus offer a dark, Heracleitan view of existence, whose utter violence, now an essential aspect of the civil society that was supposed to tame it, must be resisted. In such a world, far removed from Locke's notion of a 'state of nature,' poetry is both the means and the goal of cultural resistance.[56]

As the reference to H.G. Wells suggested, nature is in this period itself frequently likened to a sort of mechanics: in section XLI of *Ideas of Order's* "Like Decorations in a Nigger Cemetery" the image of a natural mechanics is ominously defined as a 'truth' underlying sensory experience:

> The chrysanthemums' astringent fragrance comes
> Each year to disguise the clanking mechanism
> Of machine within machine within machine. (*CP* 157)

This understanding of nature also implies humanity, which is compared to the lower ranges of animals, as in the "mechanical beetles not quite warm" of "The Man with the Blue Guitar." This notion of reified humanity is also a question of the way people live. In Robert Frost's contemporary "Departmental" (1936) the life of ants, defined by its automatism, its unethical and unfeeling bureaucracy, establishes a disturbing analogy with humanity which reflects on both the tenor and the vehicle of the metaphor: while animal existence is humanized in a negative sense, human beings are compared to mechanical, insignificant and unthinkingly obedient ants—the ideal animal representation of 'workers.'[57] Crucially, Frost's poem is an implicit critique of urban life; if human beings, like ants, are all too departmental, they also dwell too *apart*mentally.

Stevens' contemporary unease with city housing is very ambiguous, and often related to his sense of poetic language. In "The Man Whose Pharynx Was Bad" (*CP* 96), included in the second edition of *Harmonium*, the speaker's complaint of being mute, incapable of speaking poetically, is closely linked to a state of ontological imprisonment: the bad pharynx and urban isolation are intertwined aspects of his affliction. The speaker is "too *dumbly* in [his] being *pent*" (my italics) and remains unaffected by Nature's momentous seasonal changes:

> The wind attendant on the solstices
> Blows on the shutters of the metropoles
> Stirring no poet in his sleep, and tolls
> The grand ideas of the villages.

After hinting at the possibility of transcendence—"Perhaps, if winter could once penetrate / Through all its purples to the final slate" the poet might begin "spouting new orations of the cold"—the desolateness of the poet's situation is confirmed in a pounding iambic pentameter:

> One might. One might. But time will not relent.
>   x   /   x   /   x   /   x   /   x /

While this line could certainly be 'scanned' as iambic pentameter, this is made almost unavoidable by the punctuated isolation and repetition of first two identical 'iambs,' which generates a sense of integrity and monotonous succession which readers are likely to project onto the final six syllables. Pentameter, or an iambic rhythm, is clearly not semantic by itself, but its introduction into the semantic structure of this poem may function as a metrical 'coding' of an inescapable predicament. Stevens, we could say, uses iambic pentameter both 'iconically' and 'ironically' in this poem, recalling a traditionally high poetic mode—used with less irony in poems like *Harmonium*'s "Sunday Morning" and "To the One of Fictive Music"—while exposing it as inappropriate and, as such, part of the poem's image of closure. In this sense, the poem indicates an important aspect of Stevens' peculiar involvement in modernist formal change. If the man's illness, as Dennis Taylor has suggested, amounts to having "a meter stuck in his throat,"[58] or even that his vocal cords are metrical, the automatism and routine of sloppy, repetitive convention equal the impasse of expressive closure which, as the poem formulates it, produces not only a "malady of the quotidian" but expressive impotence.

A further, or different, kind of irony in Stevens' rhythmic language will be central to this study: the way that, beyond its positive or negative *associations,* a metric pattern may, as Aviram argues, yield "an unreadable physical effect (rhythm and sound)." Thus, while "the rhythm . . . is first seen as merely an allusion to a tradition . . . the degree to which its energy escapes the definition of mere tradition is revealed."[59] This rhythmic potentiality of meter, central to Slavic Formalism as well as what Aviram calls the "Nietzschean" tradition of thought,[60] is crucial for Stevens' complex re-use of metric structure—or, as above, metric "stricture"—in the rhythmic and semantic sequences of his poems: while the common meaning of conventional poetic language will be as empty of meaning as that of 'sound itself,' the latter—as for Aviram—may constitute a critique of or alternative to poetic normalcy.

The fact that the modernist "break" with the material confinements of oppressive form (timidly suggested in this poem's wistful "perhaps") was never quite realized as such in Stevens' modernism is significant. This is not least because his poetry's imagined creative space—contrary to Whitman's imperative—*is* the private sphere of the urban apartment, and because the isolation it provides, on the model of his early poetry, makes its urban quality much less visible as it causes or, from another perspective, *allows* the poet to blind and deafen himself to the exterior. Furthermore, it is essential that such privacy, like the individual 'vision' enabled by poetic language, is never to be taken for granted. These elements of Stevens' poetry of rooms—a figure of his "trials of device"—are closely related to his complex sense of the capacities and shortcomings of poetry. One of the most important explorations of this dilemma, "Mozart, 1935" implies that poetry may be made possible—while also, in Whitman's sense, made impossible—by the uncertain possession of a piece of mass-produced real estate in the midst of a threatening chaos of urban dispossession.[61]

PLAYING THE PRESENT: "MOZART, 1935"

In a letter of November 5, 1935,[62] to Ronald Lane Latimer, his most important correspondent in the thirties, Stevens mentioned a couple of poems, "Mozart, 1935" and "A Fading of the Sun," which deal with an issue "very much at heart," "the status of the poet in a disturbed society, or," he adds, "for that matter, in any society" (*L* 292). This added comment implies that the current pressure of reality was part of an eternal process or force perpetually calling for imaginative renovation and readjustment. It can be understood to naturalize, and neutralize, the particular urgencies of the particular year 1935 and, in the same gesture, the disapproving voices of his contemporary realist critics. Filreis has suggested that Stevens' argument was similar to that of The Hartford's publicity agents who argued that "[t]his particular depression was just one of many the Hartford had already endured."[63] The fact that "Mozart, 1935" (*CP* 131–2) itself defies this idea, however, can be seen in the unique verbal gesture of the poem's title—the only time, to my knowledge, that Stevens included a reference to a particular year in a poem—which implies that the poem should not simply deal with the modern world as with *any* troubled society. Furthermore, its reality is urban and, as such, cannot, in spite of the poem's efforts to this effect, easily be naturalized into an aspect of what Stevens would later call 'the weather.' Written during a business trip to Key West, it is thus crucially different from the critically esteemed "The Idea of Order at Key West" (*CP* 128–30), placed only a few pages before it in *Ideas of Order,* in which a female singer, figuring the need to humanize what Schiller called "nature's terrors," becomes able, in fluid blank verse, to become "the single artificer of the world / In which she sang."

"Mozart, 1935" shows a deep unease about the notion that art derives, or should derive, its main energy and motivation from itself, that is, from demands intrinsic to the art form, its ruling practices and traditions. This unease, combined with nostalgia of these forms and their underlying vision of art, is closely linked to an intensely social understanding of poetic language. One of the most important implications of the poem's city scene is the notion that artistic "autonomy" is preconditioned on material *qua* economic security. In its description of a separation between the exterior world and the poet, who is allowed—or perhaps forced—to dwell in a 'room of his own,' the poem thus addresses problems that are at the core of both Stevens' own poetics and the 'open road' aesthetics that is still operative in normative debates on American modernism. "Mozart, 1935" will be the first of a number of poems discussed here that describe the search for expressive vitality as predicated on a turn *away* from "the men and women of the time" toward a more original creative impulse, acting on a strongly defensive—possibly both conservative and radical—impulse to preserve the value of poetry through being ex-clusive, 'closing out.'

In the first stanza, the realist imperative defining Stevens' thirties is represented in the voice of a ponderous instructor who makes demands on a pianist/poet which the poem, as I will argue, will ultimately be unable to fulfill. [64] This voice—prefiguring the one uttering "Begin, ephebe" at the beginning of "Notes"—appears as a kind of Maecenas who has provided the poet/pianist with his instrument and an apartment located in a neighborhood of great dereliction and human misery. This predicament may recall the material plight and uncertain existence of the real Mozart, whose genius was appreciated by very few and who frequently lived in economically precarious situations, depending on dreary teaching work and the beneficence of the wealthy and powerful. The discrepancy indicated in the title's components, *Mozart* and *1935,* two distinct entities that the poem needs to bring together, is explored in a musical and sonic metaphor defining the piano's sound possibilities. The association with Mozart rather than with modern composers like Varèse or Ives,[65] is revealed as intensely incompatible with the sounds to be "played" on it.

Poet, be seated at the piano.
Play the present, its hoo-hoo-hoo,
Its shoo-shoo-shoo, its ric-a-nic,
Its envious cachinnation.

These sounds, however, have a significant history of their own. In Peter Brazeau's collection of interviews with people who knew Stevens, Judge Arthur Powell, his close friend and companion while on his Florida trips, gives a pair of clues as to their origin:

In February, 1935, we [Powell and Stevens] were at Key West again; and his poem "Mozart" . . . was forming in his mind. In the second and third lines, for sound effect, he uses the phrases, "hoo-hoo-hoo," "shoo-shoo-shoo," and "ric-a-nic." I now have in my possession a scrap of brown paper, a piece of a heavy envelope, with this written on it in his handwriting:

'ses hurlements,
ses chucuotements, ses ricaments.
Its hoo-hoo-hoo,
Its shoo-shoo-shoo, its ric-a-nic.'"[66]

Stevens' use of French and other kinds of foreign diction was not only, as Natalie Gerber has argued, an important element of both his prosody and diction,[67] but was often used ironically to feign the foppery of an effete and conventionally poetic style, a practice which could appear as strongly provocative in the American thirties, when, as Filreis has observed, French was a bold sign of cultural elitism and artistic escapism.[68] Stevens' transformation of these words, which may already be onomatopoetic, into alien sound patterns, can to some extent be understood as a radicalisation of their foreignness, making them more thoroughly intractable and un-poetic—no longer foreign as one national language is to another, but to articulated language as such. In the sense, however, that the sounds replace a familiar sign of aestheticist elitism and conventional poeticity, they may also suggest a movement toward raw, empirical realism.

Crucially, the meaning of the excised French nouns—screams, whispers and derisive laughter[69]—are brought back at different stages in the poem. In the first stanza, the "ricanements," mocking laughter, is indicated in the representation of the sounds of reality as an "envious cachinnation,"[70] which implies that the sound series is not neutral but actively hostile to the pianist. As the next stanza will suggest, this is apparently because of a resentment of his privileges, which gives the poem's sonic and musical discord its distinctly social meaning. The fact that the no longer adequate forms of the imagination are understood as firmly cemented by particular socially, culturally, and materially determined conditions, suggests an ethical as well as aesthetic impasse.

In his letter to Latimer, Stevens writes that "we all feel that there is a conflict between the rise of a lower class, with all its realities, and the indulgences of an upper class" (*L* 290). In the poem, this conflict is embodied in the piano's exclusivity, both because it suggests expressive nobility, in the figure Mozart, and because it belongs to the privacy and comfort of an affluent domestic sphere: shortly after, Stevens made his poet-figure strum a nomadic blue guitar, whose "lazy, leaden twang" (*CP* 169) was less likely to alienate the poor and dispossesed, envisaging a poetic attempt to embrace multitudes of Whitmanian proportions—"a million people on one string?" (*CP* 166).

An interesting view on the nature of these non-sense sounds is Riddel's idea in 1965 that "Mozart, 1935" illustrates Stevens' readiness "[t]o embrace the jazz discordance of his age and supply the softening but not evasive tones of the imagination."[71] Jazz is of course already an imaginative form and as such not simply real, but a modern experimental mode of expression that would contrast with older forms, such as traditional poetry. Also, while jazz could have been regarded as provocative and noisy to contemporary ears, it is not itself chaotically formless. The element of improvisation that is central to jazz is not just a free creation of a gifted subjectivity, capable (to borrow from Pound) of a "precise rendering of the impulse" but also, in its very idea, a mode in which freedom can ideally be consonant (in the root sense of this word) with the freedom of others. Its implicit ideal is, in this sense, to embody the *overcoming* of social, religious and political cleavages, rather than to indicate chaos and disjunctiveness. In Stevens' poem, the sounds represented as reaching the musician from outside (whether sirens, hooting horns, or creaking machinery) are already a poetic representation of reality, a poetic image of the anti-poetic, presented as deviant in, but part of, the internal context of the poem, and, as such, already embraced by and submerged in 'poetic discourse.' The poem has thus already 'formalized,' reduced or 'deformed' the present—which it has located in the suffering of others in the street outside—into nonsensical sound or, in Whitman's words, into "resonance."

The idea of jazz appeared already in Hillis Miller's argument in "Stevens' Poetry of Being," of 1964, where he suggests that Stevens' search for new ways of conceiving of the truth in a post-religious world, resulted in a mode of poetry equipped to deal with two, now disconnected, extremes of human experience, imagination and reality. After the impasse of the thirties, Miller argues, Stevens elaborated a more fluid, mobile and receptive kind of poetry capable of representing the fragmented, contradictory flux of modern consciousness. Miller's idea of a new "fluidity" or "openness" in Stevens' later poetry, obviously akin to the ideals of openness that unite different strands of free verse thinking, was thus based on the notion that his earlier poetry was rock-hard, closed and unreceptive: Stevens' "chief contribution to literature" was "the meditative poems of his later years" which, unlike the "finished unity of his early poems, which makes many of them seem like elaborately wrought pieces of jewelry" are more like "open-ended improvisations."[72] Miller's subsequent reference to jazz—a quintessentially American form of expression highlighting the solo improvisation—may be especially appropriate, it could be argued, at the time of Miller's essay and the decade before—the age of Parker, Monk, Davis, Shorter and Coltrane—when radical experimentation in jazz was rife. But even while invoking music as a model for poetic language, Miller's argument is scant in references to aspects of Stevens' poetry like rhythm, meter and sound patterning, possibly because of his phenomenological focus on the *correspondence* between modern art and modern reality (whether inner or outer, things *as* they are in consciousness or things as they *are*). A close look at poetic patterning, it could be argued, is likely to bring forth 'structural' relations of internal equivalence or closure rather than a representation of an unfolding psychological process. Mutlu Kanuk Blasing has argued that even Stevens' later poetic language can be understood in terms of a conflict between the "freedom" of his argumentative music, the poem "of the act of the mind," and the closures of abstract, *a priori* metrical patterns.[73] Instead of understanding "jazz discordance," like Riddel, as an aspect of chaotic urban modernity or like Miller, as an epistemological principle of artistic cognition, the notion of jazz as a hybrid, exploratory mode of expression, can enable us to grasp the rhythms of "Mozart, 1935," while keeping in mind that an analogy is being made between different cultural phenomena.

The poem often avoids definable metric patterning, but locally establishes persuasive rhythms that are subsequently destabilized or disappointed, as well as hidden, sometimes overlapping, metric figures. The stress pattern of the first line, for example, does not suggest any meter (unless the preposition "at" is 'promoted' into taking a metrical beat, which would be very strained, or if we re-read it in the light of the following lines, assuming a 'peripheral' perception of what comes next). I have notated it as a succession of stressed and unstressed syllables, without metrical beats:

Poet, be seated at the piano
/x   x / x   x   x   / x

In the second line, however, a four-beat rhythm is established, to an extent reinforced by its phonic repetition of the first line's alliteration on *p:*

Play the present, its hoo-hoo-hoo
∠   x ∠x   x ∠   /   ∠

While the third line proceeds to deviate slightly from this pattern, demanding a final 'virtual' beat, the last line strays further from it. To keep the four-beat rhythm, it requires not only an implied beat, but a promotion of a 'weak' syllable that would normally take a secondary stress (*):

Its shoo-shoo-shoo, its ric-a-nic
x ∠   /   ∠ x ∠ x x [∠]
Its envious cachinnation
x ∠ x   ⌐*x ∠ x [∠]

Without ascribing a definite semantic meaning to to the nonsensical sound patterns and pulsating, syncopatically interrupted, rhythms, they are clearly likely to convey something quite different from the beauty, poise and lightness often associated with Mozartian harmony.

In the second stanza, the disturbing noises of 1935 are imagined in more actively threatening anti-aesthetic terms, and are given tangible social and political significance by the pounding of stones hurled by a crowd outside onto the roof of the poet's attic apartment, a terrifying and anything but contrapuntal backdrop to the patterns rehearsed by poet/pianist. This situation, we could well say, is deeply *absurd*—a word we may use for its range of etymological meaning of this word, derived from Latin 'surdus,' meaning 'out of tune,' 'irrational' and, not least, 'deaf.' Such absurdity is manifest in the apparent need for the instructor to explain the turmoil outside to the ephebe, who is both 'out of tune' and 'out of touch' and appears doomed, in the Platonic predicament to be redeemed by Whitman's new poet, to take things not only 'second,' but even 'third' hand:

If they throw stones upon the roof
While you practice arpeggios,
It is because they carry down the stairs
A body in rags,
Be seated at the piano.

This intensely contradictory situation demands an unlikely capacity for simultaneity in Stevens' Mozart, who has to play the present without bursting the doors of his apartment. By itself, the insistent repetition of the injunction to "be seated" and play *in spite of* the turbulence outside, sticking to the arpeggios while listening intently to what is going on outside, may signal that the pianist has begun to find his circumstances insupportable.

Next, the poem temporarily drifts off into a wistful vision of Mozartian art, a nostalgia of the past that is also an idea of a utopian future. This train of thought is interrupted by three suspensive points between line four and five, followed by an unpleasant return to actuality.

> That lucid souvenir of the past,
> The divertimento;
> That airy dream of the future,
> The unclouded concerto . . .
> The snow is falling.
> Strike the piercing chord.

This disruption could be interpreted as a disjunction, of the kind "*but now* the snow is falling and you need to play a *different* music," but this is implausible in the poem's context: the poet is after all practicing Mozartian arpeggios in spite of the pressure of the chaotic outside. Snow in Stevens is often understood, as in many interpretations of "The Snow Man," as an image of the "essential poverty" of a world deprived of cultural order or, reversely, of the decreative imagination which covers, like snow the ground, the ever-moving reality with a coating of aesthetic emptiness. The knowledge, however, that actual people in rags are trying to survive in the cold outside, gives this poem a more ethically chilling character: the metaphorical vehicle comes threateningly close to the realities of 1935.

A few subtle but significant elements of rhythmic tension in this stanza should not go unperceived. Together, the two final lines form a regular iambic pentameter figure with a medial 'caesura':

> The snow is falling. / Strike the piercing chord.
>   x ⌣̲ x ⌣̲x   ⌣̲   x   ⌣̲ x   ⌣̲

This would have been less effective, however, had the last two lines of the preceding stanza not already established a precedent for it. While the first two (eight-syllable) lines of stanza two with some difficulty scan as four-beat patterns, line three (of ten syllables) can, with a fully pronounced beat-taking 'is' and a slight demotion of 'they,' be read as iambic pentameter

It is because they carry down the stairs
x ⌣ x ⌣ / ⌣x ⌣ x ⌣

or perhaps

It is because they carry down the stairs
x x x ⌣ / ⌣x ⌣ x ⌣

with a beat promoting the unstressed 'is' into metric prominence.

This interpretation can be projected onto the next line, where, if we elide the /i/+/i/ sequence (bod*y in*) and promote "at" into taking a beat, we have another—enjambed, or, as Finch has called it, 'split'[74]—iambic pentameter figure, straddling the line boundary as well as the syntactical break (and implicitly intonational, as the voice moves from explaining to giving orders) suggested by both the line break and the comma:

A body in rags,
x   ⌣ x-x ⌣
Be seated at the piano.
x ⌣ x x x ⌣ x

The greatest reward for this interpretive possibility, however, will come in a consideration of stanza four, where the poem continues to look for ways to solve the pianist's dilemma while further increasing its demands on him. Here, the instructor engages the Romantic urgency of Percy Bysshe Shelley's supplication to the West Wind to merge with and empower the artist—"be thou me, impetuous one." The pianist is now requested to become the expressive medium for the sufferers outside, who may (as the poem suggests) be raging precisely because they resent what he is doing. The pianist is 'besieged' or 'beleaguered' by hostile imperatives that give him no other possibility of escape but to express them:

Be thou the voice,
Not you. Be thou, be thou
The voice of angry fear,
The voice of this besieging pain.

The play on pronouns in the first sentence offers a series of interesting interpretive alternatives. The voice may be admonishing the poet to become *the voice* and stop being only himself, in Eliot's sense of an "extinction" of personality in favor of artistic expression. But since 'thou' addresses the pianist, suggesting that he is singularly apt to 'be' the voice, 'you' may, as a plural, designate the others outside, who are not. Furthermore, if the negation of 'you' is understood as a contrast on the level of diction and stylistic value, the archaic 'thou' may be appreciated for its noble sense of poeticity; it is not a simple 'you.' Not excluding any of these possibilities, the last one may explain why "be thou" works both as an injunction and as a poetically sounding phrase, whose nobility is, in turn, challenged by its reproduction as mere material, as a mere sound, moving the reader's perception, as Jameson has formulated it, beyond the "phonemic" into the "phonetic":[75] a strategy to be intensified in the noisy conflict of bird sounds in the middle section of "Notes."

A salient rhythmic feature of this stanza is its consistent 'iambic'[76] regularity, facilitated by the fact that all words except 'angry' and 'besieging' are monosyllabic. The first three lines play upon, as I would like to formulate it, intersecting iambic pentameter sequences. The first two lines together,

> Be thou the voice, / Not you. Be thou, be thou
>   x ∠ x ∠   /   ∠ x ∠ x ∠

and the stanza's enjambed second phrase

> Be thou, be thou / The voice of angry fear,
>   x ∠ x ∠ x ∠ x ∠ x ∠

constitute iambic pentameter figures. These 'figures,' once established, may appear mutually exclusive—there is, one could argue, either one or the other, depending upon what choice the reader makes—and even so they may only be perceived by readers sensitive (or hyper-sensitive) to metric patterning. The perception of such 'intersections,' however, may be part of a rhythmic competence that is likely to be exercised with ease while listening to music of some rhythmic and melodic complexity, when listeners are occasionally compelled to reinterpret an apparently integral rhythmic or melodic figure when a segment of it appears to make sense as part of another unit, or in relation to a different, as yet unrealized, overarching rhythm. As terms like 'figure' and 'pattern' suggest, a description of Stevens' poem in these terms would have to be made by way of visual metaphor: it could well be called a kind of metrical 'overlay' or 'rhythmic palimpsest.'

A poem like this one, given its absence of an all-pervading underlying rhythm, and its frequent interruptions or deviations from established patterns, could be perceived as a-rhythmical and therefore perhaps disharmonious and unpleasant. Even so, it may give us a good idea of the richness of Stevens' rhythmic language. While the total intricacy of its rhythmic, semantic and phrasal tensions cannot be described here, for reasons of "readability" and economy of argument,[77] the poem's combination of metric variation, bombastic repetitiousness and uncertainty may be a powerful source of perceptive tension that interacts with its assertion of expressive and cognitive desire in ways that may not be possible to bring to full consciousness.

In stanza V, the anger and pain of the suffering masses are, again, imagined as a sound; but now the expressive identification of the pianist-poet is imagined as a cathartic or therapeutic 'release' (an etymological meaning of 'absolve') or 'placating':

> Be thou that wintry sound
> As of the great wind howling,
> By which sorrow is released,
> Dismissed, absolved
> In a starry placating.

This transformation of the sounds of the exterior from an ill-sounding and envious "cachinnation" into a desolate but powerful wintry sound, an aspect of nature's merciless seasonal cycles, appears at odds with the poem's highly material staging. As such, it appears largely futile. It certainly does not make it into the concluding stanza, where very little appears to have been accomplished since the beginning, at least if we take the poem's central imperative to imply a need for resolution:

> We may return to Mozart.
> He was young, and we, we are old.
> The snow is falling
> And the streets are full of cries.
> Be seated, thou.

The effect of the emphatic repetition of "we" in the second line is crucial. Without it, the line would constitute a four-beat pattern, realizing the first line's prospect of a fourth 'virtual beat' (imagine: "He was young and we are old"). Instead, the pace is slowed down and given a more 'natural,' less overtly rhythmical, prosodic shape. This may function 'affectively,' both by suggesting a sense of slowness appropriate to the speech of a group of old, tired and dispirited people, and by underlining the wistfulness or melancholy of the speaker's emotional state. These aspects may also be coupled with the "associative" sense of an approximate pentameter, even though the repetition of "we," forming two contiguous stresses, appears locally to discourage a strong sense of rhythmic alternation (which is why I use 'stress' rather than 'beat'). The next two lines, however, may continue this rhythmic suggestion, as they can be experienced as an enjambed, syllabically excessive and stress-timed pentameter figure (with a strain between "*fall*ing and the *streets*" which demands a swift but not unnatural realization to bridge the syllabic distance).

What, then, can the poem's final idea of "return" really mean when the speaker, after all, has implied that a return to the past is both impossible and undesirable? Clearly, the name Mozart, invoked as a "figure of the youth as virile poet"[78] as in the title of the Stevens' Princeton lecture of 1946, represents certain *forms* of the imagination which are posited as resilient to the things as they are of 1935. Mozartian arpeggios define poetry's language as "absolute music," in the sense of referring only to itself and an 'abstract,' autonomous structure of tonal harmony: an arpeggio is a chord realized in time.[79] While the poem insists that 1935 needs the creative principle of Mozart and vice versa, the paradox is that insofar as the "we" of the poem have Mozartian forms at our disposal "we are old," since these forms are merely Mozartian *forms* without Mozart; poetic language without poetry.

The title's juxtaposition, a sort of mini-collage, does not come to signify the straightforward introduction of Mozart *as* Mozart into 1935, whereby the poverty of 1935 is either redeemed or criticized by comparison with (what nostalgic moderns may suppose to be) the youth and nobility of Mozart's era. The idea that "we may return to Mozart" can thus not be a question of cultural rebirth, of bringing back a lost past, appropriating and reviving Mozart as he was. Nor, as the apartment walls make sure, does 1935 absorb and destroy Mozart. Their relation remains, precisely by virtue of the halting juxtaposition, immeasurable and, in the words of the contemporary "Sad Strains of a Gay Waltz" (*CP* 121–2), "full of shadows." Mozart's possible 'presence' is thus not an image of the productive meeting of tradition and artistic innovation but, I would suggest, an ambivalent expression of strangeness or that which Jacques Derrida, in his analyses of "spectrality" (with reference to the same *Hamlet* passage as Eliot) has called an *anachrony:* the fact that a historical moment is defined, or 'haunted,' by imperatives by which our actions and attitudes are forcefully commanded, but which remain inscrutable to us. [80] In describing the failure of music 'lagging behind' the events of the real world, "Mozart, 1935" does not simply discard it as false but presents reality itself as a lack of correspondence between logos and language. The proposal that Mozart, and the forms of art which he represents, can still exist in 1935 suggests a form of cleavage in the present. This gap, however, may ultimately enable poetry rather than undermine it.

In terms of M.H. Abrams' inventory of historically dominant ideas of literary language (all of which are still operative in contemporary 'fictions of form') the instructor's challenge to the ephebe is made in terms of three important models for aesthetic agency. The pianist has to *imitate* reality ("play the present"), to *express* or 'give voice' to it ("be thou the voice of this angry fear") and achieve a *pragmatic* effect in, or on, it ("strike the piercing chord"). The word "piercing," as a piercing through both to reality and to readers (or, if you will, the 'reality of readers') indicates a link between the pragmatic notion and the other two: poetry can be effective not only when it is able to communicate powerfully with people but when it is able to represent or express, after accurate diagnosis, their most urgent concerns. These three theories—all preceding Abrams' consideration of the fourth paradigm, the "*objective* theories" of artistic autonomy[81]—presuppose a dualism between language and reality. Even if this is not unambiguously the case with theories of autonomy they often function as tacit mimetic conceptions: just as Eliot's idea of the 'objective correlative' should be understood in its implication with expressive and mimetic models,[82] the "autonomy" of the poet in "Mozart, 1935," is figured both by his isolation in the urban apartment and in the character of Mozartian music, and is thus strictly subordinated to the fulfillment of the other demands. It is also, of course, severely questioned by his apparent incapacity to fulfill them.

In the ambience of Stevens' thirties poetry, the presence of this *pragmatic* theory makes Abrams' scheme preferable to the one suggested in Hillis Miller's deconstructionist study, *The Linguistic Moment*. Miller argued that the "vitality" of Stevens' poetry is "generated" by an alternation of the three conflicting aesthetic theories of *mimesis, aletheia* and *creation: mimesis,* where "the structure of the poem should correspond to the structure of reality";[83] *aletheia,* or revelation, which assumes that "reality, things as they are, is initially hidden" but may come to light in poetry (understood as "act" rather than thing, "reality" or "truth"); and, finally, the idea "that poetry is *creation,* not discovery," assuming "that there is nothing outside the text," that "meaning comes into existence with language and in the interplay of language."[84] Miller stresses the last theory, whose structuralist lineage is apparent in his explanation of how Stevens' rhythmic language 'undermines' meaning: even if 'the guitar' in "The Man with the Blue Guitar" needs the existence of real guitars for the word to exist as image, "the word *guitar* in this poem, in its interplay with all the other words, effaces *in its poetic operation* any real guitar."[85]

This idea of "the poetic function" in Stevens is clearly based on an interpretation of his later poetry, and does not account for the way it can be seen from within a set of strongly ethical concerns. The "poetic operation" in the scene of "Mozart, 1935," the urge to convert reality into sound, is complicated by the simple fact that "reality" here is first and foremost the empirical realities of others. The wintry sound is a call for justice by people who are outside in the falling snow and risk becoming mere bodies in rags. In this sense, the demand to "be seated" is one that calls the poet/pianist away from a fundamental ethical instinct, to partake in reality, in order to fulfill another ethical imperative, for which he needs to remain bent over his piano in the privacy of exercise: in Stevens, Lentricchia has suggested, Pound's "Make it New!" becomes "Make it Private!"[86] The capacity to deal with reality is here based on a silent and structural counter-violence, implicit in the walls of the pianist's apartment and the cultural and economic order that keeps him there. The prospective Mozart of 1935 is able to listen *poetically* to all sides, as Whitman's poet suggested, only from within the isolation of his room, which on some level becomes the condition for art, even the aesthetic sphere itself. It is thus not only a temporary space needed for learning, but a permanent condition for poetry, which needs to 'have time' rather than be absorbed by it. In "Effects of Analogy," Stevens would defend artistic isolation in the following way:

> The ivory tower was offensive if the man who lived in it wrote, there, of himself for himself. It was not offensive if he used it because he could do nothing without concentration, as no one can, and because, there, he could most effectively struggle to get at his subject, even if his subject happened to be the community and other people, and nothing else. (*NA* 123)

This explanation would not placate the masses gathered outside the poet's apartment, or satisfy his Leftist critics. For Fredric Jameson, Stevens is a perfect example of what he calls the "fundamental paradox of the 'autonomy' of the cultural sphere." This is because in Stevens "the sign [by which I take Jameson to mean any meaningful unit, like a poem] can become autonomous only by remaining semi-autonomous, and the realm of culture can absolutize itself over and against the real world only at the price of retaining a final tenuous sense of that exterior external world of which it is the replication and the imaginary double."[87] While the full implications of Jameson's critique are too complex to deal with here (just as his apparently total separation of poetic sign and the real), his formulation appears as a fairly accurate description of the staging for poetry set up in "Mozart, 1935," where the tenuous sense of reality filtered through the constricting apartment walls is meant to enable the creation of powerful, 'piercing' music. This mode of creative response is very similar to the one we found in the house-room metaphors of Stevens' Harvard and early New York poems.

But even though the poem's scene and its inconclusive resolution may suggest a proto-Marxist understanding of artistic autonomy, it describes something missing in Jameson's critique: the feeling that the poet's isolation is extremely frail, that the fragile apartment walls are the only defense against reality, in Jameson's words, 'absolutizing itself' over and against the poet. Although the masses are hostile because the poet's unethical isolation may make him oblivious to their concerns, the poem implies that an escape from his confinement would have consequences of which they may not be aware: a) the poet/pianist would unethically leave his artistic obligations, b) his chance for individual and idiosyncratic expression would be devoured, and with it his unique possibilities of expressing their concerns, and c) he would simply cease to be a poet. It may well be that the poem exaggerates these aspects, reinforcing social superiority by invoking pity, just as the upper class speaker of a later poem compares his aesthetic plight to the hardship of workers, sighing "I am the poorest of all" (*CP* 200–1). But even though Stevens' ambivalent concern with linguistic and cognitive isolation is different from arguably more liberating versions of modernist poetics—and not necessarily more insightful—it may be a key to get a sense of his poetry's particular power.

One aspect of this is that the linkage between the artistic isolation of the apartment and the autonomous music of the urban Mozart, closely connects the ivory tower of artistic solitude to the 'devices' of traditional poetic language. Words, sounds and rhythms are poetic just because they are associated with poetry rather than because they have a particular expressive or mimetic capacity or a related social purpose. In this sense, they do more than shape the language of particular poems: they define poetry itself as a distinct cultural practice. Clearly, when the ivory tower of the poet's autonomy is safeguarded only by a rented apartment in the midst of a threatening urban chaos, this also affects the way these forms of inherited poetic language are understood and valued: and, ultimately, how they are used.

THE ABSTRACTION OF APARTMENTS:
POETRY AND WITHDRAWAL

A sense of the development of Stevens' poetics from the thirties onwards can be had by looking at changes in, and the partial disappearance of, his images of crowds. The violent, amorphous and intimidating masses of *Ideas of Order*—the "slime of men in crowds" of "Farewell to Florida," the "sudden mobs of men" in "Sad Strains of a Gay Waltz," the rioters of "Mozart, 1935"—appear to be the source of what Walter Benjamin, in a study of

Baudelaire, called "shocks of consciousness."[88] As such, they represent what Lennart Nyberg has called the arguably most common trope in "modern poetry and discussions of it . . . that of the 'pressure of the world,' that is, the sense in which the external world, with its confusing mixture of sense data, invades the mind of the individual and threatens to take over."[89] Stevens' ethically loaded way of handling this pressure was figured in "Mozart, 1935" as a question of both provisional isolation and absolute music.

Unless a mass of people are indeed temporarily moved by a singular intent, momentarily reducing their differences in common action, a crowd is a visual misprision per excellence, as it falsely, if inevitably, reduces an irreconcilable plurality of beings to a singular identity. The multitude at the beginning of the middle section of "Notes," "It Must Give Pleasure," however, figures a linguistically and musically coherent community, whose members are, as Stevens, conjuring up a pre-modern world, would nostalgically express it, "as Danes in Denmark" (*CP* 419), joined by an ecstatic organic nationalism whose most vicious aspects were at the foreground of the poem's historical moment. While this collective offers the gratuitous possibility

> To sing jubilas at exact, accustomed time,
> To be crested and wear the mane of a multitude
> And so, as part, to exult with its great throat,
>
> To speak of joy and to sing of it, borne on
> The shoulders of joyous men, to feel the heart
> That is the common, the bravest fundament (*CP* 398)

the poet's participation in this collective myth is a "facile exercise" which needs to be declined in favor of the hard-won reward of solitary freedom and poetic againstness. The poet, who "as part" could "be part" or "take part" in a jubilant cultural expression needs instead to be "apart" from it, to some extent by evading or actively disturbing, the stereotyping monotony of its "exact, accustomed time." This defines the poet's position as not only distant and unique, but a-rhythmical, and suggests that when the masses are defined as incoherent, chaotic and dissonant, poetry needs to supply coherence, order and form, in order to 'become part' of the world. When they are all too coherent, he needs to avoid cooption and become disruptively off-beat and, in a social, spatial and linguistic sense, "apart."

Notably, both positions suggest that poetry should always avoid serving practical, utilitarian purposes. Its only "use" is its accomplishment of a difference between itself and mainstream culture, between poetry and other forms of discourse, which is also a discrepancy between a poem and the desires and expectations of readers. Blasing argues that Stevens' use of the *conventional* "time" of blank verse "underlines its 'unnaturalness,'" and thus, one could add, its character of a social fact. However, "the *composing* and *experiencing* of the conventional rhythm are temporal processes and have historical reso-nance, thereby locating the experience of time in poetic form rather than in nature. In other words, time appears as a conventional human construct, and we need poetry to restore time to nature."[90] Hence, as I will elaborate further on, unconscious stereotypicality can be disturbed by a consciously assumed and conspicuous one. T.W. Adorno has argued that "[o]nly by immersing its autonomy in society's *imagerie* can art surmount the heteronomous mar-ket. Art is modern art through mimesis of the hardened and alienated; only thereby, and not by the refusal of a mute reality, does art become eloquent."[91]

No definition of these matters can account for all the evasive turns of Stevens' essayistic and poetic argumentation. In "The Noble Rider" he would both propose that the poet "has no social obligation" and develop a notion of social utility—that the poet should "help people live their lives" (*NA* 29–30). The epilogue of "Notes," a poem brimful of abstraction and metalinguistic difficulty suggests—incredibly—that "the soldier would be nothing without the poet's words" (*CP* 407–8). Stevens' complex stance both suggests that poetry's cultural centrality depends on its capacity for mimesis and defines poetic language as essentially evasive or, as critics like Blasing and Riddel[92] have called it, "eccentric." However, it is not *only* incoherent, but needs to be related to his peculiar kind of anti-poetics, and his definition of that which poetry must work 'against.'

At the time of "The Noble Rider," the most absorbing and unsettling aspect of what Stevens called the "general pressure" of reality were the news concerning the Second World War, whose world-shattering, "abnormal" events were "not only beyond our power to reduce them and metamorphose them," but stirred "the emotions to violence," engaging people "in what is direct and immediate and real." In view of the totalitarian threat to Western Democracy these emotions were concerned with "the concepts and sanc-tions that are the order of our lives" and, perhaps, "our very lives" (*NA* 22). Although the poet's faculty of resistance, the imagination, has no choice but to be attached to this pressure, which "is incalculable and eludes the historian" (*NA* 21) it will, and needs to, rally its utmost powers to resist it. The 'general' pressure of reality, however, also included what Stevens called the "normal" facets of an age in which the sceptical "spirit of negation" had "denied" all comprehensive religious and political myths. When the human subject has thus been left forlorn in the midst of a bewildering "intricacy of new and local mythologies, political, economic, poetic, which are asserted with an ever-enlarging incoherence" there can no longer be "any authority except force" (*NA* 17).

To Stevens' mind, these developments were accelerated by democratic massification, the increased accessibility of liberal education which, he complains, is superficial, levelling and stereotyping, the careless dissemination of liberal ideas, the increasing vulgarity of the mass media, and crucially, the growing intimacy in the way people live. "We no longer live in houses," Stevens complains, "but in housing projects," becoming too close, and too equal, with people with whom "we" should not be forced to have anything to do. For Stevens, the lack of privacy, the feeling that "there is no distance" (NA 18), does not simply indicate the ambivalent loathing of the lower classes denounced by Lentricchia,[93] but a modern form of rootlessnes—the understanding that one's home is not necessarily part of one's identity, but may be a milieu hostile to idiosyncrasy and individuality, creating a sense of imprisonment that, as canto II of "It Must Be Abstract" explains, "sends us back to the first idea / the quick of this invention" (*CP* 381). The sterility of civilized life compels us to search for a more original truth (even though the poet will ultimately come to work *against* this "first idea," too). The essential characteristic of the apartment, however, is that it is not a place that can, or even should, be escaped: it is the creative site that Stevens assigns to the modern poet, and which defines the very character of his idiom. Thus, even though the poet is painfully aware that his language does not allow original, primary expression, making him "homeless" or nomadic, he is bound to this domestic—or semi-domestic—image of poetry.

In "It Must Be Abstract," the "ephebe"—learning poet—dwells in an urban attic furnished with a "rented piano" and suffers from an affliction formulated as "a celestial ennui of apartments." This punningly suggests that he is both *apart* from the world, in the sense of "disconnected," and too much *a part* of it, not being able to claim individuality in speech or thought. In canto V of "It Must Be Abstract" (*CP* 384–5), his language is negatively compared to a series of instinctive and violent but also pure and purposive "barbaric yawps": the lion's roaring, the elephant's blaring and the snarling of the bear, which make the ephebe appear as a veritable anti-hero:

> But you, ephebe, look from your attic window,
> Your mansard with a rented piano. You lie
>
> In silence upon your bed. You clutch the corner
> Of the pillow in your hand.

The ephebe's silence, however, equals a tormented form of utterance that can hardly be called speech or voice, but which is extracted, pressed out, from the anguished effort to speak:

> You writhe and press
> A bitter utterance from your writhing, dumb,
>
> Yet voluble of dumb violence.

Following a series of severe negations this final "yet" signals, as often in Stevens, an inkling of hope in unbearable hopelessness. The ephebe somehow manages to overcome his expressive isolation by sounding its very depths, squeezing his ex-pression out from within the strictures (or structures) of his predicament: "writhe," suggesting to 'wriggle' or 'squirm,' is only an *h* away from 'write.' The black humour of these images is summarized in the canto's ironic ending:

> These are the heroic children whom time breeds
> Against the first idea—to lash the lion,
> Caparison elephants, teach bears to juggle.

In view of this apparent mockery of heroism, however, it should be kept in mind that the ephebe's isolation and passivity are in fact defined as a condition for poetic speech. His heroism is the outcome of a willed 'againstness' not only in the face of preexisting fictions or myths that cover or distort the 'mere being' of the natural universe, or disable his possibilities of writing justly about the urban social universe outside his apartment room. He also needs eventually to defy "the first idea" itself, the total absence of fiction which lays bare the intolerably inhuman, merciless and repetitious goings-on of nature (and, possibly, society).

The idiosyncratic 'volubility' obtained from the ephebe's muteness is ultimately a consequence of the fact that he is writ(h)ing in a time and place in which he does not really belong and which he does not own: "From this the poem springs: that we live in a place / That is not our own and, much more, not ourselves" (*CP* 383). Further on, canto VIII asks whether it is possible, "without the help of Viollet-le-Duc"—a painter, as Bloom explains, who puts false fronts on edifices[94]—to escape apartness by composing "a castle-fortress-home" (*CP* 386), an imaginary edifice providing a sphere of nobility (a castle), a defense (a fortress) and offers, unlike the rented apartment, a sense of identity (a home). Even if these images, which recall an organic and hierarchical

feudal society, are only metaphorical projections of an imaginary nobility—
"less time than place, less place than thought of place," as in "The Owl in the
Sarcophagus" (*CP* 433)—they clearly correspond to Stevens' skepticism about
and experience of actual apartment living.

The idea in "Notes" is to substitute the ephebe's particular form of
'apartness' with a stronger sense of belonging, bound up with a voluntary,
and thus more complete, withdrawal from others. Such an isolation would
accomplish a belonging on one's own terms, of which the rented apartment
is at least an approximation. Thus, even though "Notes," in view of the
place where the ephebe lives, is a city poem, it is one in which the city
is hardly visible, except as "roofs," which, as Bloom suggests, may signify
"all dualisms, all imbalances between subject and object, concept and per-
cept."[95] While the city thus incarnates a modern dissociation of sensibility and human reification, its social and cultural fragmentation may also
be an opening to idiosyncrasy and individuality. Stevens' poetry suggests
an essentially paradoxical understanding of the modern city itself, which is
not part of Lentricchia's idea of Stevens' falsifying street-room-mind process. For Stevens, the city itself includes, as much a part of its essence as the
streets, spheres of possible psychic and creative escape: private rooms only a
few steps away from the street which can be purchased or rented if one can
pay for them.

ABSTRACTION AND THE SOUND OF WORDS

Many critics regard the success of Stevens' post-Depression poetry as a result
of his elaboration of new modes for dealing with the pressure of reality in a
poetic idiom that was argumentative, tentatively open-ended and musical
at once. This mobility, I would argue, also marks a transition in his concept
of evasion from being an ethical and political concern to a more individual, ontological one. In "The Noble Rider" lecture, the 62-year-old Stevens,
emerging victorious into what can be considered his artistic 'maturity' while
his poetry gained in critical appreciation, was bold enough to state—half can-
didly, half provocatively—that the poet will, and should, always instinctively
"address himself to an élite" and that "the poetic process is psychologically
an escapist process" (*NA* 30). The provocative power of these formulations is '
partly due to the fact that the polemical charge in the idea of escapism is not
only ethical but epistemological: the refusal or unwillingness to face reality
equals averting one's face from the truth. Modern Anglo-American criticism,
not least in its intimate connection with modernism, has been nothing if
not interested in formulating a solid epistemology of literary form, possibly

because of a deep-seated sense that art's peculiar capacity for truth is fundamental to the capacity for knowledge in literary scholarship.

A possible answer to the ethico-epistemological quandaries of the "Noble Rider" is the suspicion that the "mind pressing back," the very act of 'evasion,' does not really mean what we may immediately think it does. Instead, Stevens expands the usual sense of the word while exploiting its original meaning for polemical purposes. In her discussion of "lyric resistance,"[96] Melita Schaum quotes Stevens' idea in "The Irrational Element in Poetry" (*OP* 224–33), published in *The Hartford Agent* in 1937, that

> Resistance is the opposite of escape . . . Resistance to the pressure of ominous and destructive circumstance consists of its conversion, so far as possible, into a different, an explicable, an amenable circumstance. (*OP* 230)

Resistance, this implies, does not simply mean a refusal to deal with historical, social and geopolitical reality, but the very act of dealing with it poetically. If the term 'escapism' in Stevens' later development of the idea would, by implication, also mean the opposite of its habitual meaning, then Stevens' evasion would itself be closely regulated by the demands of reality. As an immediate consequence of that reality's most urgent imperatives, a poem simply cannot help adhering to, bearing the imprint of, the pressure of reality: 'expressing' reality would also mean to 'press it out.'[97] While Stevens gives an apparently problematic normative dimension to his idea, adding that poetic evasions cease to be vital when they do not "adhere to reality," his rhetoric suggests that this lack of adherence may actually follow from too placid and acquiescent an adherence: in one of Stevens' Adagia we read that "Reality is a cliché from which we must escape through metaphor" (*OP* 179). This 'escapist' movement of metaphor adding itself to, and perhaps covering, the real is part of the larger ambivalence of his poetics, which in the later poetry becomes precisely a question of rhetorical magic or sleight-of-hand. The astounding section IX of "An Ordinary Evening" emphatically and elaborately insists that "We seek / The poem of pure reality, untouched / By trope and deviation . . . We seek nothing beyond reality" only to effect an astonishing 'turn' of rhetorical trickery, incorporating this "beyond" (including the deviant movement of metaphor) in reality itself: "Within it, / Everything, the spirit's alchemicana / Included, the spirit that goes roundabout / And through included, not merely the visible, / The solid, but the movable, the moment"(*CP* 471).

The frequent understanding that Stevens' dissociation from the real—whether positively or negatively regarded—is a consequence of the *abstract style* of his poetry's imagery and sound patterning, points to another important circumstance. The image of the poet confined in his apartment is connected to a notion of escapism and artistic isolation and, as such, is strongly bound up with his ambiguous and critically volatile concept of "abstraction." The contention that "It Must Be Abstract" is in this way central not only to an understanding of "Notes" but of Stevens' poetics as a whole. In the Latin root sense of 'abstrahere,' 'draw away,' abstraction may refer both to poetry and the poet, both artwork and consciousness. In "The Noble Rider" Stevens argues that the modern poet's "own measure as a poet . . . is the measure of the power to abstract *himself* and also to abstract *reality,* which he does by *placing it in his imagination*" (*NA* 23 My italics). To "abstract oneself," however, does not necessarily mean to "de-personalize" oneself. Stevens argued, possibly against Eliot, that "there can be no poetry without the personality of the poet" (*NA* 46). It does however, appear to suggest a personal withdrawal, a retreat from the public effected precisely in order to be able to become *more* rather than less personal. In "Mozart, 1935" such a withdrawal, intimately bound up with the urge to *abstract reality,* on some level involved a dehumanization of that which one withdraws (which also meant: 'from which one withdraws').

B.J. Leggett has singled out two dominant but conflicting ways of understanding Stevens' concept of abstraction, "depending in part on whether [Stevens] is viewed as the Poet of the Imagination or the Poet of Reality."[98] For critics who believe that the primary focal point for Stevens' poetry are the creations of the mind or imagination, abstraction comes to carry its most common meaning, that which is only immanent and, in the words of "It Must Be Abstract," is "never to be realized"; or as Leggett formulates it, that which is "disassociated from the concrete, the specific, the sensuous—that is, abstraction as artifice, idea, concept or generalization."[99] This has often, he argues, informed understandings of Stevens' poetics as disembodied and philosophizing, and, as such, has been a point of censure as well as praise. Jameson, studying Stevens' representations of landscape, typically argues that they create a dehumanized, abstract landscape of the mind only and thus "launder" landscapes of their "cultural and social semantics."[100] Altieri, to the contrary, understands Stevens' abstraction as a process of sifting out—abstracting—the aspects of reality which are not subject to immediate decay, and in which one can therefore believe. This process is one which, in a sense, can be understood as a search for reality rather than an escape or evasion from it.[101] On the other side, Leggett argues, the opposite sense of the word has been applied by many critics. The pre-deconstructionist Hillis Miller, for example, believes that Stevens abstracts in order to "annihilate mental fictions and reach the uncreated rock of reality behind."[102] In this case, 'to abstract' means clearing the thing perceived or expressed of its entanglement with a conventional context which has deprived it of sensuous individuality and particularity. Thus, as Leggett puts it, "in a strange turnabout, the abstract is associated with the concrete."[103]

Re-reading "Notes" in the light of I.A. Richards' *Coleridge and the Imagination*, arguably Stevens' greatest influence at the time of writing the poem, Leggett points out that it was Richards' purpose to overcome the Romantic subject-object (Stevens' imagination-reality) problem by indicating how it was in fact created by fictitious, inherited, language problems. This can become visible by considering the simple fact that all levels of intelligible experience are in some sense abstractions. Richards' psychological 'materialism'—and by the same token Stevens' poetry in "Notes"—thus tries to exhibit the essential link "between the artificiality of our doctrines of experience and what [Richards] calls the 'facts of mind' from which these doctrines originate." In Legget's view, however, this proves that Stevens (through Richards through Coleridge) was already 'beyond' the divide which has polarized his interpreters. This means, he argues, that once "these rival doctrines [the poet of the imagination vs. the poet of reality] are harmonized through the conception of abstraction, the artificial notion of 'reality' is no longer a stumbling block for the imagination. The 'unabstracted and unrepresentable' view [valued by those who see Stevens as the poet of reality] *is indeed present* in the 'concrete fact of mind' [the abstracted mental representation of reality]. However, recognizing the fictive nature of all our efforts to articulate it, the imagination is unconstrained in its pursuit of the myth that, to revert to Stevens' terms, [in "The Noble Rider"] 'gives to life the supreme fictions without which we are unable to conceive of it.'"[104]

I would argue that Legget does not really prove that Stevens ever dispensed with the inside-outside metaphor in which the notion of a gap between imagination and reality is embedded. Nor does his argument refute the fact that the power of Stevens' poetry appears to an extent to stem from its insistence on this trope and its dramatic force. Stevens' rhetoric of the imagination's capacities for inclusion and interdependence does not only imply escape and evasion (his odd synonyms for adherence) but *violence*. The poetic act, in the words of "The Noble Rider," is "a violence from within that protects us against a violence from without" (*NA* 36).[105] Also, 'the fact of the mind' would itself, one could argue, have to be imagined, in the sense that it would have to be represented in order to be apparent. Leggett's notion of Stevens' transcendence is in this sense entirely mental and/or theoretical. The problems of the 'material' of language, which may be both enabling and obstructive for the cognition of 'the fact of mind,' are *real* problems and require insistent work to be, if fleetingly, overcome. Stevens' complex struggle with language, visible not least in his insistent focus on falsity, repetitiousness and sham, looms large to the very end of his poetic career, even if it later appears subordinated to other concerns and managed in a rhetorically flexible medium for linguistic illusionism. "It Must Be Abstract," for example, imagines the abstract in terms of deviousness and sham, as "False flick, false form," but is still indirectly related to the otherness it is charged to reach: it is "falseness close to kin" (*CP* 385). Such tense, loaded images of transcendence imply a simultaneous sense of contiguity and distance rather than the incarnations of anagogy or the participation of synechdoche; Stevens' 'close' is often very close to meaning 'closed.' This is bound up with the ethically ambiguous intuition that poetry, if it is to be understood as valid and true, needs an inside, an autonomy, which means that on some level it needs to *exclude,* close out, even as it wants to get close. What of "the *fact* of mind," for example, in a city full of others who make different, perhaps mutually exclusive claims to the same reality?

It is very instructive to compare Leggett's evaluation of Stevens' abstraction with one which is utterly opposed to his—but nevertheless based on similar assumptions—such as Kent Johnson's comparison of Carl Rakosi's Objectivist poetry and Stevens' poetics. Johnson describes Rakosi's poetry in almost the same terms as those which Leggett applies to Stevens: "[Rakosi's] poetics proceeds from epistemological inclinations that are quite removed from the Kantian antinomies that underlie the bulk of Stevens' verse; instead [of Stevens' language-mind-room abstraction] 'subject' and 'object,' text and world, are held to be fully co-extensive, and mutually implicated, in an unfolding phenomenal field."[106] Crucially, Johnson understands this difference as directly related to their different prosodies: Rakosi's verse, unlike Stevens', is undetermined by the foreclosures of metric patterning, and is thus shaped according to its object or, which is the same, the 'fact' of the poet's 'mind.' While Johnson's idea of the essential connection between prosody and mind is by no means unusual—it underlies, in fact, much of the discourse about free verse—it is clearly difficult to argue that the avoidance of metric form signifies an elimination of constraint on his expression.

Marie Borroff has also linked the problem of Stevens' abstraction to poetic prosody (but without assuming that Stevens' prosody is essentially different from other kinds):

> Poetic statement is language set into form, sequences of words which are and must remain fixed, so that the mind's attempt to give definite expression to its sense of an "always incipient cosmos" . . . is doubly

self-defeating. 'It must be abstract'; 'it must change'; these two equally important dicta regarding the supreme fiction meet each other head-on. The very word *abstract,* it should be noted, is in origin a past participle, designating the result of an action that has already taken place; it properly applies neither to natural nor to mental process.[107]

In terms of Stevens' concrete use of rhythm and sound patterning, the idea of abstraction can be linked to either of the exclusionary positions defined by Leggett. Language may both be experienced as more concrete, in the sense that the word itself stands out in its physical 'materiality,' enabling a form of direct, but semantically hollow apprehension, and as more abstract, in the sense that, as such, it is to some extent withdrawn from the historical world of contextual meaning, when its intended object, or structure of meaning, appears to disappear from view. The sensory quality of poetic language can, as Anca Rosu has argued, be understood precisely as a kind of abstraction, in the sense that it displaces the attention "from representation to pattern," a "transfer of emphasis" which often entails "an *apparent* loss of meaning at a semantic level."[108] While Stevens' abstraction in the sense of the foregrounding of the 'material' of signification, may frustrate 'decoding,' accomplishing a 'defamiliarizing' moment of radical deception and bafflement, it may also, perhaps simultaneously, produce a sense of integration and participation, a heightened experience of language as the physical and semantic aspects of a poem appear to work together.

What rhythmic and linguistic approaches have brought to Stevens studies is the possibility of understanding the process of abstraction pragmatically, in terms of the co-creative experience of readerly response, in light of which the mimetic and expressive aspects of language are likely to recede in importance or change. In this way, Maeder's work is enabled by a more radical attempt at bracketing the imagination—reality problem. Suspending Stevens' and our every-day notion "that the prime task of language is to represent thought, perception, or imagination or . . . that language is the human subject's way of making sense of the world and his or her complex relation to it"[109] she investigates Stevens' manipulations of his printed linguistic medium, "the material body of the poem's trajectories," taking "a hard look" at what she calls "the non- or extra-ontological implications of his particular uses of English lexis and syntax."[110] Even if Maeder's model, happily, cannot help being ontological in the sense that Stevens' poems belong to a particular cultural and historically detemined language, poetry's claims to knowing the world external to it is willfully "banished, or at least attenuated."[111] This emphasis on the non-representational is related to Maeder's interest in the way Stevens' poems offers the "sensuous and nonconceptual pleasure of the direct apprehension of patterns, which we can call aesthetic pleasure."[112]

However, among the metaphors into which Stevens, as Maeder puts it, performs "basic research," the above oppositions are extremely real and constitute a formidable, defining concern for many of Stevens' poems, pervading them all the way down to the significance of its most 'concrete' elements. The 'pleasure' of the constructive abstraction of sound from semantic and contextual sense and, as Bakhtin formulated it in his critique of Russian Formalism, "the elimination of the ideological meaning of the word"[113] is in Stevens' poetry, as I will try to show, tied to a sense of anxiety at the price paid for this elimination, which may itself be understood as an essential component of its creation of meaning.

Chapter Two
Motion and Voice

. . .

His self and the sun were one
And his poems, although makings of his self,
Were no less makings of the sun.

It was not important that they survive.
What mattered was that they should bear
Some lineament or character,

Some affluence, if only half-perceived,
In the poverty of their words,
Of the planet of which they were part

"The Planet on the Table" (*CP* 532–3)

GESTURE WITHOUT MOTION: IMAGINING THE ABSENCE OF THE IMAGINATION

It appears natural to interpret Stevens' first collection of the 1930's in terms of what has often been understood as the fundamental endeavor of his project, memorably—if ambiguously—expressed in "The Idea of Order at Key West": to give coherence to the threatening flux of contradictory modern experience, and provide consolations of aesthetic wholeness. Crucially, "The Idea of Order" imagined this external chaos in terms of nature, rather than, as in "Mozart, 1935" of society. While a 'naturalization' of modernity has 'already' taken place, as it were, 'outside' or 'before' the metaphoric staging of "The Idea of Order," "Mozart, 1935" acted out this ethically difficult procedure in its metaphors and rhythms, with a degree of explicitness which by itself implied that the sound of printed words and human otherness may be contrary, mutually exclusive, even inimical. In "Sad Strains of a Gay Waltz" (*CP* 121–2), its protagonist "Hoon," who in *Harmonium* had "found all form and order in solitude" (*CP* 65) now gloomily discovers that his forms "have vanished." This feeling is closely related to the notion that the "shapes" he had dealt with in creative solitude had not been "the figures of men," whereas now, in a world of "sudden mobs of men" and "sudden clouds of faces and arms," "there is order in neither *sea* nor *sun*."

This replacement of troublesome others with the already "mimic motion" of the sea should, I believe, be recognized as a fundamental aspect of Stevens' imaginative work towards order, and not least because of another implication of this metamorphosis: the way global or collective ideas of order are privatized into affirmative modesty. Art, as in "The Noble Rider," is at crucial points formulated in medicinal (or, as Marx would say, narcotic) terms, as helping people live their allotted lives rather than changing them on a larger scale. Seeing Stevens' "rage for order" as an aspect of his life, Joan Richardson understands *Ideas of Order* as the starting point for a more conscious aesthetics, creating a musical order out of arbitrary historical and natural time:

> Melody, harmony and counterpoint came from events that were not predictable: changes in the weather; the movement of national and world affairs; contact with others, each with particular and different needs. The work of the imagination was to order these "chance" elements against the ground established by the regularly occurring others. This would produce a pleasing whole, a symphony of psalms to the fact of merely circulating with the gift of consciousness.[1]

This suggests that even though poetry's origin is the unpredictable demands of others, and the frighteningly uncontrollable and unstable movement of historical events, this creates a predicament that must itself be redeemed— or be made amenable—by a musical and rhythmizing imagination which 'begins' in unpleasant disorder and 'ends' in shapeliness and harmony. To circulate "with the gift of consciousness" thus implies a state of cognitive mastery, in which the impingements of reality are no longer experienced as disagreeable or challenging. Along these lines, critics have posited that structural order is a property not only of Stevens' *Collected Poems* but in some cases of the methodologies they apply to discover or formulate it.[2]

Such an approach, I believe, is dubious when applied to *Ideas of Order.* Here, its intrinsic tensions, "among" and "in" its individual poems, will not be understood as resolved by, in Stephen Knight's words, an artistic "craft of contradiction," an authorial mastery in perfect control of its materials.[3] Instead, I have understood it as an expression of an aesthetic in crisis, responding in catachrestic ways to difficult but non-ignorable cultural imperatives. This means that its discords will not be understood as complementary, as though different poems describe different phases of the poetic act, nor (in musical terms) as a contrapuntal circling around an essential theme. I will be interested in the way poems employ poetic devices like metaphor, diction, and rhythm to grapple with primary productive dilemmas for Stevens' poetry; and how in this way they may exemplify different facets of the larger historical attempt of modernist poetics to fulfill difficult, perhaps impossible, demands on poetry.

To begin with, I will engage with two poems which assess their own cultural and rhythmic repetitiousness as well as its possible overcoming and, in doing so, clearly propose a withdrawal from a reality shared with others, a social reality, and its languages. Such poems are highly interesting because they link the spatial idea of closure—of the poem, the poet's linguistic dwelling and self-representation, as a closed sphere—with stasis, the opposite of the temporal-kinetic idea of movement. Further, these ideas are linked both to the idea of monotony, which had been scrutinized in one of the dark poems added to *Harmonium* in 1931, "Anatomy of Monotony" (*CP* 107–8), and with a pictorial sense of one-dimensionality, implicit in the lack of shadows in "Sad Strains of a Gay Waltz."

In "Waving Adieu, Adieu, Adieu" (*CP* 127–8) the iambic repetitions of the poem's title initiates a disconcerting meditation on a sense of expressive deadlock. Even if this is a predicament that poetry finally needs to transcend, this poem is chiefly concerned with imagining it, digging deeper into it and confirming it rather than accomplishing a purposive motion 'forward.' In fact, the very notions of "forward and backward," of movement itself, are complicated from the outset.

> That would be waving, and that would be crying,
> Crying and shouting and meaning farewell,
> Farewell in the eyes and farewell at the centre,
> Just to stand still without moving a hand.

Unless the deictic "that" of the first phrase "*that* would be waving" has an implied but unspoken referent (in which case the poem's utterance is part of a larger, unknown, context) it can only be understood as either referring 'back' to the "waving adieu" of the title, thus establishing a tautology—"waving is waving"—an absence of reference which is a mere repetition, or as referring cataphorically to the fourth line, "just to stand still without moving a hand." The 'empty' deixis suggested by the first alternative indicates an absence of the differential and expansive aspects of signification, which are central to the way language can be conceived of as metaphoric, thriving on the deviant movement and perceptual change promised by one of the root senses of metaphor, *metapherein:* the 'transfer' of signification which Aristotle's *Poetics* defined as one of its most important functions.[4]

The fact that there is no longer any 'back' or 'forward' of signification, however, is at odds with the dramatic sentiment attached to "waving adieu," which is intensified in a sequence of incremental verbal substitutions: a desperate "crying" is followed, more desperately, by "shouting," until the effort collapses into a silent and implosive "meaning farewell." As the culmination of this crescendo, "meaning farewell" can be understood both as triumph and bathos, as *more* or *less* than actually being able to 'communicate' or 'perform' the farewell. It appears as *more* if seen as its very emotive core—a "farewell at the center"—its pure intentional content, absolved from the contextually framed, possibly falsifying, contingencies of interpretation and communication. In this abstracted state, 'meaning farewell' not only represents, but *is,* an essential truth, the very core of an act of pure expressive volition, which Jean-Jacques Lecercle argues can be aptly captured by the standard French equivalent for 'mean,' *vouloir dire.*[5]

In the communicative, pragmatic, sense of language, however, 'meaning farewell' is clearly *less* than 'taking farewell': it is a sign without interior referent, without, as in Stevens' very late "Of Mere Being," "human meaning." As an empty gesture or sound disconnected from any *vouloir dire,* it would be alien to all effective truth. "Meaning" would be meaning 'without meaning,' and the one who 'merely means' expressively impotent. In the poem's mixed metaphor, this equals an inability to move, a "standing still": the waving is performed without "moving a hand": an image strikingly akin to the human paralysis envisioned in Eliot's "The Hollow Men" of 1925, where reality is experienced (in a similar sonic-visual-kinetic metaphor) as "Shape without form, shade without colour, / Paralysed force, gesture without motion."[6]

The conditional "would" adds complexity to the poem by situating the action, or non-action, in a sphere of potentiality or possibility rather than actuality. The idea that "waving would be waving" may both mean that 'to wave adieu, if one did it, would be a fruitless waving' and 'if we succeed in seeing reality in a certain way we would see that the movement of waving, as we do it, has neither cause nor purpose.' These interpretations may in fact work together, since the poem's representation of imaginative vacuity is intimately connected to images of indolence or lethargy. This conditional 'hollowness,'[7] however, is the other side of a peculiar form of presence produced by the ways in which the material aspects of language obtrude in the signs and gestures of leave-taking.[8] Presence, activity and movement, we could say, are manifested grammatically and rhythmically in the repeated present continuous verbs indicating leave-taking precisely because these farewells are essentially non-final. In this sense, the poem's agency is to an extent conditioned on its own muteness: its failure to communicate gives it a present of its own.

In a collection of essays on how to teach Stevens' poetry, P. Michael Campbell and John Dolan have called attention to its frequent use of the rhetorical strategy of 'praeteritic antithesis,' by which something negated or subordinated is given prominence in the linguistic space created and occupied by the act of negation.[9] A formulation of "Waving" in these terms would be abysmally complex. It would have to account for how something merely potential becomes present in the act of articulating its potentiality—which in this case would be the presence of a potential absence, perceived by virtue of an 'absence of the imagination,' which, as the late "The Plain Sense of Things" suggests, needs "Itself to be imagined" (*CP* 503). In "Waving," such a sense of absence is not only created by the manipulation of syntactic and semantic structure, but in close relation to its rhythmic movement:

> That would be waving, and that would be crying,
> ⌐ x   x ⌐ x   x ⌐   x   x ⌐ x
> Crying and shouting and meaning farewell.
> ⌐ x   x ⌐ x   x ⌐ x \ ⌐

The first stanza is constituted by a single sentence in which all line-endings coincide with syntactical breaks and/or intonational pauses indicated by commas. The second and third lines begin by anadiplosis, repeating the word ending the preceding lines, signaling an expansion of the preceding statement. The stanza is unrhymed, but rhythmic cohesion between line-endings is provided by the correspondence of falling ('trochaic') endings in line 1 and 3, and rising ('iambic') ones in 2 and 4. In the first line, the deictic 'that' is given intense syntactic and semantic prominence by virtue of its position in a heavily regular rhythmic pattern, taking the first of the two heavy beats in the 'stychs'—two-beat units—of the four-beat line. By drawing perceptual attention to the form of the pointer itself as well as its pointing, this configuration underscores the poem's sense of self-referential vacuity.

Even though there is a statistical dominance of 'falling' stress units in these two lines, the fact that the stanza as a whole—and every second line—

concludes with an iamb, and thus 'returns' to a rising stress unit, suggests a *structural* 'dominance' of a rising rhythm. If we experience the 'trochaic' gerunds as variations on a dominant iambic pattern, which is rhythmically released in the 'iambic' 'farewell,' they may signal a strain or effort in the desire to express and consummate a leave-taking. Insofar as "farewell" and "adieu" are 'expressed' by the actions indicated by these verbs—waving, crying and shouting—they also appear "set off" from them, as though between quotation marks, a factor which may further heighten the sense that the repeated 'farewell' remains nothing more than itself, and only, in the end, 'means' itself. On a more general level, the rhythmic regularity of the stanza may underline the sense of rhythmic structure, on the model of tension-and-release or counterpoint, as confirming the 'endlessness' of stasis evoked in it. A tune, as Wittgenstein observed, "is a kind of tautology" in the sense that "it confirms only itself,"[10] just as the 'waver' "stands still without moving a hand," and 'farewell' is a word or gesture repeated without any significance beyond—before or after—itself.

The second stanza explicitly describes this state as a *predicament,* evoking, like Eliot's poem about 'hollow men,' a 'fallen' world where central fictions have ceased to provide existential coherence. The resulting absence of order, a chaos, is here manifested as an intense experience of immobility and one-dimensionality. The complex work of describing a lack of order, and imagine an ending which is not also, on some level, a beginning, is acted out in different manipulations of the heavy four-beat pattern passed on to it from the first stanza.

> In a world without heaven to follow, the stops
> x x ∟   x   /   ∟ x x ∟ x x   ∟
> Would be endings, more poignant than partings,
>   x   x ∟ x   /   ∟ x   x   ∟ x
> profounder,
>   x ∟ x
> And that would be saying farewell, repeating fare-
>   x ∟ x   x ∟ x \ ∟ x ∟ x \
> well,
>   ∟
> Just to be there and just to behold.
>   ∟ x x   ∟ x   ∟ x x ∟

There is now an increase in grammetrical tension between syntax and rhythmic patterning. The metric isolation of the final iamb ("the stops") which syntactically belongs to another four-beat phrase ("the stops would be end-ings, more poignant than partings") draws attention both to the significance and the sound of the word, and thus underlines its sense of interruption. As a disconnected subjective noun phrase that syntactically needs to "run on" to its verb, it is both left hanging—enjambed—at the end of a line, *and* syn-tactically crosses over into the phrase it belongs to. As such, it is the center of a strain that destabilizes an interpretation of the poem's rhythmic shape, bringing about a hesitation of whether to give perceptive primacy to the unit of the line or the unit of the phrase.[11] A similar pressure is condensed in the modifier "profounder"—'hanging' below, yet part of, the second line—whose apartness is intensified if we experience it as belonging, as a late addition, to the phrase beginning "the stops."

This is not to say that an interpretation of the first two lines as four-beat units is simply 'false': it would certainly be justified by a sense of rhyth-mic regularity passed on from the first stanza, as well as the stress-timing possibilities of English. However, the syntax now works against this inter-pretation, disturbing the rhythm established by the first stanza, even if we may feel that the new the strains put on rhythmic perception to some extent highlight and reinforce the initial rhythm. Taken as a whole, the third line is likely to be experienced as a five-beat sequence since its five primary stresses conform to an established triple rising pattern. However, the stanza's initial repetition of the poem's deixis,

> And that would be
> x   ∠   x   x

appears to indicate what succeeds it as an integral, separate, four-beat segment:

> saying farewell, repeating farewell
> ∠ x   \ ∠   x ∠ x   \ ∠

a figure that is repeated in the four beat phrase of the last line, which also echoes the rhythms of the first stanza:

> Just to be there and just to behold.
> ∠ x x ∠   x ∠ x x ∠

In the idea that "the stops would be endings," the 'would' is again sig-nificant as it points to one of the essential difficulties of Stevens' project.

Indicating possibility or potentiality, it tells us that the world without heaven 'to follow' (possibly meaning both 'that which can and should be pursued or strived for,' and that which, in religious terms, will 'come after' worldly existence) *is* not, does not yet exist, but can only be imagined and, the poem implies, *should* be imagined. In this view, the intent of "Waving Adieu" would not primarily be to create order in an a-human world in which it is lacking, but to defictionalize, de-humanize, an existing human order in an effort to imagine its chaotic absence, which is also to imagine the absence of the contextualizing, connecting force of the synthetic imagination. Having accomplished this, we may reach a pure seeing, just to "behold," a notion that would either contrast with, or complement, a 'humanist' view that the poem expresses a melancholy produced by the incapacity to move and to say good-bye. There seems to be an attempt to communicate a lack or impossibility of melancholy as such, an incapacity, even of the poem itself, to perform tearful farewells: the endings, we have learnt, are "not partings," but a sort of freezing of motion and the eradication of any spatial relation of distance or nearness.

Logically, any attempt to give meaning to a chaotic existence deprived of its central fictions first needs to validate itself by claiming that there *is* no 'real' or 'true' order to be found in the remnants of those fictions. Since the 'order' they provide, insofar as it at all exists on some level, is not 'poignant' or 'profound' enough, reality needs to be peeled down to "The Plain Sense of Things," which, in Stevens' later poem with this title (*CP* 502–3), "Had to be imagined as an inevitable knowledge, / Required, as a necessity requires." The 'sense' of this title may both indicate that which is (humanly) meaningless and a fullness of sensory experience, but also that phenomena which are divested of cultural meaning by the operation of the human imagination may come to mean more fully and more truly. Stevens was to formulate this ambiguity of modern creativity in a letter to Hi Simons on February 18, 1942:

> When a poet makes his imagination the imagination of other people, he does so by making them see the world through his eyes. Most modern activity is the undoing of that very job. The world has been painted; most modern activity is getting rid of the paint to get at the world itself. (*L* 402)

A poet, as his poetry suggests, may not only create or imagine—i.e. 'paint—but also, if understood as part of "most modern activity," undo previous imaginative work, get rid of the paint. In "Waving," the word "behold" recalls *Harmonium*'s "The Snow Man," where to "have a mind of winter" was needed in order to perceive the presence of an utter imaginative absence, "nothing that *is not* there and the nothing that *is*" (*CP* 10). Even though the word 'behold,' as Bloom has pointed out,[12] suggests activity, motion and participation rather than passive reception, the fact that in "Waving Adieu" it contains a phonemic-phonetic echo of "be there" suggests that it is also approximate to "be hold," or (as the poem will later confirm) to "be beheld," obliquely suggesting the idea of being "held" captive. Thus, it implies that what is apparently actively and thus, in a sense, "freely" imagined is really an inevitable necessity.

Stanzas 3 and 4 initiate a shift in both rhetoric and prosody that enables a sense of verbal exploration or groping for resolution. Together, the two stanzas consists of a single sentence and replace the forcible, 'closed' rhythmic repetitions of the first two stanzas, tenser in the second one, with a principle of repetition (prepared for at the end of the second stanza) based on the reiteration of infinitive phrases at the beginning of lines and phrases. However, the fact that the end of the sequence returns to the vocabulary ending the second stanza suggests that the sequence of infinitive phrases is subsumed into the repetitiousness of the 'conditional present continuous' of the preceding ones. Thus, what may first appear to indicate a change or opening finally leads back to the point at which the poem started. The poem closes, we may say, without conclusion.

> To be one's singular self, to despise
> The being that yielded so little, acquired
> So little, too little to care, to turn
> To the ever-jubilant weather, to sip
>
> One's cup and never to say a word,
> Or to sleep or just to lie there still,
> Just to be there, just to be beheld,
> That would be bidding farewell, be bidding farewell.

To be one's "singular self," *if one could* (the poem suggests one should), would not only be to bid farewell but perpetually to "*be* bidding farewell," to "*be* waving adieu": the gerund is now part of a non-finite infinitive clause, defining these de-personalized activities as constitutive of existence. Defining the individual as isolated in self-identity, the phrase "To be one's singular self" turns the copular use of 'to be,' which would normally link two different terms, into an existential one: it is just to be.[13] This inward turn is simultaneously envisioned as a turn to the natural world. It is "to despise the being that yielded so little" and, finally, "to turn to the ever-jubilant weather." The "being that yielded so little" ('being' should be understood as a verb as much as a noun here) must therefore be different from or in between the 'weather,' the purely exterior, and the 'singular self,' the purely interior (what one of Frost's poems called "inner and outer weather"), neither purely the one nor the other. What it must indicate, then, is 'being' in complex involvement with a reality of others, a common yet discordant world of collective but conflictive fictions and languages.

The last stanza describes this perpetual leave-taking as a form of 'practice,' distinguishing the speaker's kind from that of others:

> One likes to practice the thing. They practice,
> Enough, for heaven.

It is not immediately clear who those who practice "for heaven" are, but the formulation clearly implies a separation between people who still have a heaven to follow, and the poem's speaker whose 'practice' of 'the thing,' 'waving adieu,' is non-final and constant: the to-God of the poem's à-Dieu is, as I have argued, either pure meaning or mere gesture, either more or less than the purposive practices of other people. The difference between the atheist speaker and the religious others is also formulated as a difference between necessity and pleasure, vocation and vacation, between those who *need* to practice the thing, since their final leave-taking (as they believe) will initiate a transport into heaven, and one that, although the sense is also that he *has* to do it—and cannot *but* do it—tries to claim to enjoy doing so.

The individualist naturalism opposed to religious belief in the successive invocations of the "singular self" and the "weather" implies that the poem's repetitive 'waving' receives a purpose and sanction somewhere in its likeness to the repetitiousness of nature. As a kind of resemblance that is part of what it resembles, then, we could call it *anagogic*. However, the poem's final affirmation, in the form of a rhetorical question embedded in a stylistically abrupt hyperbaton, comes at the price of excluding the possibility that "spirit" can be found anywhere else than in pure, extra- or a-human nature:

> Ever-jubilant,
> What is there here but weather, what spirit
> Have I except it comes from the sun?

Edmund Wilson, one of Stevens' sharpest contemporary critics, claiming that his objection to the poem was "not so much an aesthetic one as a moral one," declared that the poem's ending was "distasteful."[14] The idea that common, conventional fictions are 'lies' to be cleansed by a

more original language would of course have (and has had) dreadful consequences when transferred to politics, even if the utter lack of heroism in
"Waving Adieu" makes it not very daunting. Indeed, the poem suggests
a privatizing, indolent withdrawal that implies a renunciation of cultural
influx and, along with it, any possibility of exerting cultural influence. It
is certainly quite unlike the experienced yielding to necessity at the end
of tremendous effort central to Vendler, who sees Stevens' final achievement as a dignified, merited old-age disconnection from worldly concerns
in his late poetry,[15] a maturity which encapsulates the energy of all previous exertion. The turning away of "Waving Adieu" indicates nothing
but infirmity: the "being" that has not yielded anything is simply avoided
(or evaded, but without the synthetic connotations of his later idea): the
speaker merely gives up instead of 'trying again.' Thus, his silence is not
a harmonious, transcendent, semantically loaded one—a speech cleared
of its material mediation—but the muteness of somebody who wants to
speak but cannot, who merely sleeps or "lies there still" and, unlike the
bed-ridden but paradoxically voluble "ephebe" of "It Must Be Abstract,"
remains silent.

EXPUNGE THOSE PEOPLE: POETRY'S EXCLUSIVE MOTION

To some extent, "Waving Adieu, Adieu, Adieu" suggests that the naturalist turn 'away' from modern social being is both difficult to imagine and
ultimately insufficient, not least since at this point in Stevens' career it is
difficult to imagine a turn from the 'form' that the sun takes in common
discourse—as conventional myth, metaphor or wasted and all too material
poetic device—to the sun itself, worshipped by the pagan ring of men at
the end of "Sunday Morning" (*CP* 66–70). The feeling that the romantic
turn to nature in search of truth and power is already a commonplace of the
collective imagination is central in another poem in *Ideas of Order*, "Sailing
after Lunch" (CP 120–1), which also deals intensely with a sense of stasis.
Unlike "Waving," however, which describes an elaborate repetition of itself
(since what could be taken for its predicament is actually the thing sought
for), this poem, which Stevens placed first in the original 1935 *Alcestis Press*
edition of *Ideas of Order*, makes a distinct claim to movement, visible in the
change between stanza one through four and the rest of the poem. While
the first part states the poem's predicament, the second suggests a way of
moving out of it; a 'movement' toward closure in a double sense—both in
terms of 'resolution' and of a 'sealing off' of poetic language from social
discourse. This movement, as I will show, is effected both in its rhythmic

motion and its rhetoric, which also effects an alteration of the scene, the basic coordinates for the poem's metaphorical agency.

At the poem's beginning, its speaker is caught up in the sad dilemma of riding an "old boat" that goes nowhere, stuck in a circular motion that is more like a non-motion, and merely confirms the inescapability of its stasis. This bind, barring the poet from artistic truth, has an important ethical aspect: the speaker is imprisoned in a 'reality' determined by others, *of* others, to which his discourse is both bound and responsible. If the poet, as in "Waving," can be "beheld," both seen and seized, by others and their discourses, the spirit of the romantic—in its etymological sense of 'wind'—is also 'held' back, or down, by these people. This anxiety about the public's encroachment on the private sphere has been explored by Louis A. Renza in the context of *Harmonium,*[16] but I would argue that it becomes intensified as Stevens' poetic language faces more insistent ethical and ideological demands. In this sense, "Sailing after Lunch" relates directly to Stevens' concern with a revaluation of the idea of the 'romantic' to which, as he explained in a letter to Latimer on March 12, 1935, he wanted to give a less pejorative sense (*L* 277). Much like his poetry's re-use of traditional device, Stevens' theoretical discourse often attempts to squeeze new—less 'pejorative'—meanings from (or into) concepts like "romanticism" "escapism," "evasion" and "abstraction," rather than inventing new vocabularies.

The boat's crippled movement at the beginning of "Sailing after Lunch" is due to the feeling that the word 'pejorative' "hurts," meaning that the bad sense heaped on the word 'romantic' by common opinion is what inhibits poetry.

> It is the word *pejorative* that hurts.
> My old boat goes round on a crutch
> And doesn't get under way.
> It's the time of the year
> And the time of the day.

Although the syntactic relation between the first three lines and the last couplet is not clear, the penultimate line's "it" can either account for a state of things for itself, or, more probably, serve as an explanation of the cause of the circular movement of the old boat: 'it' (the above) 'is to be blamed on' this particular time. In both cases, however, "the time of the year" and "of the day" lack a clear reference (the time of the year that . . . or the time of the day when . . .). This suggests that it simply designates "the time" . . . , a time that merely ticks on, unrelated to anything but itself, and which, moving with an impervious and monotonous regularity, does not really move at all. This monotony, however, is not simply a chaotic monotonous repetitiousness of primeval nature, the frightening naturalist sublime of "Anatomy of Monotony," but the monotony of convention, the predictable happening of the all too expected, and the habits of thinking that prevent us from seeing anything else: the anathema of the Slavic Formalist ideas of "perceptibility" and "deautomatization."

In this sense, the "time" of "Sailing after Lunch," codified in the rising triple rhythms of the stanza's last couplet, is not just what Frank Kermode, in *The Sense of an Ending*, called *chronos*, a pure succession of natural time that needs to be humanized[17] and which he, frequently quoting Stevens on the purposes of modern poetry, identifies with the 'fallen' state of a modern world without, as it were, 'heaven to follow.' Kermode's idea of 'fictionalization' describes a desire to make a differentiated, rhythmical "tick-tock," humanly meaningful time—*kairos*—out of what would be a repetitious and non-differential sequence of tick-tick—a 'mere successiveness' which is *in*human in the sense of 'raw nature.' Stevens' later "The Pure Good of Theory" (*CP* 329–33) describes the struggle of the mind, "silent and proud . . . that knows it is destroyed by time," defined as "the hooded enemy, / The inimical music" to be overcome by an imagined "large-sculptured, platonic person" free from it. Here, his rhetoric—frustratingly for those who want to use it as a set of defining propositions—not only contradicts his recurrent repudiation of sculptures as unreceptive to the incalculable changes of historical time, but also goes against a different, complementary but perhaps more significant notion of time: that a clock, such as the one Kermode refers to, is *already* a human tool for cognitive measurement of time as something that we need to understand and order. Part XLVI of "Like Decorations in a Nigger Cemetery" (*CP* 157) invokes a world in which

> Everything ticks like a clock. The cabinet
> Of a man gone mad, after all, for time, in spite
> Of the cuckoos, a man with a mania for clocks.

An archaic meaning of 'cabinet' is a small room, and it may here metaphorically suggest the man's mind. It follows that to humanize and rhythmicize the clock's 'real' sounds we need first to have dehumanized it, imagining it outside of any perception or, in Heidegger's terms, outside of any context of use. As a matter of raw nature, the clock's ticking would signify the reverse side, as Adorno and Horkheimer argued, of the rationalist project of modern civilization taken to its 'natural' extreme: time is an all too human tick-tock that has itself become static and "without motion," like the relentless time of "The Man Whose Pharynx Was Bad." Thus, in order for the poem's boat to start moving, its fictive forms need, as Kermode suggests, to be 'humanized.' However, we also need to understand this to mean 'de-humanized.'

In the second stanza, the *mal* of the poem's sailor is figured as a gastric discomfort, the result of a bad meal: "Perhaps it's the lunch that we had." This ailment, the poem suggests, is produced as a disappointment: the speaker has eaten but feels that he should have had better food ("the lunch that we *should* have had"). This lack of appropriate nourishment, the poem suggests, is a consequence of inappropriateness, of being out of place:

> But I am, in any case,
> A most inappropriate man
> In a most unpropitious place.

If the poem's space, as Kenneth Burke proposes, constitutes a 'scene' for poetic agency, the idea of inappropriateness suggests that there is something wrong either with the scene or the agent, with the poet's place or the poet himself. Since the need for the romantic, as Stevens explained to Latimer, was "constant," and since "without this new romantic one gets nowhere" (*L* 277), the effort at making the inappropriate man appropriate will be to change the scene and not its agent, "to create," as in "Of Modern Poetry," "a new stage." After imploring "Mon Dieu" to "hear the poet's prayer," the poem envisions the romantic's way of empowering itself as an effect of a constant dissolution of its own exclusivity. The demands made on the 'new' romantic are severe, suggesting a radical necessity for discursive resistance and perpetual critique. In order to achieve a new form of centrality it must lead a nomadic existence, effecting an ever-elusive motion, a perpetual movement 'away':

> The romantic should be here.
> The romantic should be there.
> It ought to be everywhere.
> The romantic must never remain,
> Mon Dieu, and must never again return.

The limitlessness and ubiquity of the new romantic, implying the inclusive extension of the imagination and the subject matter of poetry to all, even the "impure," forms of life, is thus conditioned upon an increased elusiveness. It must be removed from the intersubjectivity of common perception, and thus into another form of more ex-clusive 'purity.' What "one is always doing" in order to create the necessary 'new romantic,' Stevens told Latimer, is to keep "the romantic pure; eliminating from it what people speak of as the romantic."[18] To salvage and safeguard its 'nobility,' poetry has to be as omnipresent and elusive at once as the Scarlet Pimpernel, the foppish character saving French aristocrats from the guillotine in the British motion picture from 1934 with the same name, based on the Baronness Orczy's novel of 1904. In the film, shown in American theatres at the time, Sir Percy Blakeney (famously played by Leslie Howard) says tauntingly about his *alter ego,* the Scarlet Pimpernel, that "they seek him here, they seek him there, those Frenchies seek him everywhere. Is he in heaven, or is he in hell, that damned elusive Pimpernel?"

To make the romantic invulnerable to "what people speak of," to withdraw it from any taint of convention and thus make it more difficult to recognize, to de-familiarize it and yet affirm its panoptic presence "everywhere," is to make a simultaneous claim to the universal (the imagination is present everywhere and all the time) and the individual (the uniqueness of poems is an effect of their elusiveness and exclusivity, their capacity to resist to common perception). Both aspects of poetry, whether ex- or inclusive, involve a kind of 'clusion,' a closing 'in' and/or a closing 'out,' that are themselves both *mutually* inclusive. They are *both* each other's condition *and* exclusive of each other, since they are opposite, incompatible effects of the same act. In *Spurs,* Jacques Derrida defines writing as a process of force that 'closes in,' both in the sense of welcoming, giving space to (which may also mean to domesticate and imprison) and the ex-clusive process of cleaving, sundering and forcing out. "The style," which in French puns with *stylo,* a ball-point pen, "would seem to advance in the manner of a *spur* of sorts (éperon)."[19] Derrida exemplifies this with the image of a boat that needs to *force* its way ahead: the 'style' is "[l]ike the prow, for example, of a sailing vessel, its *rostrum,* the projection of the ship which surges ahead to meet the sea's attack and cleave its hostile surface."[20] Stevens' boat metaphor in "Sailing after Lunch" is deeply troubled by its 'style,' or lack of style, as an incapacity for both closure and openness.

Before moving toward its final solution, the poem provides an ekphrasis of the anachronistic romantic imagery that people "speak of" pejoratively. The boat's preposterous 'heaviness' suggests both that the new romantic poet carries a heavy traditional burden and that the size and weight of the boat makes it awkward and inappropriate, relating to its scene in a clumsy and ridiculous way. It is not even traversing a painted ocean but a "musty" (as in the colors of a worn-out painting) *lake;* suggestively rhyming with *fake.*

This heavy historical sail
Through the mustiest blue of the lake
In a really vertiginous boat
Is wholly the vapidest fake . . .

Stevens had exploited the difference between lake and romantic ocean
in *Harmonium*'s "The Doctor of Geneva," whose bourgeois protagonist, a
"lacustrine man"—a man of lakes—"had never been assailed by the long-
rolling opulent cataracts" of the sea, but is now overwhelmed by its power, so
that "the steeples of his city clanked and sprang / In an unburgherly apoca-
lypse" (*CP* 24), an image which recalls his early sonnet to Santayana. The
later "Esthétique du Mal" suggests that while lakes "are more reasonable than
oceans" the 'logic' of lakes" (*CP* 325) may lead to a lunacy of self-confirmation. The vertiginous movement in "Sailing after Lunch" is more like the
dizziness of merely going round than forward movement, and the poetry it
describes is neither inclusive nor exclusive, but merely 'clusive,' an ill-fated
perpetuum mobile which mechanically perpetuates itself. Artistic convention
is thus understood as an inhuman but humanly wrought mechanics. The
image of the boat, and the sail moved by the spirit of natural wind are themselves worn-out images of poetry.

A decisive 'heave' to break with this predicament is announced by
replacing the visual metaphor, according to which poetry should not only
'behold' but (unfortunately) 'be be-held,' with a poetry of emotions:

It is least what one ever sees
It is only the way one feels.

Filreis understands this phrase as a result of Stevens' current interest in
Richards' Coleridge study, in which he argued that "[f]eeling is sometimes
a more subtle way of referring"[21] and proposed a move from denotation to
emotion that promised a degree of freedom from communicative require-
ments. Thus, Filreis explains, "It is indeed the effort of exchanging 'people'
for pupil, submitting to the gorgeous sounds of words even (evidently) at
the expense of sense, finding the 'Awareness of words as *words*,' as Richards
insists was Coleridge's idea, that immediately precedes the sudden rising
light wind of the imagination, the wind that will fill the new romanticized
sail of the boat of modern poetry."[22] Following the pattern explored in
"Waving Adieu," however, the turn to the 'sound of words' is also formulated as a turn away from the socio-cultural to the natural world. In order
for the poet

to say

Where my spirit is I am,
To say the light wind worries the sail,
To say the water is swift today,

it is necessary

To expunge all people and be a pupil
Of the gorgeous wheel and so to give
That slight transcendence to the dirty sail,
By light, the way one feels, sharp white,
And then rush brightly through the summer
Air.

Apparently coming from nowhere, the repeated infinitive "to say," a means of pure creativity or a 'deus ex machina' enables the poem, as Stevens explains to Latimer, to make "the most casual things [to] take on transcendence, and the poet [to rush] brightly, and so on" (*L* 277). In his groundless and spontaneous self-creation, the speaker now recalls *Harmonium*'s Hoon, who 'finds himself' in his own creations and who does not become 'less himself' because "in purple" he "descended / The Western day." To say that where "my spirit" is "I am," is also to say that where "I am" is the place where the wind comes from. One—one's singular self—has only "to say" that the wind grabs the sail for it to actually do this. Public opinion, to which poetry would also be opposed in a 'scientist' sense,[23] is thus an inauthentic and oppressive construct of an immediate historical present, whose present forms of poetry forbid it to make contact with reality: poetry, as it is, is always untrue in relation to the present, which means that what is (or should be) really present in the 'present' does not become present enough, since the available linguistic forms for imaginative perception are not able to represent it. Thus, poetry will remain perpetually false in relation to its other unless it manages to abnegate its inherited poeticity, destroying 'the romantic' with the destructive force of the romantic itself.

Stevens' use of the very uncommon word 'expunge' explicitly defines the possibility of this motion in the very material vocabulary of writing, and is highly suggestive of the ethical implications of the poem's pivotal event (more so than "exchange," for which Filreis curiously substitutes it). Derived from Latin 'expungere,' it literally means to 'erase' or 'blot out' undesired elements in ones text. People are "ex-punged," blotted out from the script or canvas by means of the pen—as in Derrida's 'style' or 'stylo'—since what has hampered the boat's motion is the weight of their opinion, crystallized in the *pejorative* sense of the romantic that it has needed to drag around like a ball and chain. "Farewell to Florida," the poem which replaced "Sailing After Lunch" at the beginning of the 1936 Knopf edition of *Ideas of Order,* would make further aesthetic use of this violent, cleaving movement of the boat's—metaphorically poetry's—creative progress.

In *Harmonium,* the self-creative character Hoon was clearly not obliged to understand his creative autonomy as conditioned upon 'expunging' anything or anyone. The difference between the two poems, however, is also a question of their difference in scenic 'props.' The sumptuous paraphernalia of Hoon, the "golden ointment" sprinkled on his beard, the "blowing hymns" and the sea of which he was "the compass," contrasts with the old boat, its dirty sail and the musty coloring. The "purple" atmosphere of Hoon's Palaz—in "Of Hartford in a Purple Light" (*CP* 226) purple was to be defined as a feminine color—is substituted for by a 'sharp white,' a striking absence of imaginative colors belonging to a poetic language that needs both to be revived and constantly transcended. In "Sailing after Lunch" the very 'material' and technological image of editing a printed page is also imagined as a turn to a natural principle 'beyond' language: the poem's self-going and static motion, its vicious circle, is 'opened up' for a kind of autonomy understood as a freedom from 'what people speak of,' which is ideally both individual and natural at once: the speaker can now be "taught" directly by the sun, or "the gorgeous wheel." However, this formula is evidently complicated by the sense that present languages (the present forms of the romantic) are indeed inescapably *present*. The fact that the romantic will remain and does return indicates a cleavage in the actual that cannot simply be redeemed by a cleansing of preceding fictions. Stevens' poetry thus works both on the utopian notion that poetry may accomplish pure naming and with the acute conscience that even the new itself has a form, that, indeed, new forms can only be perceived as 'new' insofar as they are repetitions of something which already exists.

The poem's catachrestically defined 'turn'—its graphic, 'stylistic' erasure of otherness which is also a 'turn' to the sun which, as Derrida has argued, can be regarded as the condition of possibility for all metaphor[24]—coincides with a substitution of what could (with caution) be called 'closed' rhythmic patterns for a 'freer' prosody. This may be best understood as a cumulative 'loosening' of metric binds. While the anaphoric repetition of infinitives lets the new poetic verve happen grammatically by 'expunging' personal conjugation, it also allows rhythmic phrases to develop without ending in conformity with the preceding line, giving an impression of an improvisational, spontaneous, speech act. This approximates a poetry of 'process' that "Of Modern Poetry" would name "the poem of the act of the mind."

The four-beat rhythm of the first part determines even the more deviant penultimate one, whose rhymes are less predictable. The strong enjambment in the first line, isolating and emphasizing 'to say,' highlights this stanza's new emphasis on spontaneous and self-propelled imaginative 'saying':

> It is only the way one feels, to say
> x x ∟x x ∟ / ∟   x ∟
> Where my spirit is I am,
>   x   x ∟x ∟/ ∟ [x∟]
> To say the light wind worries the sail,
>   x ∟ x ∟ /   ∟ x x ∟
> To say the water is swift today,
> x ∟ x ∟x x ∟ x ∟

While the third line above could be experienced as pentameter, the context provided by the preceding lines is likely to encourage a perception of four beats in it. In the last stanza, however, there is a definite expansion both of syllabic quantity and phrasal length, giving the reader a clear choice of rhythmic interpretation. All its lines can be realized both as four-beat lines and as pentameter. I have suggested a possible interpretation, indicating with * syllables that could take a rhythmic beat. While promotion may appear slightly artificial in line 2, or fall on a syllable immediately preceded or followed by beat-taking syllables in line 1 and 4, demotions could be the more strained alternative: 'all' and 'sharp' in lines 1 and 4 carry emphatic weight, and in line 3 and 5 a demotion would strain the established rising duple rhythm, which would be especially problematic in 5 due to the phonetic slowness of '*th*rough':

> To expunge all people and be a pupil
> x--x ∟ /* ∟x   x ∟ x ∟ x
> Of the gorgeous wheel and so to give
> x* x ∟ x ∟ x ∟ x ∟
> That slight transcendence to the dirty sail,
> /   ∟ x ∟ x x* x ∟x ∟
> By light, the way one feels, sharp white,
>   / ∟ x ∟ / ∟   /*   ∟
> And then rush brightly through the summer
> x ∟ / ∟ x /*   x ∟ x

Air.

$\angle$

Even though there is hardly a more conventional metric convention than iambic pentameter, its (possible) closural function in "Sailing after Lunch," as an aspect of the poem's total cumulative movement as well as its rhetorical struggle for resolution, can be sensed in two different ways. The first is contextual: it allows for a greater sense of natural speech by evening out the heavy rhythmic peaks of a four-beat structure and thus comes to represent or, in a more immediate rhythmic sense, *present* a sense of release and determinate movement. The second aspect is 'associative,' as the stylistic, connotative value of a pentameter line may by itself, in more or less conscious ways, introduce a nobility of diction lacking in the first stanzas. In both senses, pentameter may function as what Herrnstein Smith has called a "non-structural" closural device, a device that produces a sense of closure—and, as she argues, a sense of truth—while it does "not necessarily follow from the poem's [established] structural principles."[25] In "Sailing after Lunch" its closural function would rather be an effect of its difference from those principles. While it is essential to Stevens' rhythmics that his meters are volatile and essentially open to interpretation, the work of pentameter 'sneaking' into the final stanza may be an important part of the trickery by which the poem shapes its kinesthetic illusion of motion.

In the sense that the boat of "Sailing after Lunch" is both a conventional metaphor for poetic composition and a 'metaphor of convention,' the image of the dirty sail is a verbal gesture intended to bring it closer to reality through revitalizing old symbolic forms by de-sublimizing them. Thus, although the poem's final suggestion is to attain solitary yet universal speech, this is achieved by way of the debasement of a classical image of noble style—even if the quintessentially noble style of pentameter is, as I have suggested, brought back to resolve the poem's linguistic impasse. The normatively potent discourse of Mikhail Bakhtin can thus be used both *against* the poem, in the sense that its resolution is tied to an assertion of unconstrained monologue, and *with* it, by recognizing how the poem's language works to parody itself, acknowledging its entanglement in collective discourse. This aspect of Stevens' poetics has been persuasively argued for—against Bakhtinian censures—by Michael Keith Booker.[26] By virtue of what Derrida has called the waste or 'usure' of metaphor, when he puns both on "use" and on how interest, or excess of value, can be derived from the 'exchange' of signification created in the process of metaphorical movement, the old boat is made to yield new value.[27] While old forms (which, it should be kept in mind, are also understood as collective) are exposed as non-profitable, value is obtained not only despite them but in the process of using them, of wasting them even further. This 'recycling' of poetic debris will be discussed more closely in the next chapter.

The notion that the turn to the sun as to an absence of (all too) human meaning can only be *figured* as a turn to 'the gorgeous wheel,' suggests that the sun is 'always already' metaphorized, and never a 'pure' source or 'motive' for new metaphor. In this sense, the "pupil" of "Sailing after Lunch" prefigures the learning "ephebe" of "Notes" who is told see the sun "again with an ignorant eye . . . clearly, in the idea of it" while making sure that it receives "no name"; an imperative which is right away contradicted when the instructor himself calls it "gold flourisher" (*CP* 381). If we concede that "the gorgeous wheel" of "Sailing after Lunch" is a 'new' name for the sun, the naming, even if it is not a mute seeing, would not, at least, be 'unoriginal.' Idiosyncrasy can itself be seen as a kind of originality, although we would have to conceive of this originality only as permitted by and from within the regularized, conventional historical languages. In *Harmonium*'s "Gubbinal" (*CP* 85), the sun (so frequent in Stevens' poetry that it would be a huge undertaking to chart all its appearances) provokes a series of metaphorical descriptions of itself: it is a "strange flower," a "tuft of jungle feathers," an "animal eye," a "savage of fire," and finally, a "seed," a display of exuberant metaphors that works against the poem's final concession to those of dull imagination: "Have it your way. / The world is ugly. / And the people are sad."

If the sun is a 'dehumanising' agent, in the sense that it is alien to the discourses of the people expunged, it is also, according to this logic, the mobilizing force for the creation of new language. In the sense in which it is anthropomorphized or personified, the humanization of the sun is thus part and parcel of a (de)humanization *of* the sun. Its natural sublime throws our language into a need to reformulate itself (an aspect of Stevens' relation with otherness explored by Lakritz).[28] Many of Stevens' poems alternately propose and forbid seeing truth and encouragement in natural symbols like the sun, the moon, the sea, the air, the weather, which can only be potent, it seems, as long as they do not petrify into anthropomorphist convention. When *Ideas of Order*'s "The Brave Man" (*CP* 138) calls the sun a "brave man," that gives courage and makes "fears of life and fears of death, / Run away," it also clearly goes against the earlier imperative against pathetic fallacy in *Harmonium*'s "Nuances of a Theme by Williams" (*CP* 18), which was directed *against* the idea that the moon of Williams' poem (another astral symbol) gives "a strange courage" to the speaker. Stevens' response demands that it reflect neither "my face nor any inner part / of my being" and mirror "nothing," and that it lends "no part to any humanity that suffuses you in its own light." The limits of conceiving the sun as a brave courage-giver are exposed in the poem immediately following "The Brave Man" in *Ideas of Order*, "A Fading of the Sun" (*CP* 139), where the sun is declared impotent as a source of instruction or delight in the anguished modern world.

> Who can think of the sun costuming clouds
> When all people are shaken
> Or of night endazzled, proud,
>
> When people awaken
> And cry and cry for help?

In a world where everything and everyone grows "suddenly cold" the "tea is bad, bread sad," and joy is "without a book" (presumably a central fiction like the Bible), people will have to "look / Within themselves." By doing so, the poem claims, not very convincingly, "they will *not* cry for help" and "will *not* die."

THE EMPTY SPIRIT IN VACANT SPACE: POSING THE SUBLIME

Tracing Stevens' development into a modernist, George Lensing has discerned two basic modes defining his poetic diction: the "ironic" one where Stevens "relied on the poem's effect, which was often wry, witty, and opaque," and the "prophetic" one "where the voice was one of instruction and admonition."[29] The movement of "Sailing after Lunch" could be understood as exhibiting a stylistic transition from an ironic mode into a prophetic, or sincere one. Lensing further suggests, however, that it was "[t]he very *convergence* of the portentous and the playful, sometimes ironic, [which] set Stevens apart as a poet and fixed him securely on the path to modernism."[30] This would mean that the playful risks at any moment tainting the prophetic, portentous or sincere, or that these modes may become practically indistinguishable. Thus, the 'play' in Stevens' poetry between high seriousness and playful irony, although often drawing on 'lower' forms of expression, is also a 'serious play' of endless parody which increases the feeling of a discrepancy between the imagination and reality, subject and object, even as this disorder is lamented. In view of Lensing's 'voice' metaphor, we could also understand this play as an interplay between a sense of natural/individual voice and a kind of non- or anti-voice effected by the devices of conspicuous rhythmic repetitiousness and anachronistic diction.

Bloom defines "the lasting impression of *Ideas of Order* as a book" as "the note of the American Sublime, a hyperbole overthrowing the ironies that attempt to work a catachresis upon it."[31] The irony operative in the short "The American Sublime" (*CP* 130–1) is exposed as a predicament of the present artistic language of sublimity, mocked by a derisive populace. Here, the revitalization of the sublime is linked to a search for a *style* or *form* of the sublime, and the superficiality of pose and gesture rather than the sublime itself.

> How does one stand
> To behold the sublime
> To confront the mockers,
> The mickey mockers
> And plated pairs?

The question is thus not primarily about *where* to stand to gain perspective or insight (which also means to lose perspective and insight, as the sublime would be that which exceeds vision and rational grasp)[32] but *how* to stand. To 'behold' the sublime equals being 'beheld' by the mockers in a certain way that enables one to elude their pejorative discourses, resisting the determinations of common discourse. In poem XVIII of "Like Decorations in a Nigger Cemetery" (*CP* 153) the speaker asks whether to "grapple with my destroyers / In the muscular poses of the museums?" receiving a negative answer, since these destroyers "avoid the museums." The notion that the real culture wars take place outside museums, in the mockers' home ground—'reality'—calls for other strategies.

Whether the mockers in "The American Sublime" are museum-goers or not the poet's discourse is imagined in terms of plastic form, and the poem's initial question can be rephrased into "how does one make oneself into a statue without being ridiculous?" In Stevens' mixed metaphor, the inappropriateness or catachresis of the statue makes it an appropriate image of what is too solid and static and thus both too visible and perishable in relation to ever-changing inner and outer realities. The representation of solid and therefore breakable "metal heroes that time granulates" (*CP* 250), is countered by the idea that the hero, as is suggested in *Part of a World*'s "The Examination of the Hero in a Time of War" (*CP* 273–81), is "not an image. It is a feeling." In fact, this poem asks, "How could there be an image, an outline, / a marble soiled by pigeons?" (*CP* 278). In *Ideas of Order*'s "The Dance of the Macabre Mice" (*CP* 123), poor and hungry mice dance in mock-celebration around the statue of a "monsieur on horse back," "The Founder of the State." In doing so, they devalue the pathos of the statue's "arm of bronze outstretched against all evil": for, "Whoever founded / A state that was free, in the dead of winter, from mice?" And in "Notes toward a Supreme Fiction" a General Du Puy is found to be only "rubbish in the end" (*CP* 392).

The speaker of "The American Sublime" describes a feeling of shared experience between himself and the statue's object, "Du Puy"'s forerunner, the founding father and creator of the ideal of the common man, General Andrew Jackson.

> When General Jackson
> Posed for his statue
> He knew how one feels.
> Shall a man go barefoot
> Blinking and blank?

The General appears to have known how one feels, that is, when the sublime one tries to achieve is public property, and can therefore never again be sublime in the same sense. In order to satisfy the public's hunger for the sublime, one is made to repeat gestures that are theirs, not one's own, since the populace would deride any conception of the sublime that they are unable to recognize, or in which they are unable recognize themselves.

As one of the "noble riders," the statue of General Jackson would play an important part in Stevens' "Noble Rider" lecture. This essay begins by arguing that the central image of Plato's Phaedrus, "a pair of winged horses and a charioteer" traversing the skies, has become "merely the emblem of a mythology, the rustic memorial of a belief in the soul and in a distinction between good and evil," even though the figure had in fact been "as unreal for Plato as he is for us" (*NA* 3–4). The difference, Stevens suggests, is that "we" are "not free to yield ourselves to this gorgeous nonsense" (ibid.) and that the strength of modern art is "a strength of reality or none at all" (*NA* 7). Stevens continues by comparing three works of art which contain, like Plato's image, horses and riders. The first one, Verrocchio's Renaissance statue of Bartolomeo Colleoni, is too much a thing of the imagination, too noble to serve in the present. Even as "a thing of nobility responsive to the most minute demand" it "seems, nowadays, what it may well not have seemed a few years ago, a little overpowering, a little magnificent"(*NA* 9).Verrocchio, whose idea of nobility "was an affair of a noble *style,*" is contrasted with Cervantes, for whom "nobility was not a thing of the imagination" but "a part of reality," "something that exists in life" (Ibid.). If 'reality' and 'life' in Stevens' argument do not simply suggest an absence of style, an absence or outside of literary form, Stevens appears to imply that the nobility of Cervantes is an effect of the dynamic and ironic interchange between the knightly ideas of Don Quixote, a kind of "Bartolomeo Colleoni in Spain" who lives in a world composed in the noble style of romance, and Sancho Panza, whose common sense realism has its own conventions. Just as the low life encountered in Cervantes' novel debases and falsifies Don Quixote's idealized idea of the world, the very genre of the picaresque novel overturns, in Bakhtinian terms, the epic, at the same time as it nourishes itself on it, making it live on.

The second work is the one of "The American Sublime," the statue in Washington's Lafayette Square, facing the White House, of General Jackson "riding a horse with one of the most beautiful tails in the world" and "raising his hat in a gay gesture, saluting the ladies of his generation" (*NA* 10). This sculpture, Steven suggests, "is a work of fancy," referring to Coleridge's famous distinction between the imagination, which is "essentially vital" but also deconstructive in the sense that it "dissolves, diffuses, dissipates, in order to recreate" or "where this . . . is . . . impossible . . . struggles to idealize and unify," and fancy, which "has no other counters to play with but fixities and definites" and "must receive all its materials ready made from the law of association."[33] "Fancy," Stevens clarifies,

> . . . is an exercise of selection from among objects already supplied by association, a selection made for purposes which are not then and therein being shaped but have already been fixed. We are concerned then with an object occupying a position as remarkable as any that can be found in the United States in which there is not the slightest trace of the imagination. Treating this work as typical, it is obvious that the American will as a principle of the mind's being is easily satisfied in its efforts to realize itself in knowing itself. The statue may be dismissed, not without speaking of it again as a thing that at least makes us conscious of ourselves as we were, if not as we are. To that extent, it helps us to know ourselves. It helps us to know ourselves as we were, if not as we are. The statue is neither of the imagination nor of reality. That it is a work of fancy precludes it from being a work of the imagination. A glance at it shows it to be unreal. The bearing of this is that there can be works, and this includes poems, in which neither the imagination nor reality is present. (*NA* 10–11)

If "there is not the slightest trace of the imagination" nor, as a mere "glance" at it will show, "reality," this would, as far as the statue of General Jackson is concerned, make it conceivable as a pure product of a hegemonic ideology.

As such, Stevens appears to 'dismiss' it from artistic consideration, defining it as a suitable object of the discipline that is today called 'Cultural Studies,' the study of how cultural identities and stereotypes are created through ideological mechanisms, including art and literature. The statue "helps us to know ourselves as we were, if not as we are": its conventionality makes it lag behind actuality in a way that a truly imaginative work of art should not. General Jackson, then, would 'know how it feels' to be part of a stereotyping mechanism of static and narcissistic self-confirmation.

The third work of art is "a painting called *Wooden Horses*" by Reginald Marsh, an artist who, Stevens quotes, has "'turned his back on the aesthetic whims and theories of the day, and established headquarters in lower Manhattan'"(*NA* 11). The painting is of "a merry-go-round, possibly several of them," a bustling scene of horses "prancing" or going "lickety-split," one of them "struggling to get the bit in his teeth," and a number of robust people riding them, apparently with some difficulty. [34] "We are here," Stevens writes, "not interested in any aspect of this picture except that it is a picture of ribald and hilarious reality. It is a picture wholly favourable to what is real. It is not without imagination and it is far from being without aesthetic theory" (*NA* 12). Thus, although Marsh's painting is not an image of 'nobility,' it is an example of an imaginative work conspicuously informed by artistic theory. It is crucial that its representation of the lower aspects of reality has beenmade deliberately, or that the spectator will experience that it has. It is less important that Marsh's painting is 'real' or 'realistic' than that it is 'favourable to what is real.' While the image of 'not-so-noble' riders magnifies the gross and bawdy this is not done simply at the expense of a noble style. Rather, (as Stevens' argument suggests) it establishes a relation to it, communicating with it.

Hence, the reason why General Jackson and the speaker of "The American Sublime" share a sense of 'unreality' is not just because they do not represent something very real, in the sense of very public and common, but because 'the real' of the statue is an idealized real which is common property. A 'swift glance' immediately recognizes it as what it is, by those—the 'we' of Stevens' essay—trained to recognize it as such and to expect this style to be art. This amounts to an absence of artistic theory, which Stevens formulates hyperbolically as an absence of both reality and the imagination. Thus, the 'presence' of theory (and art), rather than an obvious set of propositions stated by the work, would be an effect of its capacity to challenge perception, resulting in the need to pay more attention to it than a cursory glance. It would require a fuller kind of attention involving what we could call *interpretation*.

Obviously, Stevens' improvisational argument is based on swift abstraction and generalization. One could of course take an artistic interest in General

Jackson's statue if one chose to, as people have in Duchamp's urinal or Warhol's Mickey Mouse images. In fact, the statue's predicament is analogous to the ambiguous role played by repetitious form, in terms of rhythm and meter as well as diction and imagery, in the poems analyzed in this chapter: think of the gestural repetition and monotonous rhythms in "Waving Adieu, Adieu, Adieu," the endless and pointless circulation of the romantic image in "Sailing after Lunch" and the idea of the sublime as 'pose' in "The American Sublime." While this poetry exudes a delight in the comic aspects of repetitiousness and sound-play, parodying the high genres of poetry, the use of lower styles and genres—a sort of 'pressure of reality'—also imply a desire for nobility, a kind of nostalgia. Thus, Stevens' plunge into the decrepit and false—yet compellingly material and thus to some extent actual and true—world of common discourse, is performed in order to 'return' to an expression of sublimity, after changing these conventional patterns in the use of them (which, as we have seen, may include 'expunging people').

In "The American Sublime," moving slowly onward in steady two-beat lines undisturbed by the accelerations of enjambment, a 'turn' in the argument is initiated by casting doubt on the feeling supposedly shared by General Jackson and the speaker. The sudden question "But how does one feel?" is responded to, but not fully answered:

> One grows used to the weather,
> The landscape and that;

This may refer back to the assumed need to walk barefoot, "blinking and blank," in a weather which by implication is inhospitable. Attaining the sublime now becomes a question of assimilation to the climate or, in Whitman's words, "the atmosphere," looking straight but blinkingly into the sun, rather than the redeployment of a falsely noble style. The last line indicates that the impasse of sublimity is not to be solved by replacing it with a new content of consciousness, but by creating a vacant space, a process described by Frye as a willed "arrest of a flow of perceptions without and of impressions within."[35]

> And the sublime comes down
> To the spirit itself,
>
> The spirit and space,
> The empty spirit
> In vacant space.

It is possible to experience a 'dipodic' hierarchy of beats[36] in these lines, making the first beat heavier than the second, and the first beat in each four-beat figure heavier than the third. This may underline the sense that 'come down to' may not only mean 'depend on' but also carries the implication of a downward movement. The final long, twice qualified phrase appears to move the self inexorably deeper into imaginative emptiness. The 'spirit itself' is expanded, made more precise, in 'the spirit and space,' and is further deepened in an '*empty* spirit in *vacant* space,' where the adjectives are emphasized by taking the heaviest beats. It is possible to experience a falling beat hierarchy all the way from the first line to the third one, a dipodic rhythm moving downwards along with the insistent semantic amplification of the sense of emptiness. The 'emptiness' or 'hollowness' of pose and vacuous forms is replaced by an emptiness purposively sought for, imagined. *In* this movement, (whether from motion to stasis, or stasis to motion) a sort of change is intuited. The sublime as mere stylistic pose or gesture, already exposed as a language without human meaning, is further dehumanized, but by human imaginative agency.

The poem, however, reverts to interrogation. The idea of art as pose or gesture is replaced by the metaphor of nourishment, asking about "the meal that one should have had."

> What wine does one drink?
> What bread does one eat?

With these questions the poem terminates in a form of anti-closure. Since this spiritual ingestion, a post-religious communion of bread and wine, would be needed chiefly in order to perceive the sublime, it appears to have progressed very little from its beginning. Perhaps, however, these precise questions could not have been asked before the emptying out, but signal a renewed hunger and thirst of and empty imagination which needs to nourish itself again, filling the void or vacancy that it itself has made.

THE PORCELAIN CRIES: BROKEN VOICES IN "OWL'S CLOVER"

The ambivalent, ironic and nostalgic debasement of poetic language at work in many of Stevens' thirties poems is a crucial part of the long blank verse sequence "Owl's Clover," written between the end of 1935 and the beginning of the next year, first published in 1936 and republished, after considerable revision and some abbreviation, in *The Man with the Blue Guitar* in 1937. My discussion will only be dedicated to the first two parts, "The Old

Woman and the Statue" and "Mr. Burnshaw and the Statue" (*OP* 75–101).[37] It will draw on the first version, clarifying, when this can be valuable to know, that the parts discussed were excised. The second part (renamed "The Statue at the World's End" in the *Blue Guitar* version) was a direct response to the Leftist critic and poet Stanley Burnshaw's famous review of *Ideas of Order* in October 1935, which discussed the problems of Stevens' kind of poetry in a troubled age that demanded political engagement. Burnshaw later admitted that if he "had known about" "The Old Woman and the Statue" he "probably would have written the review in a different way,"[38] suggesting that Stevens' response in "Mr. Burnshaw and the Statue" was already implicit in the first poem. Critics have since pointed out that Burnshaw's review has been influentially interpreted as more negative than it really was, perhaps most influentially by Frank Kermode.[39] Burnshaw not only explicitly opposed the "cliché" which had "crept into left-wing criticism . . . that contemporary poets have all tramped off to some escapist limbo where they are joyously gathering moonshine,"[40] but clearly suggested that the "turmoil" in middle ground writing was not only instructive but artistically and culturally important. The words of the middle-ground writers he reviewed, Stevens and Haniel Long,[41] "have intense value and meaning" not only "to the sectors within the class whose confusion they articulate. Their books have deep importance for us [socialist writers and intellectuals] as well."[42]

The governing image of the first section, a statue in an urban park depicting "a group of marble horses" which "rose on wings" is revealed to be aesthetically potent only in disconnection or withdrawal from social and political reality, as the presence of a poor old park-roaming woman of the first part invalidates its cultural and aesthetic value. It is only, the argument goes, able to be alive and interactive in relation to a nature understood as abstracted from the social world, i.e. 'before' and 'after' the woman's presence. The "Old Woman's unfulfillment," as Cleghorn argues, "is the energy driving the argument of the poem."[43]

> Without her, evening like a budding yew
> Would soon be brilliant, as it was, before
> The harridan self and ever-maladive fate
> Went crying their desolate syllables, before
> Their voice and the voice of the tortured wind were one,
> Each voice within the other, seeming one,
>
> Crying against a need that pressed like cold,
> Deadly and deep. (*OP* 77)

The social sphere of the park, as Cleghorn suggests,[44] is a contradictory scene. It is a pastoral haven, offering relief and recreation for such victims of urban modernity as the old woman, but also an idealization of nature, a classical ideal as unreceptive and exclusive of the woman's discordant presence as the statue at its center.[45] In a series of accusations and counteraccusations, arguments and counterarguments, amid a play of voices that are frustratingly difficult to tell from each other, the poem negotiates an ethical dilemma of artistic autonomy. In the first sections, a bizarre group of muses are requested to dance around the statue, surrounding it with the low expressive forms of dance and song, celebrating it while revealing its historical decay.[46]

At the beginning of "Mr. Burnshaw and the Statue" a voice declares the statue dead, just as "everything is dead, except the future." This follows from the notion that "Always everything / That is is dead except what ought to be" (*OP* 78). The statue, as a thing of the past, does thus not really exist, since only what 'is to be' does: a satire of the most dogmatic Marxist thinking, which, like the statue, needs to do away with whatever does not fit in with its ideal. In section two of "Mr. Burnshaw" it is proposed that in "The stones that will replace" the statue "shall be carved"

> "The Mass
> Appoints These Marbles of Itself To Be
> Itself." No more than that, no subterfuge,
> No memorable muffing, bare and blunt. (*OP* 80)

The inscribed marbles that replace the statue are intended to be a piece of reality rather than a distant imaginary ideal, but they come to *re-place* the monument in a monumental way that the speaker may not have intended. Their utter materiality is meant to be a complete expressive transparency, a literality, but in the end becomes a narcissistic idealization—or, which is the same here, materialization—of the masses striving towards an identification of themselves and their historical purpose. They are both "what is" and "what should be." This means that the stones are as impenetrable to actuality as the statue ever was. A future that is entirely predetermined, already materialized, ceases to be future, just as the present, the intersection of past and future (composed, in Husserl's words, by retention and protention) ceases to be present. The literal inscription of the narcissistic mass, then, merely repeats them as they are—or, to be grammatically correct, '*it* as it is'—and does not change anything. The vacuous self-reference of the copular 'to be' is highlighted by its inscription in a deceptive enjambment. The flip-side of this process is that the marbles, designed to represent the people, not only merely repeat themselves but absorb the mass into its material (the word 'mass' as a metaphor for people—as in Burnshaw's *The Masses*—may already suggest a kind of 'materiality').

In section VII, omitted in the later version, the speaker calls upon a group of muses to dance around the remains of the crumbling statue, "and with sharp voices cry" while turning their backs on it. Although the statue is their pivotal center, their averted dance projects the attention away, towards the sky, "that possible blue." It is perhaps intentionally unclear which of the two monuments is the object of their ritual, the statue or the stones replacing it, and whether the significance of the dance is to celebrate them or to celebrate, even contribute to, their decay:

> In the glassy sound of your voices, the porcelain cries,
> The alto clank of the long recitation, in these
> Speak, and in these repeat: *To Be Itself,*
> Until the sharply-colored glass transforms
> Itself into the speech of the spirit, until
> The porcelain bell-borrowings become
> Implicit clarities in the way you cry . . . (*OP* 83)

The violent catachresis of these vocal images—the glassy voice, the porcelain cry and the alto clank—brings what is solid, material, and exterior, into problematic coexistence with that which needs to be interior, personal and human. The speech or song of the muses takes place in the confrontation between vocal expression and that which appears inherently hostile to it, i.e. solid material. The muses (who are not sources of inspiration here but actual singers) are told to speak in these anti-vocal voices, as though they could have chosen to do otherwise. The porcelain of their cries recalls Stevens' early play "Three Travelers Watch a Sunrise" (*OP* 149–67)[47] in which porcelain is an ambivalent symbol of artistic autonomy and abstraction: "There is a seclusion of porcelain / That humanity never invades . . . As abstract as porcelain . . ." (*OP* 151–2).[48] The figure of glass is more recurrent in Stevens' work. An interesting reference to it can be found in Burnshaw's review, which linked Stevens' apparent urge for aesthetic autonomy to a drive for scientific precision, more often associated with the poetics of Eliot and Pound. Steven's poetry, Burnshaw writes, was grounded in "'scientific,' objectivated sensuousness separated from its kernel of fire and allowed to settle, cool off, and harden in the poet's mind until it emerged a strange amazing crystal." Reading such "verse that people concerned with the murderous world collapse can hardly swallow . . . except in tiny doses" thus "becomes a venture in crystal-lography."[49] Burnshaw's phrasing points forward—perhaps as an unacknowl-edged source—to the conclusion of "Notes," where canto X of "It Must Give Pleasure" envisions the moment when his "green, fluent mundo . . . will have stopped revolving except in crystal"(*CP* 407).

Porcelain and glass are solid, finished materials that cannot be molded or wrought and whose only way of yielding to exteriority is to break, to frag-ment. As such, they refer back to the statue, which section V of "Mr Burn-shaw and the Statue" describes as "Parts of the immense detritus of a world / That is completely waste, that moves from waste / To waste, out of the hopeless waste of the past / Into a hopeful waste to come"(*OP* 81). This waste can to some extent be understood as fragments of a ruptured past, but it is not brought into a 'fallen' present as a metonymic trace of a past wholeness, shored *against* the ruins of the present. Rather, the rupture has revealed that there never was a wholeness in the first place. This, in turn, does not suggest that truth is the *absence* of these invalid fictions, but that it is something that can only be attained in the attempt to relate to them. Even if the statue's crumbling, "topple, tumble, tip / In the soil and rest," is related to its lack of grounding in the real—manifested ethically in its exclusion of the old woman—the fragments produced in its crumbling *are* nevertheless real.[50] The fragments, however, are not simply themselves, do not speak a lost historical truth with a voice of their own, but need to "be spoken," to be mobilized into artistic speech. In this way, the very idea of voice as speech or song is challenged by Stevens' image, which makes it extremely difficult to imagine an eventual attainment of "implicit clarities." The muses are singing while ripping their throats apart with fragments of glass and porcelain and, at the same time, the stubbornness of the porcelain and the glass is, along with the statue, challenged and mobilized by their speech.

This difficult image certainly suggests a dead end not only of the kind of poetry it strives for, but of the realism as conceived by intellectuals like Burnshaw. Accordingly, critical valuations of "Owl's Clover" have until recently been negative, largely due to a dissatisfaction with the impropriety of the rigidity and unreality of the statue as both inappropriate and located in an unpropitious place. Vendler, whose ideal Stevens is vocally fluent and at ease, claims that in "compelling the Muses here to sing the maudlin meridian in such an exalted way," Stevens "exceeds their vocal range, and the strain shows, as he knew, in the overpitch of his rhetoric."[51] Similarly, Kermode argues that "[o]ne sees what Stevens meant by using the term 'rhetoric' pejo-ratively here; there is much random noise, the dry clatter of uninterestingly queer diction and stiff rhythms."[52]

These assessments conspicuously replicate Stevens' own. On what was to become the dust jacket to *The Man with the Blue Guitar and Other Poems* Stevens claims that the purpose of "The Man with the Blue Guitar," which dealt with "the incessant conjunctions between things as they are and things imagined," was an attempt to make up for the failure of *Owl's Clover*, whose ultimate "effect" had been to "emphasize" this opposition and thus "isolate" poetry (*OP* 233). Referring to this comment, Maeder agrees that "Owl's Clover" does not meet Burnshaw's indictment that Stevens would "sweep his contradictory notions into a valid Idea of Order,"[53] but stresses "the cleavage between a language reserved for art and the languages of everyday life."[54] In "The Man with the Blue Guitar," "contrary to what he does in 'Owl's Clover,'" Stevens would find a way to "juggle with the system."[55]

Stevens wrote extensive comments on the poem in four letters to Hi Simons between August 27 and 30, 1940. In the first one, he explains that the first section, written before Burnshaw's review, "deals specifically with the status of art in a period of depression" and is "*when generalized*, one more confrontation of reality (the depression) and the imagination (art). A *larger* expression than confrontation is," however, "a phase of the universal intercourse. There is a flow to and fro between reality and the imagination" (*L* 368 my italics). This generalizing 'enlargement' of the poem's 'particular' theme itself implies a de-historicizing or decontextualizing of its relation to its historical moment. The exchange of *confrontation*, which suggests a clash of sorts or a face-to-face encounter between separate entities or spheres, for the sexual metaphor of *universal intercourse* indicates a change from the imaginative mechanics of Coleridge's "fancy" to a more supple kind of creative principle. Thus, Stevens felt, he had gone from "building the world out of blocks" to

> think more of the energizing that comes from mere interplay, interaction. Thus, the various faculties of the mind co-exist and interact, and there is as much delight in this mere co-existence as a man and a woman find in each other's company. This is rather a crude illustration, but it makes the point. Cross-reflections, modifications, counter-balances, complements, giving and taking are illimitable. They make things inter-dependent, and their inter-dependence sustains them and gives them pleasure. While it may be the cause of other things, I am thinking of it as a source of pleasure, and therefore I repeat that there is an exquisite pleasure and harmony in these inter-relations, circuits. (*L* 368)

Stevens' formulation of the poetic process as a mystical, spontaneous creative process bringing opposites together is what has been celebrated by many critics as the great achievement of his post-Depression work. In "Notes" Stevens' would write the prime example in his work of this ontology of universal intercourse, the fourth canto of "It Must Change" where "Two things of opposite natures seem to depend / On one another, as a man depends / On a woman, day on night, the imagined / On the real" (*CP* 392). But the fact that his idea of the imagination, as Maeder has argued, "is only tangentially an aesthetic one" and "primarily a construct of epistemology"[56] has naturally distracted attention from his poetry's keen sense of the materiality of its verbal language. To make a long and highly eventful story short, the remaining parts of "Owl's Clover" present figures such as the "portent" and the "subman," who may replace the rigid statue and prefigure the abstract yet potent "major man" of "Notes." They come to represent the imagination as a kind of immanence, an essence residing in its representation yet not equaled by it, which is also an imminence of what is not yet but will be—just as the "seclusion" of porcelain in the dialogue of "Three Travelers" was finally granted the power of imminence: "It is the seclusion of sunrise, / Before it shines on any house" (*CPP* 603).

A heavy stress on these aspects, however, may obscure "Owl's Clover"'s alleged *failure*, its way of "isolating art" against its own intentions. The noisy malfunction of the established forms of the imagination, bringing the poem even farther away from 'reality,' also implies a description of history as a form of violence between incompatibles or a plurality that does not close or cohere, rather than as a process of cross-fertilization. In a sense, thus, two different theories of language, interpretation, and history are at stake. In more specifically aesthetic terms, they suggest, on the one hand, the importance of the alienating moment implicit in art as an encounter with semantic impenetrability or otherness and, on the other, what may well be the final purpose of this event: the possibility of (re)interpretation. Cleghorn's reading, which focuses on how Stevens 'deconstructs' the oppositions between art and reality, 'creation' and 'rhetoric,' suggests that deconstruction is itself a Hegelian enterprise. Stevens, in such a view, transcends the narrow antitheses of his time and, insofar as these oppositions or new manifestations of them are still prevalent (which they are), his work goes 'beyond' these too. Insofar as "deconstruction" implies a process of learning, its debt from Hegel is undeniable, and the negative work of "Owl's Clover" would accomplish, if not a resolution or synthesis, a positive new understanding of the oppositions between which it pretends to mediate.[57] Even so, Stevens' troubled engagement with his realist opponents in the thirties stresses the negative phase of 'deconstruction' according to which reality, understood in terms of chaotic violence, is understood as failed intercourse itself, as the originary violence of signification.

In the *Prefatory Note* to his comments to Simons, Stevens writes that the statue, in the first section of "Mr. Burnshaw and the Statue," signifies not only its own failure, but "the failure of an era," suggesting that the historical reality he was describing was out-of-joint with itself. As "a manifestation of the civilization of which it was a part," the statue was not alone to blame since, he implies, any art would be constituted as a gap between itself and its 'era' (*L* 366). In a letter to Latimer five years earlier (November 5, 1935) Stevens had explained the statue's significance as follows:

> It is difficult for me to think and not to think abstractly. Consequently, in order not to avoid abstractness, in writing, I search out instinctively things that express the abstract and yet are not in themselves abstractions. For instance, the STATUE about which I am doing a great deal of writing now-a-days was, in the poem which appeared in the SOUTHERN REVIEW, a symbol for art, art being a word that I have never used and never can use without some feeling of repugnance. In MR. BURNSHAW, etc., the same statue is also a symbol, but not specifically a symbol for art; its use has been somewhat broadened and, so far as I have defined it at all, it is a symbol for things as they are. (*L* 290)

The "broadening" of the statue, from a symbol of the excessively unreal, into functioning as a symbol of reality would imply, it appears, a total change of meaning. Five years later, Stevens would write to Simons that the statue, as "a manifestation of foppery" stands for "[t]he imagination (civilization etc.) as decoration, with its mementoes of things never achieved (observe that I am not trying to write English)" (*L* 366). From being privileged as something per definition extra-artistic, then, reality is seen in relation to art and, importantly, as relating not only to the artistic manifestations which successfully reflect or express it, but to those which fail to do so (although at this point 'fail' could be put between brackets).

Stevens' curious remark at the end of the last sentence suggests that the poet is trying to write something different from English as a common, familiar language. Artistic language, in this view, is a kind of dia- or idiolect, in the sense that it needs to radiate a sense of foreignness. In the poems studied above, this has chiefly been accomplished by using very *familiar* forms of poetry in ways that make them appear and function differently. Stevens would describe this as an effort to "compound the imagination's latin with the lingua franca et jocundissima," (*CP* 397) a compounding which is not only a merger of high and low diction, but an estrangement of both and the opposition which they constitute. Linguistic and, by analogy, formal inadequacy, is not *only* a flaw in poetic language that should be redeemed, but the mark of an age which is essentially not master of itself. This age is, in fact, not 'one age' or 'one history':

> The failure of an era is as if a man was trying to find a word in his mind and could not formulate it: as if the word was *artichoke* and he get no nearer to it than *inarticulate,* rather an heroic pun. The imagination, a toy unworthy of its reality, incapable of unconsidered revelations (sequels without thought). (*L* 366)

While modern poetry's movement "from enclosure to liberation," as Donald Wesling argues, is closely linked to the way the ideal of poetic language moves "from song to speech,"[58] Stevens' trials of poetic device suggest both the necessity and pervasiveness of this movement and formidable, but artistically productive, problems with it.

Chapter Three
Rejections
Poetry Against Poetry

BEATING FOR BELIEF: THE REJECTIONS OF
"THE MAN ON THE DUMP"

In 1934, the year before *Ideas of Order* was published, William Carlos Williams asked Stevens to write an introduction to a collection of his earlier poetry, the *Collected Poems 1921–1931,* published by the Objectivist Press in the same year. Stevens agreed somewhat reluctantly, writing an essay in which he called Williams a "romantic poet," something that he suspected "would horrify him." Although "the proof" of this romanticism, Stevens argued, was "everywhere," he added that Williams was only "rarely" romantic in the "accepted sense" (what people speak of as romantic) but first and foremost in his search for what Stevens called the "anti-poetic" (*OP* 213–15). Thus, although "all poets are to some extent romantic poets," Williams' romantic temperament was primarily visible in the fact that he had "spent his life in rejecting the accepted sense of things," among other things the traditional senses of the romantic.

Albert Gelpi has taken these remarks to suggest a hypocrisy in Williams' poetics: Stevens' introduction, he argues, insinuated "that Williams *vacillated* between his sentimental proclivities and his antipoetic, realist, 'Imagist' side."[1] While in Gelpi's view, "the adjectives with which Stevens labeled Williams' work . . . 'romantic,' 'sentimental,' 'antipoetic,' 'realist' . . . caused understandable offense,"[2] I would argue that it is far more important to consider how Stevens in fact showed an appreciation of Williams' work. Also, the review enabled him to establish a connection between ostensibly opposed tendencies in poetic modernism, and not only between competing poets, like himself and Williams, but *within* their respective poetics. In this way, it was only through upsetting the terms central to the poetics of Williams and other post-Imagists that he was able to discuss issues of crucial importance to his own project. Clearly, since Gelpi's intention was to describe a distinct divide between the "epistemologies"[3] of Williams' Imagist/Objectivist modernism and Stevens' Romantic Symbolism, it was essential to retain a stable referential content in the words that Stevens' played with and re-connected in provocative ways: "romantic," "modernist," and "realist." Similarly, Kent Johnson has understood the fact that Stevens showed appreciation for Carl Rakosi's poetry (in a letter to Rakosi in 1953) as "perplexing" since Rakosi was interested in "actual objects and people." This, he argues, "can hardly be seen as a vital quality of [Stevens'] own work."[4] Johnson's assumption was that Stevens' uninterest in the "outside" world was either the cause or effect (this is unclear) of his metrical prosody and archaic diction. That such a sense was also part of Stevens' own sense of aesthetic 'trial' can be seen in the way his poetry often appears to devalue, deprecate or criticize its own language. In the context of democratizing or liberatory modernist ideas of free verse Stevens' less utopian way of envisaging aesthetic change, however, is itself too easily interpreted as simple conservatism or nostalgia.

One of the important provocations of Stevens' introduction was the notion that Williams' writing was nurtured by a longstanding sense of cultural and linguistic privilege attached to poetic art. The contemporary romantic, Stevens suggests (meaning simultaneously, of course, the contemporary *anti*-romantic)

> happens to be one who still dwells in an ivory tower, but who insists that life there would be intolerable except for the fact that one has, from the top, such an exceptional view of the public dump and the advertising signs of Snider's Catsup, Ivory Soap and Chevrolet Cars; he is the hermit who dwells alone with the sun and moon, but insists on taking a rotten newspaper. (*OP* 214)

The romantic poet à la Williams, unlike that of the speaker of "Sailing after Lunch," is *already* with the sun and the moon, but *insists* on taking a "rotten newspaper," an 'anti-poetic' act which, Stevens' image suggests, can only be performed by a poet and from within poetry itself, closely identified with the ivory tower. This idea appears quite opposed to the admonition of "The Man with the Blue Guitar" not to "use the rotted names" (*CP* 183) as well as the initial phenomenological imperative of "It Must Be Abstract." Stevens' poetry, however, also frequently suggests that the poet, *any* poet, *has to* and *does* use the 'rotten' names of inherited poetic diction, images, metaphors and rhythms. As far as Stevens' figure of Williams is concerned, such rotten names are as likely to be the sun and moon, pertaining to the ambience of poetry's ivory tower, as those of old newspapers and other items found on the dump. They are all to be found in the piece where Stevens made maximum use of the central image of his essay on Williams, "The Man on the Dump," published in *Parts of a World* in 1939, but in many ways part of the ambience of *Ideas of Order*.

Gelpi, who prefers to see Stevens' image as a critique only, rather than an indication of an irony central to both Williams' and Stevens' modernisms (and perhaps in modernist realism as such), suggests that "Stevens' description of the romantic as an idealistic solipsist in a shabby, commercialized society . . . befits him more than Williams." It is, after all, "Stevens who would write 'The Man on the Dump' from an ivory tower elevation that permitted the exotic figurations and highfalutin language of that poem."[5] While the contemporary romantic was not yet a man *on* the dump in Stevens' essay, but one looking at it intently from a safe distance, my reading of "The Man on the Dump" will focus on its conception of the poet's proper ambience, his poetic language—*especially*, we might say, the 'highfalutin' sort—as trash on a dump. Hence, since the poet's language and his dwelling, as I have argued, are nearly interchangeable terms, the poem will be analyzed insofar as it describes the dump as a locale for poetry, as the place in which poetry is created, even as the dump itself is, in the poem's own vocabulary, "rejected." This complexity can not only be made more understandable in relation to the essay on Williams, but may also add depth to our discussion of the early poetry studied in chapter I and the poetry of *Ideas of Order*.

Dwelling on the cyclic movements of sun and moon, the first stanza describes nature itself in terms of mechanical mass production.

> Day creeps down. The moon is creeping up.
> The sun is a corbeil of flowers the moon Blanche
> Places there, a bouquet. Ho-ho . . . The dump is full
> Of images. Days pass like papers from a press.
> The bouquets come here in the papers. So the sun,
> And so the moon, both come, and the janitor's poems
> Of every day, the wrapper on the can of pears,
> The cat in the paper-bag, the corset, the box
> From Esthonia; the tiger chest, for tea.

The 'creeping' alternation of sun and moon suggests a loss of vigor, freshness and peculiarity, as they are coming and going with the automatized predictability of the machinery of "mechanical reproduction" shaping modern culture understood by Walter Benjamin, in the famous essay published in the same year, as resulting in a loss of the "aura" of the work of art.[6] In Stevens' poem, this notion is juxtaposed with an eccentric, 'highfalutin' diction that imagines the sun to be a 'corbeil,' a sculpted representation of a flower basket placed at the top of a portal's 'capital' pillar. This French word joins the moon "Blanche" (possibly an echo of Matthew Arnold's "moon-blanched shore" in "Dover Beach") and the French derivative "bouquet" in providing a sense of artificiality and strangeness, whose stylistic opposite, the nonsensical exclamation "ho-ho"—used in *Harmonium's* heavily ironic "Depression Before Spring" (*CP* 63)—further augments the stylistic disagreement. These bouquets come, as in "The Emperor of Ice-Cream" (*CP* 64), *Harmonium's* eccentric death poem, "wrapped in last month's newspapers."

Just as speaker of "The Man with the Blue Guitar" feared that he might have to say that "the sun no longer shares our works" (*CP* 168) and appears on some level to *imagine* this state of things by refusing to anthropomorphize the sun, the one in "The Man on the Dump" can be seen to make an elaborate metaphorical effort at expressing a state of ontological disconnection—of terminally 'dead metaphor'—if only to escape or evade this state. The word 'creeping' also recalls poem XVII of "Like Decorations in a Nigger Cemetery" (*CP* 153), which describes the sun's westward movement as a loss of its life-giving powers in the spiritually deadening ambience of the West: "The sun of Asia creeps above the horizon / Into this haggard and tenuous air, / A tiger lamed by nothingness and frost." Patricia Parker has framed a discussion of Stevens and metaphor in Derrida's discussion in "White Mythology," of metaphor as an ancient teleological 'plot'—echoed in Stevens' title "The Westwardness of Everything" (*CP* 455). Derrida scrutinized the discourses according to which the movement of the sun itself, the sensible kernel of metaphor, from East to West, from origin to civilization, sense to signification, should finally—ideally—return to its original, full sense and place of origin.[7] Significantly, a "tiger chest"—suggesting the power and spirit of the Asian animal—lies on the dump in the form (possibly) of an empty tea box.

The word 'image' plays a curious but highly important role in the poem, not least in light of its centrality to the poetics of Imagism, where it functioned as the crucial outcome of poetic art: "It is better," Pound famously argued, "to present one Image"—"that which presents an intellectual and emotional complex in an instance of time"—"in a lifetime than to produce voluminous works."[8] The 'images' on Stevens dump are of course essentially non-original replications. The epiphanic promise attached to Pound's Image, accomplishing "that sense of sudden liberation; that sense of freedom from time limits and space limits; that sense of sudden growth, which we experience in the presence of the greatest works of art,"[9] is nevertheless exactly what Stevens' poem tries to achieve. A crucial difference between the poetry of Stevens and Pound (and Stevens and Williams) lies in the status given to 'inherited,' 'traditional,' 'conventional'—'dead'—poetic device and the role such elements are given in the texture of his poems. Even if the dump presupposes another, superior (*prior*, *anterior*, *exterior* or *interior*) reality attainable through, say, Romantic epiphany or a Poundian Image, this reality or truth is not conceivable without that which appears to obstruct or conceal it: the images on the dump. The fundamental problem with these images is that, even as they clearly stand for the inorganic and inauthentic, they are supremely, compellingly real. In Stevens' poetry the visual and material aspects of poetry are both foregrounded and distrusted.

The painterly metaphor for poetry, which Stevens makes frequent use of,[10] may thus be misleading as a way of understanding his ideas of poetic language. Bonnie Costello has argued that Stevens' relation to painting "is a far more figurative and conceptual one" than that of a poet like Williams, who "takes the analogy of painting literally and strives for an equivalency of effect in words . . ."[11] Stevens' poetry often suggests that poetry does not operate wholly in the world of light and clarity, and should not only 'present': the poet is a "priest of the invisible" (*OP* 195). In "It Must Be Abstract," the first section of "Notes," the demands for visibility and invisibility are simultaneous imperatives whose relation is formulated with intentional complexity. "It," the poem or 'supreme fiction' projected in "Notes," "must be visible or invisible, / Invisible or visible or both" (*CP* 385). Here, the absence of an 'either' lays the whole pressure of 'must be' on the disjunctive 'or,' which is forced to work both exclusively and inclusively, as both disjunctive and conjunctive. Dis-closure, the way things are brought to light, thus implies a closure, since that which can be seen always indicates more than itself, a surplus that will remain unformulated but operative.[12] In this way, "The Man on the Dump" tries to accomplish a poetry which is not reducible to the images on the dump, but which would be impossible without them.

"The Man on the Dump" is not metrically regular, but its general syllabic and visual 'frame' (most lines consist of 9–12 syllables) may encourage a readiness to experience pentameter, a 'spectral' possibility which may add rhythmic and semantic depth to the poem's combination of ironic and serious diction, its insistent sound repetitions and dizzying, semantically hollowing, circulation of poetic device. The very first line of the first stanza, however, appears to demand four beats:

Day creeps down. The moon is creeping up.
∠ / ∠ x ∠ x * x ∠

The verb phrase "creeping *up*" would normally receive its primary stress on "up," unless a speaker wants particularly to stress the mode of movement, and the alliteration on "day" and "down" in the first phrase may reinforce the sense of distinct rhythmic beats and thus encourage us to project the same rhythmic relation to the corresponding words in the second one—"moon" (metonymically indicating night) and "up"—and thus to bridge the syllabic distance between them by stress-timing. The prosodic and syntactic pause indicated by the point, replacing a conjunctive 'and' or a causal 'therefore,' may also heighten the syntactic and rhythmic integrity of the two sentences and establish them relationally, as possible antitheses. The consequential 'up' and 'down' movement of sun/moon day/night is further underscored by the similarity of the two phrases in rhythmic shape. (A "promotion" of the first syllable of 'creeping' into taking a metrical beat, which I would suggest is very unlikely, would be experienced as a drastic, even unpleasant, "slowing down" of the pace established in the first phrase; and perhaps as an emphatic 'representation' of the creeping motion of day and night). As we shall see, stress-timing rather than syllabic regularity is crucial in this poem, as it enables a perception of syllabically excessive pentameter or, more correctly, five-beat lines (c.f. line 8 above). This possibility will enable us to discuss the possible 'semantic'—associative and affective—functions of pentameter in the poem's drama.

This is especially relevant in the second stanza, where the dump is revealed to consist of poetic language, or to be more precise, the images, vocabularies and rhythms conventionally associated with it. In accordance with Stevens' tendency to identify poetry with "the romantic," the dump's word-images are, in Stevens' words, "what people speak of as romantic." As such, they become involved in a sickening rhythm of "puffing" and "smacking."

> The freshness of night has been fresh a long time.
> The freshness of morning, the blowing of day, one says
> That it puffs as Cornelius Nepos reads, it puffs
> More than, less than or it puffs like this or that.
> The green smacks in the eye, the dew in the green
> Smacks like fresh water in a can, like the sea
> On a cocoanut—how many men have copied dew
> For buttons, how many women have covered themselves

With dew, dew dresses, stones and chains of dew, heads
Of the floweriest flowers dewed with the dewiest dew.
One grows to hate these things except on the dump.

The wind, as in the moralizing tales of the Roman chronicler Cornelius Nepos, is a "blowing" that merely "puffs." Nature's green "smacks" rudely onto vision, and the freshness of water is seen in terms of the oxymoronic freshness of spring water which has been canned up—"smack" may here be extended from meaning a 'blow' or 'smacking sound' sound to its Old English meaning of 'flavor' and 'smell,' as in today's 'to smack of.' The sea is seen on a label stuck on a cocoanut. Prosodically, the wind's iambic "puffing" is located in positions where it performs rhythmic and sibilant 'release,' and 'the dew,' suggesting the virginal and fresh (Bloom points out its reference to one of "Sunday Morning"'s climactic moments),[13] is repeated into nauseous indistinctness, a euphony (or 'dewphony') gone cacophonic.

This ironic foregrounding of the 'poetic function,' a frontal assault on the aura of poetic language, takes place in the ambience of a rhythmically and semantically volatile relationship to the poem's pentameter frame. The presence of iambic pentameter here is difficult to validate in absolute terms (the poem is simply too open to rhythmic interpretation), but it is quite plausible in view of the preceding and following parts of the poem, as well as Stevens' general proclivity for this mode. Assuming a pentameter rhythm will also enable us to suggest a few remarkable effects. The first line can be pentameter only if the noun phrase "long time" takes two beats, and thus takes a 'long time' to pronounce. The 'falling' ('trochaic' or 'dactylic') variations at the beginning or in the middle of lines often lead to a final rising rhythm (an 'iamb'). We need to compensate for the syllabic surplus of the penultimate line (a maximum of fifteen syllables) by way of elision (flow*er-ie*st) if the five-beat rhythm is to be maintained. The very strong enjambments create powerful 'grammetrical' tension between syntax and verse rhythm, on occasion using the line break to create a sense of deception or heightened reification ("like the sea / On a coconut," "dew / For buttons").

But why does one hate these things everywhere *except* on the dump? On the dump these devices—these objects—become visible as what they really are—trash, inert material and cannot be seen in the unreflective, unconscious ways induced by advertising agencies. To some extent, this will recall Pound's modernist admonition to poetic ephebes to "Consider the way of the scientists rather than the way of an advertising agent for a new soap."[14] The idea that the dump reveals these forms as they are, in an imagined absence of conventionalized imagination, and the man itself in his state of destitution, makes it function as a place of purity, even truth. The poet can only reuse, recycle, or repeat these images by first acknowledging (which, again, would mean imagining) their essential inertia and uselessness. It is not only that their dense 'material' exteriority is impenetrable to active consciousness, but that the poet's consciousness is composed of them. He *is*, to make a Heideggerian compound, a *man-on-a-dump*.

In the third stanza, which signals that a movement towards change is being initiated, the restoration of poetic language is enigmatically formulated as a *rejection*:

> Now, in the time of spring (azaleas, trilliums,
> Myrtle, viburnums, daffodils, blue phlox),
> Between that disgust and this, between the things
> That are on the dump (azaleas and so on)
> And those that will be (azaleas and so on),
> One feels the purifying change. One rejects
> The trash.

The "now" announced in the first line indicates the very instant of purifying change that the poem has lost (but is looking for while negating the images that represent it). Coming to terms with its meaning is central to understanding both this particular stanza and the poem as a whole, as it will allow us to sound the depths of the dilemma articulated on the dump. The time of spring, the 'now' of rebirth and epiphany, is figured in the midst of a disgustingly repetitive catalogue of flowers, possibly echoing a passage in the essay on Williams. Referring obliquely to Williams' *Spring and All*, Stevens writes that a poet who, like Williams "is more of a realist than is commonly true in the case of a poet . . . might, at this point, set [himself] up as the Linnaeus of aesthetics" (*OP* 214), thus relating the realist drive of Imagist poetics to the encyclopedic naming of flowers and plants of the Swedish natural scientist. [15] Initially, these enumerations suggest that the 'now' of spring, as a new beginning, is itself on the dump of wasted device and musty convention. Even so, it is different from the two 'disgusts' of spring, those that "will be" on the dump but still circulate in the every-day life of contemporary society, and those that are already on it. In this sense, it is very unclear where this 'between' would itself be located or, indeed, if it can be *located* at all. Referring back to the "now" of spring, it can itself be or happen nowhere but on the dump which, we are now able to see, stretches beyond itself. Even the means to go elsewhere are not to be found anywhere else but on it. It follows that the *rejection* that is announced cannot simply mean an elimination of the dump, a going somewhere else. The dump is, simply, what there is.

An important clue to its meaning can be found in the morphemic composition of the word 'reject,' which could mean to 'throw back,' and thus to 'throw' or 'dump' *again*. This suggests that somewhere in the reuse or repetition of the worn out language of the dump, a kind of activity or motion allowed by the dump, its waste may yield something not reducible to its own materiality. Later, the speaker will perform another 'jection,' another throwing; he will e-ject, which (as I will come back to) means pulling "a day [which, we have been told, is like a paper from a press] to pieces." The man, the poem's speaking sub-ject, is himself *on* the dump with his images, part of this world as it is part of him. He is thus himself imagined as 'thrown' into a world, as Heidegger's analysis of the *Geworfenheit,* or thrown-ness of being-there, *Da-Sein,* proposes. In the Heideggerian sense (which I will only take as far as the similarity of terms takes us) the re-jection of the device on the dump is also a re-casting or re-composition of one's self.

The later "Esthétique du Mal" (*CP* 313–26), deeply concerned with a revision of the sublime, announces a "Panic in the face of the moon" which is due to the sense that the moon no longer conveys anything but "comic ugliness / Or a lustred nothingness." This implies that "he who has lost the folly of the moon becomes / The prince of the proverbs of pure poverty." Thus,

> To lose sensibility, to see what one sees,
> As if sight had not its own miraculous thrift,
> To hear only what one hears, one meaning alone,
> As if the paradise of meaning ceased
> To be paradise, it is this to be destitute. (*CP* 320–1)

Such 'miraculous thrift' is badly needed in the fourth stanza of "The Man on the Dump," when the projected moment of epiphany, the 'now,' which has been made excruciatingly hard to locate, receives a challenging description. A vision of a very artificial moon is accompanied, as on a stage or in a film, by orchestral music.

> That's the moment when the moon creeps up
> To the bubbling of bassoons. That's the time
> One looks at the elephant-colorings of tires.
> Everything is shed; and the moon comes up as the moon
> (All its images are in the dump) and you see

> As a man (not like an image of a man),
> You see the moon rise in the empty sky.

Even in this moment of elevation the moon is initially "creeping up," as a stage prop elevated by stage machinery. Perhaps, in the context of the poem's particular drama, it is a bit too *ex machina*. Its newness can neither be justified by the language in which it 'happens' (which is not new or more real) nor in the images (which remain the same). Hence, it must come from elsewhere, yet be an effect of the poem's desire to move toward it. Again, as in "Sailing after Lunch" the poetry of poetry is not, because it cannot be, what is seen, but what is felt at what is seen. There is a 'feeling' of purifying change, required by the formal push towards truth of the poem's trajectory itself, and thus produced by will rather than discovery, in sheer defiance of the sameness and repetitiousness of the images. In this ambience, even looking at old tires can produce epiphany. A miraculous and entirely irrational capacity for imaginative falsification is suggested in the perception of African natural sublime in the colors of a disused car tire. The idea that 'now' "everything is shed" contrasts with the idea that this 'now 'is spring, since it is an image pertaining to autumn which in Stevens' seasonal imagery is a passage to the emptiness of winter. The forms of spring are themselves overlaid with, and subject to, the decreations of autumn.

Even if the diction changes toward the end of the stanza, as the moon goes from "creeping up," to "coming up" to majestically "rising" in an "empty" sky, allegedly free from props, the essential problem remains: if all the images of the moon are on the dump, the moon actually seen must be one of those images. This dilemma is contained in the preposition *as* in the phrase 'the moon comes up *as* the moon,' which could certainly be seen as tautological—'the moon comes up as the moon comes up,' 'you (a man) see as a man sees'—and thus as somehow pointless. To achieve a significant difference, we need to allow for a change of intonational and emotional emphasis, stressing the second term of the comparison: the moon comes up as *the moon*, as *itself*, not as an image. Just as the falsifying music of the blue guitar was justified if it was a "*man* who plays a blue guitar" (*CP* 166) we need to stress *man* in "you see as a man." [16] At all events, the image of the moon can no longer, as the poem pushes towards closure, be allowed to be a *mere* image, but needs to be believed to be the moon and retain all its sublime power, even if the very 'emptiness' of the sky, achieved by rejecting the images on the dump, is itself an image used again, re-jected.

This precarious epiphany of stanza four is followed by a very complex last section working to encapsulate the poem's preceding parts. Its initial figure initiates a sequence of comparisons that draw attention to the discrepancy between the device and that which has to be expressed. The dump is now not only a figure of poetic language in terms of lifeless waste, but of noise:

> One sits and beats an old tin can, lard pail.
> One beats and beats for that which one believes.
> That's what one wants to get near.

The humbleness and poverty of the (one imagines) rusty tin can and its primitive metallic noise, endemic to the dump, as opposed to harmonic or euphonic ideals of poetic diction, has a parallel in the modest but inclusive jangling of rusty strings on the blue guitar. While the primary meaning of 'for,' in "for that which one believes," is 'in search of' this object, or the lack of it, it can also mean 'because of,' signifying both end and origin of poetry's "beating"; an origin which is not only as yet unformulated but in principle unattainable. It, whatever it is, will not let itself be possessed, but remains something one "wants to get near." Dennis Taylor has suggested the meta-metrical potential of line two, where the falling ending of the first line is followed by a sequence of five steadily iambic "feet," which appear to establish the iambic pentameter not only as part of the poem itself, but as part of the dump. In this way, the dump becomes part of the poem as we read it: the first two 'beats' are also rhythmic beats perceived by the reader. Such a gesture is thus not only intellectualizing, requiring a specialized metrical competence, but may force itself into the experience of the reader who, in experiencing the pentameter, may be 'living,' i.e. re-jecting, the old language of the dump in its linguistic materiality and repetitious motion.[17]

The remainder of the stanza is constituted by a series of questions which, as both Bloom[18] and Vendler[19] argue, can best be defined as suggestive and semi-rhetorical, exploiting the juxtaposition between the items and noises of the dump with images of articulated voice, either speech or song (an "either-or" which, as I will argue, is significant). The first question implies that "what one wants to get near" is not a sublime truth located elsewhere, but one's own self. It initiates a dispute between different kinds of bird song:

> Could it after all
> Be merely oneself, as superior as the ear
> To a crow's voice? Did the nightingale torture the ear,
> Pack the heart and scratch the mind? And does the ear

Solace itself in peevish birds? Is it peace,
Is it a philosopher's honeymoon, one finds
On the dump?

The 'superiority' of the ear, of the poetic self, to the voice of the crow, a typical denizen of dumps, can be understood as the creative power of active hearing to imagine harmony and order in disorder and disharmony. To be 'merely oneself,' then, means being alone, talking only to one's singular self, which "In Sailing after Lunch" meant 'expunging' other people and their languages. This formulation contains the gist of much modern and postmodern ethical criticism of Stevens' poetry, directed against a 'conservative' strain in the modernism that nostalgically wanted to fill the void after the supposed loss of central fictions and traditional hierarchy. The dump, in this case, is a predicament to be deplored and transcended, since its images and noises, or images of noise, are merely hostile and undesired. But Stevens' dump is not just a vision of a fallen civilization to be redeemed, in which case rejection would mean substitution or simply going elsewhere. It is, we have learnt, a place *to which* one escapes, a truth one seeks, if only to reject it again, escape from it; this, in turn, cannot be done without, or apart from it. It is not only a figure of things rejected, but contains even the means of imaginative rejection itself. Thus, the dump and its sound ambience function in ways that cannot only be understood as negative, without losing a good deal of what the poem is about.

While the poem's desire, as the last stanza will confirm, is largely formulated in epistemological terms, its imagery and its enactment of the "poetic function" makes the dump a powerful figure of what we could call 'non-sense,' verbal signs that can no longer fulfill their proper semantic or grammatical function, but circulate unrealized as homeless phrases, sounds and noises. To the extent that the dump as a metaphor for 'modernity' is also a metaphor for 'poetic language' this language is clearly not one that can be structured "like a grammar," an idea which Bruns associates with Stevens' "epistemological" poetry, as opposed to Bakhtin's dialogic notion that "language is structured like a conversation."[20] The special character of Stevens' use of noise and nonsense lies, I would argue, in its difficult combination of a desacralization of notions of the real, and thus of poetic language as well, and the opposite implication of this process; a drive to attain pure perception and true speech by this very process.

In the sense that Stevens' dump is a metaphor of 'the times'—the dump is (like) the modern world, or the modern world is (like) a dump—we could understand it as an effort at imagining explicitly (rather than just being) what

Bakhtin calls a *chronotope*.[21] As a way of understanding the spatio-temporal formal matrix of any narrative event Bakhtin's concept, as Lecercle proposes, conceptualized the idea that the essence of language does not reside in what Saussure named *langue,* the transhistorical storeroom of signifiers ready to be used, but in the historical and temporal use of these signifiers. Thus, Lecercle argues, it implies that "there is no simple reflection of reality in the work of art, but . . . no linguistic closure either."[22] In this sense, however, the dump of Stevens' poem is both an attempt to figure an *achrony,* in the sense of the disconnected, ahistorical inertia of its linguistic material—it is a *langue* without *parole,* or a *parole* without *langue*—but also of *anachrony,* in the sense that history, the times, and thus one's modern subjectivity is composed by things older and other than 'itself.'[23] Stevens' imagined lyric *ana-chronotope* (which is challenged by the very fact that it *can* be read and interpreted *dia-chronically,* 'through' time) is also imagined sonically, as a dissonance produced by romantic sound images of euphonic bird song being assaulted by other birds or repeated into mere noise.

The 'superiority' of the ear is to some extent already contradicted by the fact that the crow's voice is in fact what the man/poet on the dump seeks, at least insofar as he is on the dump out of free will (which appears to be at least partly the case). The dump's devastating metonymic reference beyond itself to all forms of language thus unsettles the poem's ornithological hierarchy. The ear now takes pleasure in the plaintive noise of "peevish"—querulous—birds like the raucous crow, while Keats's image of perfect mellifluous harmony, the song of the nightingale—itself, in "Ode to a Nightingale," a "plaintive anthem"—forms part of the dump's repetitious cacophony. In his Williams essay, Stevens wrote that "to a man with a sentimental side"—by which he means not only Williams, but himself too—"the anti-poetic is that truth, that reality to which all of us are forever fleeing" (*OP* 213). The 'realist' urge of "The Man on the Dump" is thus a form of escapism, but *from* the reality of the ivory tower, or the traditional imaginative forms which constitute it, towards the 'peace' offered by the dump (even though the ivory tower is brought along as well).

The last six last lines continue asking questions which rhetorically suggest that being on the dump means to live in contradiction, to do things plainly inappropriate to the place one is in:

> Is it to sit among mattresses of the dead,
> Bottles, pots, shoes and grass and murmur aptest eve:
> Is it to hear the blatter of grackles and say
> Invisible priest; is it to eject, to pull

The day to pieces and cry stanza my stone?
Where was it one first heard of the truth? The the.

To sit on the dump and insist on what Gelpi (assuming the point of view of Williams' modernism) calls 'highfalutin' poetic language is to maintain the ivory tower in the midst of its destruction, to stick to a noble ideal of poetry even when everything suggests that it no longer exists: the death of the ivory tower—much like the death of 'the book' which, as Derrida has suggested, is caused by "a convulsive proliferation of libraries"[24]—results from the feeling that it exists everywhere.

The contradictory activities of the man on the dump are indicated in a verbal series—it is to sit among the garbage, to hear the grackles, to pull the day (which is like a paper from a press) to pieces, to e-ject it—which is corresponded to by verbs of a rising vocal intensity: to *murmur*, to *say* and, finally, to *cry*. These acts are only contradictory, however, to the extent that this is also *what one does* on the dump, which is essentially a place of contrary activities. Whether the elevation of vocal pitch implied in these verbs suggests desperation or triumph is an open question. We may recognize this dilemma in "Waving Adieu," in the stuttering "ephebe" of "Notes" and in "Sad Strains of a Gay Waltz," where the lack of modes of expression may be restored by the very expression of the desperation felt in the need to restore it: "Yet the shapes / For which these voices cry, these, too, may be / Modes of desire, modes of revealing desire" (*CP* 122).

The italicized words—*aptest eve, invisible priest* and *stanza my stone*—are uttered illogically, in spite of a hostile context, and appear as prayers or mantras calling upon a semi-magical power intrinsic to the phrases themselves. Uttered against the decay of the dump, however, they are themselves necessarily part of its non-sense fabric. Cook has described Stevens' use of repeated words and sounds as "charms,"[25] an idea derived from the work of Northrop Frye[26] which has been developed by Rosu, who sees the charm's incantatory magic at work in Stevens' sound-patterning.[27] As such, these phrases reveal durable propensities in his sense of poetic language. Stevens' Journal entries from his last Harvard year are full of poetic sketches like the following, written on a holiday in Berkeley, Pennsylvania, on August 1, 1899:

Thought for Sonnet: Birds flying up from dark ground at evening clover: clover, deep grass, oats etc. to circle + plunge beneath the golden clouds, in + about them, with golden spray on their wings like dew. Produce an imaginative flutter of color. (*L* 32)

Here, Stevens takes the sounds, colors and capacity for suggestiveness of words, rather than its subject matter, as his starting point; somewhat like Poe recounting his composition of "The Raven."[28] While this was certainly part of a process of poetic apprenticeship, learning the craft by sensitizing himself to its formal elements, Stevens' fascination with suggestive (rather than semantically purposive) sound and color is a central element even in his later poetics. His later discourse on abstraction and evasion of the pressure of reality—itself, as Maeder has argued, rather 'evasive'—as well as his poetic practice, are tied to the notion that poetry is a question of the "sound of words" (*NA* 31–3). The poetic use of sound becomes not only a challenge to ideological meaning but anagogic, as part of the sound of nature 'itself.' In *Transport to Summer*'s "The Pure Good of Theory" the sound of words is exposed as ultimately more a question of sound 'itself' than the sound of words: "the weather in words and words in sounds of sound" (*CP* 332), a sort of circular implication of the poetic function. Words arise from the subject's metaphysical attempt to relate to 'the weather,' Stevens' later image of the exterior, and contain in their sound a physical presence which makes the weather, the physical world, metonymically accessible through perceiving their semantically and ideologically 'emptied' or 'vacant' physical shape and sound.

Another, more obviously ironic, aspect of Stevens' practice of the sound of words as "imaginative flutter of color" can be seen at the end of his Harvard period in the poem "The Ballade of the Pink Parasol" (*CPP* 496). Here, Stevens used antiquated, foppish and eccentrically decorative poetic diction in highly idiosyncratic ways that would lead him to the stylistic irony of many *Harmonium* poems. The poem's nostalgic *ubi sunt* is clearly itself an object of mockery:

> Answer me, where is the painted fan
>   And the candles bright on the wall;
> Where is the coat of yellow and tan—
>   But where is the pink parasol?

The anti-ending accomplished by the disjunctive "but" which interrupts a continuous series of questions—implying an implausible difference between the last question and the preceding ones—points toward Stevens' later manipulation of syntax. Even if Stevens would later parody the kind of poetic sounds and images he lists in his Journal, it is essential never to understand his parody as wholly ironic in a distanced way, i.e. satirical: Lentricchia has argued that "the master timbre of his voice" is "half-irony."[29] Clearly, this marks an important difference between him and other poets revolting against the Romantic-Victorian poetic idiom, who were hostile to gratuitous, artistically unmotivated, poeticity.

Barbara Fisher has argued that Stevens' use of parody as a "double agent" enables him "both to establish a link with traditional sources and to maintain a distance, separate himself, from those same sources."[30] This is because parody, Fisher suggests, is "one sort of permissible discourse with institutions of the past whether it be the 'Rock' of early religious training or Stevens' other theology, the 'romantic tenements' of aesthetic form and poetic utterance."[31] Stevens' employment of archaically sounding diction in "The Man on the Dump" can be called parodic, but his allusion to Keats' "Ode" also permits him to turn its imagery of invisibility into poetic profit. In the "Ode to a Nightingale," Keats' "listener" "*cannot see* what flowers are at my feet" stooped as he is in the "embalmed darkness" of creative night or twilight, but is still able to "*guess* each sweet" among which there is "the coming musk-rose" full of "dewy wine."[32] The man on the dump also needs to defy what is visible to the eye and become a "priest of the invisible," but he can only do this by bringing the dusky forms of the sublime inherited from Keats into complete visibility, exposing their very surface and sound, repeating, italicizing and thus visualizing the phrase *invisible priest*.[33]

This material sense of poetic 'device' is forcefully suggested in the alliterative phrase "*Stanza my stone*," which imagines the destructive urge to rip newspapers apart as simultaneous with a desire for new poetic form, latent in the phrase's prosodically and phonetically chiastic shape (recalling how Emily Dickinson's persona slammed shut her doors of attention "like *stone*"). The implicit analogy between poetic language and natural material is based on the idea that the stanza is a crucial material, graphic sign of poetry, which carries a sense of closure and finality in itself. As one of the defining features and cognitive markers of written or printed poetry, the stanza makes the reader recognize a poem or part of a poem as a spatio-temporal semantic unity, promising resolution, closure, satisfaction, even truth, in a way that its 'raw material,' ordinary language, is unlikely to provide.

The italicized phrase *Stanza my stone* may touch on two crucial ideas of imaginative language, both assaulted and desired on the dump. The phrase itself recalls Plotinus' Neo-Platonist argument which, as Abrams has explained, was an important influence on Romantic poetics as it to some extent was conceived against Plato's relegation of art to insignificance, thus giving artists a cultural dignity approximate, or even greater, than that of the philosopher.[34] Plotinus' argument envisioned art in the image of a stone sculpted by the agency of human 'intellectual beauty,' bearing the imprint of a power intrinsic to the human soul. This, however, is a gift that exists *before* the trace it leaves in the rock and it will therefore remain different and superior to the material on which it makes its mark: the most important task being to 'follow' the trace back to its origin. In the sense that the philosophical consequences of the linguistic nihilism implied by the dump should not be understood as its endpoint or its lesson, the poem-as-dump can clearly be related to Platonic theory, even if (or because) it makes a Platonic pursuit appear impossible. Although the dump is a figure of the *truth* of the contemporary, the man on the dump simultaneously locates truth 'beyond,' 'above,' or 'before' the dump.

The stanza itself, in the sense that it has been a visual icon of expressive elevation and formal integrity, can also be related to Aristotelian theory. For Aristotle, imitative form, whose most important aspect was "the genius for metaphor," was not simply a mere copy, but a means to discover a potency inherent in nature itself, accomplished in the dynamism of human nature's 'instinctive' creative interaction with it: in this sense, it is strongly akin to the Kantian idea of the 'synthetic' imagination which Stevens inherited from thinkers such as Coleridge and Richards. The Aristotelian legacy in Anglo-American criticism has above all been modeled upon his idea in *The Poetics* that the creation of mimetic form is visible in the internal coherence of the work of art, rather than in a more or less adequate relation to something beyond it. In Stevens, the imagination's work on reality is often understood as making reality, as "The Irrational Element in Poetry," more amenable, improving on it: "The poet," one of his *Adagia* suggests, "makes silk dresses out of worms" (*OP* 184). In the Aristotelian sense, then, the image of the stanza is that of a natural material hard as rock, but one that has been shaped by human agency.[35]

Lakritz has argued against an understanding of Stevens' poetics as an Aristotelian search for mastery over resilient material.[36] *Ideas of Order*'s "Mud Master" (*CP* 147–8) appears to confirm this view: the title's wished-for master, a god-like shaper of clay into human form, "The peach-bud maker, / The mud master, / The master of the mind" remains distantly vague, a "shaft of light / Falling, far off, from sky to land," itself a form of a shaper not quite shaped by a mind still muddy, "snarling / Under muddy skies." Stevens poetry in "The Man on the Dump" and elsewhere is simply too temporal, mobile and catachrestic—too linguistic—to give the impression of shaping mute material into something articulate. This study has taken the material—but not necessarily the 'subject matter'—of Stevens' poetry to be primarily linguistic, verbal, and, as such, already saturated with problematic meanings, in the sense of 'physical' as well as 'ideological' material.

In the introduction to *The Necessary Angel,* Stevens defined "poetry itself, the naked poem" as "the imagination manifesting itself in its *domination of words*" (*NA* viii. my italics.). This can be understood as rooted in a sense that unless the imagination dominates words, they (and the people whose culture they reflect) will end up dominating, even obliterating the very idea of, the individual imagination.

In the context of modernist formal change, the stanza may both be seen as giving spatio-temporal shape to ordinary language, or to fragment or do violence to it: this may even be part of the same process. Hence, in the legacy of free verse, the stanza and what is often called the fragment share common characteristics. The 'fragment' can not itself be understood only to indicate an abysmal groundlessness as the (non)essence of the post-religious world, or imitate a disordered perception of the modern mind (which itself would be a creative achievement). As in Eliot's shoring of fragments against the ruins of the present, the fragment may itself be a metonym or synecdoche for a lost unity that can be traced back through it. In Pound's sense, modernist fragmentation may accomplish a writerly and readerly 'vortex', compelling readers to expand one's historical and linguistic consciousness by solving a trans-temporal puzzle: a process, which the sociologist Charles Taylor has argued makes us "reach somehow between them and thus beyond them."[37] However, as Taylor adds, modernist fragmentation is not only a form of objectivism, implying the presence of a superhuman, transhistorical principle. Pound's and Eliot's fragments "come indexed to a personal vision," which means that to be moved by The Waste Land "is also to be drawn into the personal sensibility which holds all these [fragments] together."[38] While the phrase *Stanza my Stone* establishes the stanza as part of the fragmentation of the dump, as an old item of poetic device, it also implies its association with integral, solid and transhistorical truth.

Christopher Prendergast has argued, in *The Order of Mimesis,* that Plato's repudiation of art was not only a stage in a search for truth in and for itself but a question of *order.* It was even "less," he argues, "an anxiety about duplicity than about duplication, or less a question of truth than of taxonomy. For what is at risk in the endless proliferation of 'images,' the endless play of representations made possible by mimesis, is a proper sense of 'division' and classification."[39] In Stevens' "Anglais Mort á Florence," a poem in *Ideas of Order,* the speaker's vision of the moon (like that of the man on the dump) is no longer vividly real, a predicament which is linked to the loss of a time in which he "stood alone" without the help "of God and the police" (*CP* 148). If the juxtaposed activities of destroying newspapers and crying "*stanza my stone*" are seen as two aspects of the same coin, as each other's consequence, it would imply a sequence of events: the man *first* seeks (or, if a poet, imagines) the dump, in order to embrace essential poverty and decreate false essences, and *after* this move, a sort of phenomenological epoché, gains the capacity of fresh creation, of transcending it. Another, darker, way of seeing it is that the activities on the dump, once it has been established, become contradictory, incompatible, and occurring without any temporal or hierarchical order. Stevens' dump, which is full of images—visual, material, sonic and vocal—not only describes an endless reproduction but a destruction of hierarchies and is, in this sense, a 'lawless' ambience where there can be no policing of the order of things: the ivory tower is no longer a poetic panopticon, but lies shattered among the debris.

Prendergast addresses a historical opposition between a conception of mimesis as "health," the human feat of creatively orienting oneself within the world valued by Aristotle, and two major anti-mimetic positions, the first of which is the Platonic idea of imitative form as a 'poison' intervening between truth and the perceiver. The second aspect, which Prendergast names 'nausea,' is exemplified by Roland Barthes, "for whom the mimetic text is 'sickening' . . . not because it troubles an order in which everything is in its proper place, but . . . because it *confirms* that order."[40] This, Prendergast argues, indicates an "ambiguity and instability in the concept of mimesis which enables it to produce diametrically opposed interpretations, to gather itself into notions of both norm and transgression, conservation and subversion."[41] In view of Stevens' poem, the difference between the ideas of poison and nausea is that the former describes a sort of epistemological medical diagnosis—it implies both "truth" and "health" as its contrary—whereas the latter refers to an experience or a symptom (as, we could say, an image of the psycho-somatic) and is thus more a question of aesthetic effect, readerly reception or 'taste.' Clearly, both poison and nausea are implied in the image of the dump: the man on the dump is looking for truth in the midst of chaotically proliferating images, and experiences a nausea, despairing at the impossibility of the fresh: his desire is simultaneously epistemological and aesthetic.

Yet even as an image of dissatisfaction, the dump is a creative response to a desire for truth. It is more than a merely negative, 'deconstructive' image of non-originality. Its nonsense does not only indicate a simple lack of meaning—or, reversing it, a new fullness of meaning intentionally eliding the restrictions of linguistic normalcy.[42] The ironies of its use of 'highfalutin' language is not an irony of distantiation and denunciation, but an irony, we could say, in irony itself, since the ironic use of useless poetic device cannot but be affected by its positive energy. One of the most powerful challenges of the image the dump, I would argue, is that it is both nostalgic (desiring a beyond, a 'before' or 'after' the dump) and realistically pragmatic (the man will have to start where he stands): two apparently mutually exclusive attitudes which nevertheless relate to each other in different ways.

The poem's unanswered last question, as to where the truth was first heard of, where the desire for truth was raised, remains unanswered, suggesting that this origin is simply not to be found. The question's very existence, however, the fact that it has been raised at one point can itself be seen as evidence that the 'truth,' although it cannot simply be found or 'discovered,' operates in powerful ways that cannot simply be neglected: the question itself, like Heidegger's *Seinsfrage,* indicates or implicates it. In "Questions are Remarks" (*CP* 462–3), Stevens would in Wordsworthian fashion compare a child's pure questioning when confronted with the universe—"Mother, what is that?"—to that of "drowsy, infant, old men" who doubt the essence and identity of things—"Mother, my mother, who are you?" If both the origin and desire of poetry is truth and if poetry, desiring to know its origin, needs to return to it but cannot, it still has to begin afresh, be original, in the middle of things already begun and beginning: Stevens' end of epistemology is still "in" epistemology.

At the very end of the poem's movement towards closure, the final iamb 'the the,' a gloss both to "the truth" and "that which one believes," formulates what needs to be ultimate sense as utter nonsense: the phrase intensifies the very articulation or deixis of the definite article, its movement of signification, but also gives the impression (as a sign without any signified except signification itself) of a stuttering incapacity to get to the point of reference. The different grammatical status and metric positioning of the two 'the's—one does the pointing while the other is pointed at—is simultaneously questioned and intensified by their identical sound, shape and lexical meaning, which brings about a tense, loaded simultaneity of phonemic and phonetic perception. As such, it can both be seen as a form of ultimate closure and ultimate disappointment.

THE STILLNESS OF EVERYTHING GONE: "AUTUMN REFRAIN"

The battle on the dump between noisy, anti-poetic birds and Keatsian bird song has a series of precedents in Stevens' oeuvre. The sound of grackles appeared already in *Harmonium*'s "Banal Sojourn" (*CP* 62–3), a poem of disillusion and disgust which describes a scene of tropical tumescence, overripeness and putrefaction in which "one feels a malady." In this antithesis to the stark landscape of "The Snow Man" "The sky is a blue gum streaked with rose," "The trees are b*lack*," and "the *grack*les *crack* their throats of bone in the smooth air." In *Ideas of Order,* the grackles also appear in "Snow and

Stars" (*CP* 133), another poem of disillusionment, perhaps with the natural symbols indicated in the title, which the speaker wishes that the "devil take." Here, they are very irritating heralds of the coming of spring:

> The grackles sing avant the spring
> Most spiss-oh! Yes, most spissantly.
> They sing right puissantly.

The neologism "spissantly," possibly derived from Latin 'spissus,' meaning 'dense,' 'thick,' 'solid' and 'tightly packed'—suggesting a consonant-packed, throat-cracking sound—the invented Frenchism "puissantly," and the French preposition "avant" not only convey ridiculously affected style by themselves, but work with the humpty-dumpty four-beat rhythm to produce an impression of home-spun pretentiousness. The affected enchantment over the "puissance" of the vulgar and anti-vocal grackles suggests the ironic stance of a disenchanted aesthete lamenting a surrounding lack of poetry. The implicit comparison between what is unnatural (French in an American poem) with what is felt to be all too natural in the sense of common, implies the one between beauteous, poetic birds and the American grackles, who are strikingly rude heralds of spring and make its coming seem part of a bothersome routine.

The grackles of "Autumn Refrain" (*CP* 160), a crucial intertext to "The Man on the Dump," are more complex. Just as in the later poem, the nightingale and the moon in "Autumn Refrain" can be taken to refer to the imaginary scene of Keats's "Ode to a Nightingale."[43] But rather than simply bringing positive semantic values to bear on the poem, the allusion may be most important insofar as it signifies convention or "traditional poetry" in its Romantic form as such.[44] As Hollander suggests, the nightingale may also refer to the bird of Milton's first sonnet, "To the Nightingale," which warbles "at eve, when the woods are still" and is asked to "timely sing, ere the rude bird of hate / Foretell my hopeless doom."[45] In "Autumn Refrain," however, the rude sound of grackles becomes involved in the poetical song of the nightingale in a way that makes the two birds very difficult to tell apart at the end of the poem: a change suggested in the later poem XXV of "Like Decorations in a Nigger Cemetery" (*CP* 154), written after "Autumn Refrain," where the musical oriole (putatively both as an effect of the phonetics of its name and its origin: 'golden') is relied on to be realist.

> From oriole to crow, note the decline
> In music. Crow is realist. But, then,
> Oriole, also, may be realist.

Whether Stevens exploited the idea that the oriole is a transatlantic bird—different kinds of orioles are found in both the Old and New World—is an open question, but the idea of the nightingale as coming from a geographical and cultural elsewhere is crucial to "Autumn Refrain." In the *Adagia* Stevens wrote that "Nothing could be more inappropriate to American literature than its English source since the Americans are not British in sensibility" (*OP* 201), suggesting something of a postcolonial aspect of his language problems. In response to a *Modern American Poetry* questionnaire on American and English poetry Stevens would write that since American and English poets lived in "two different physical worlds" they would naturally be different, but also suggested that American poetry was enriched by its English models: "We give ourselves up to [English poetry] not at all because it is English, but because in the minute differences between it and our own poetry we find something that has a poetic value in itself" (*OP* 316). In "Autumn Refrain" the strangeness, which also means the oldness and unreality, of the English bird is turned into poetic value.

The poem takes place in a scene of, at least initially assumed, stillness and contemplation where, following sunset, the grackles have stopped cracking their throats. The poem's central motivational opposition between the nightingale and the grackles, with its associated oppositions—silence and sound, harmony and dissonance, fluency and obstruction, the imagined and the real—is enacted in the phonetic difference between the noisy sibilants and plosives of the sounds of the grackles (including the name 'grackle' itself) and, at the other extreme, the rounded mellowness of "moon," whose very sound is related to the nightingale in a catachrestic image that combines color, symbolism and sound. During a visit home in Reading, Pennsylvania, while living in New York in 1900, Stevens had a romantically sublime experience of nature, which ended disappointingly in disaffection, apparently because he realized the banality and conventional rhetoricity of his own efforts at representing it, a discovery which portends his sensibility at the time of writing the poems studied here.

> A delicate night—most gorgeous, golden stars + the air as fresh and pure as the air of the moon. I have a great affection for moonlight nights somehow + could cry "moon, moon, moon" as fast as the world calls 'thief' after a villain—What a treasure house of silver and gold they are + how lovely the planets look in the heaven—Bah—mere words. (*L* 46–7)

In "Autumn Refrain" the moon is indeed a question of its word and its sound rather than itself. The poem explicitly defines its scene as taking place 'after' sunset, which is also after the sound of the grackles has subsided. But even as the moon enters the scene, the imagined silence of night is challenged by the poem's phonetic texture, which continues to reverberate with the ruckus of grackles.

> The skreak and skritter of the evening gone
> And grackles gone and sorrows of the sun,
> The sorrows of the sun, too, gone . . . the moon and moon,
> The yellow moon of words about the nightingale
> In measureless measures, not a bird for me
> But the name of a bird and the name of a nameless air
> I have never—shall never hear.

Cook has argued that the reader is, on some level, "expected to cut the sound effects [of the grackles] abruptly with the last word"[46] of the first line. The word 'gone,' however, signifying the end of the grackle's noise, and thus the silence of night, is itself further repeated without apparent semantic motivation. The word signifying silence and peace is thus itself brought out as a repeated sound, while retaining the 'sense' of its semantic meaning, and creates, like Poe's "Nevermore," a sort of suggestive atmosphere. (Hence, it appears the reverse of the anadiplotic repetition of "forlorn" in "Ode to a Nightingale," whose repeated ringing makes it become "like a bell," waking the speaker from reverie as its more sinister meanings, involving the poet's own self, are realized.) Thus, even if the grackles and the sorrows of the sun are supposed to be gone, the word 'gone,' itself enabling the transition into the night of the nightingale, does not seem less melancholic or sorrowful.

As very often in Stevens, the poem's manipulation of syntactic and grammatical form plays a major role. Syntactically, the first three phrases, all ending with 'gone,' beg to be interpreted as a temporal complement to a verbal predicate. This predicate, however, is replaced by three suspensive points, which means that the element which would order the discourse into a syntactical hierarchy is missing. The poem's deployment of opposites nevertheless ensures that it maintains the shell of syntactic form by inducing and enabling a reader to 'fill in' the missing parts. If we replace the lacuna where the verb should have been with 'there is,' 'there appears' or 'I can hear' the first seven lines can (provisionally) be reformulated into: 'Now that the noise of the grackles is gone, and the sorrowful sun too, there is the sound of the nightingale, which is nevertheless not really out there, does not exist, in the same way as the grackles do.'

Rosu's reading of "Autumn Refrain," reflecting her argument as a whole, suggests that the difference between the noise of the grackles and the sound of the nightingale, as symbols of the "real and imagined, natural and artificial," is occluded because the poem's sound patterning makes the physical aspects of language obtrude to an extent that makes this "analytical" distinction impossible.[47] This "frustration," however, is at once redeemed by the language that accomplishes it: "the very poetic form, which through repetition of sound has given the poem the status as a self-contained aural unit makes us forget the expected failure."[48] Rosu assumes that this change between poetic and communicative/denotative/representational language, is enabled by a sudden change of perception (enforced by the poem itself) in the demands readers put on it. As such, her idea is based on the idea that the poem's language is *first* entrusted to make sense, and *then,* after a momentary frustration, we give this up in order to enjoy the fact that 'poetic language' does not have to make sense at all or (which is similar) has a sense, or reality 'of its own.' Understood as 'non-referential,' 'poetic language' thus constitutes or at least implies a sphere free of the demands of referentiality, as syntactic order is replaced by the very fact of the poem's implicit sense of beginning and ending, the way vision moves in time over the graphic space of the poem and its contingencies. In "Autumn Refrain," the missing verb is immediately followed by the repetition of "the moon and moon," which is further repeated in the next line, following a pattern that Rosu, seeing it as pervading the poem as a whole, calls "incremental."[49] Retrospectively, then, even the first three lines in which the demand for syntactic resolution is established, can be cognized as mere unfoldings of sounds and printed surfaces.

I would like to formulate this central aspect of the poem differently.[50] If, as Paul de Man has argued (precisely in connection to modern theories of poetic language), a poem's resistance to unitary meaning "can only be perceived by a reader willing to remain within a natural logic of representation"[51] at least long enough (I take him to mean) to have become *involved* in the poem's semantic expression and perceive the peculiar stakes of a poem's particular indeterminacy. The attention to the rhythmically unfolding surface features of words, and their implied sounds, as I see it, stands in a relationship of tension and simultaneity with the 'synoptic' function of syntactical order and semantic depth sought for in an effort to visualize the poem's scene and course of events. In this sense, Stevens' sound repetitions are neither simply triumphant nor clearly 'alternative,' but indicate a productive ambiguity of repetitious form in Stevens which is not only pleasurable but often signifies the circular reproduction, a form of nausea, of present, ideologically saturated forms of the imagination. The binary distinctions grafted onto the concept of poetic language in much modern theory, often related to the attainment of a sexual, social or political utopia—serious language vs. play, masculine vs. feminine language, the 'semiotic' vs. the 'symbolic,' the physical vs. the mental, etc.[52]—are different from that defined by "Autumn Refrain"which, in turn, to some extent governs the 'sense' of its rhythms. Just as in the essay on Williams's poetry, the distinction between the poetic and the anti-poetic is mobile, pragmatic and strictly non-essentialist, questioning the borders between poetic language and the un-poetic, even if this is itself understood as a poetic questioning

A crucial source of tension in the rhythm of "Autumn Refrain" is, again, the ample syllabic possibilities for pentameter. Initially, however, the first two iambic and decasyllabic lines may promote a sense of four-beat rhythm, chiefly as an effect of the configurative powers of its strong alliterations, which are likely to encourage a projection of equivalence onto the rhythmic level as well. Thus, I propose, it appears plausible not to promote either of the 'of's (*) into taking a beat.

> The *skr*eak and *skr*itter of the evening *g*one
> x / x   / x x* x / x /
> And *g*rackles *g*one and *s*orrows of the *s*un,
> x   / x   /   x   / x x* x /

The third and fourth lines extend the rhythm into six stresses per line (although a reader could get a sense of pentameter by demoting (*) in the third and (**) in the fourth):

> The sorrows of the sun, too, gone . . . the moon and moon,
> x / x x x / /* /   x / x /
> The yellow moon of words about the nightingale
> x / x / x /   x /**x / x /

Line five, however, is difficult to experience as anything but pentameter, and the triple rising ('anapestic') rhythm of the sixth line is concluded by a final 'iamb,' which resolves the heavy emphasis put on the beat-taking words— "name," "bird," "name," "nameless"—by stress-timing, giving a sense of an increase in expressive effort. The end of this extensive rhythmic and syntactic sequence modifies or adds to the paradoxical negation/evocation of the nightingale, by its rhythmically disruptive foregrounding of the auxiliary 'shall,' which begs for abrupt emphasis indicated by the hyphen.

In measureless measures, not a bird for me
  x ∠   x   x   ∠   x   ∠   x ∠   x   ∠
But the name of a bird and the name of a nameless air
  x   x   ∠   x x ∠   x   x   ∠   x x   ∠   x   ∠
I have never—shall never hear.
 /   x   ∠ x   ∠   /   x   ∠

The energetic insistence that the nightingale is "unreal," and does not belong to the speaker's world, intensifies the poem's strategy of invocative negation by saturating the poem with its presence. In the creative night, where the poet's own voice should be allowed to resound after the grackles are gone, there is only the name of a bird whose song the speaker has never heard and never will. Its 'measures,' suggesting musical as well as metrical measures, are 'without measure'; without verifiable, visible form and therefore of palpable reality. But it is precisely by virtue of this that these measures, which may refer both to the bird's song and the song *about* the bird, defy or overwhelm finalizing and reifying cognition. They exist only as a presence beyond words, a rhythm beyond meter, or a meter beyond rhythm, yet manifested in it. The 'air' that the bird sings *has* a name, but one that has to name a music that resists naming. Even so, the poem's assertions of immanence are challenged by its vivid materiality: "Autumn Refrain" is not only *about* refrains but composed *of* refrains, in their most 'material,' 'superficial' and iterative aspect. The very name of the bird and its sounds indicate the bird's lost song: the nightingale is an invisible priest whose name is a priest of the invisible (priest . . . and so on).

The part of the poem just analyzed consists of either one or two sentences, depending on whether the points of suspension are taken to indicate an ending or a hesitation in the middle of one single phrase. In line eight, however, there is a definite signal of a *turn* in the poem's argument, an "and yet"—qualified by the directional preposition "beneath"—which indicates that the nocturnal silence, "the stillness of everything gone," resounding with the mute song of the nightingale, is not final. The noun 'stillness,' derivated from the adjective 'still,' meaning 'calm,' 'motionless' or 'silent,' pervades the poem's semantics, but may also imply the contextually opposite sense of 'still' as adverb, thus expanding the poem's concessional 'and yet'—the nightingale is 'nevertheless' here—as well as its related temporal sense: the sound of the grackles is 'still' residually present, having lingered on after nightfall, to 'grate' the words of the nightingale:

> And yet beneath
> The stillness of everything gone, and being still,

Being and sitting still, something resides,
Some skreaking and skrittering residuum,
And grates these evasions of the nightingale
Though I have never—shall never hear that bird.
And the stillness is in the key, all of it is,
The stillness is all in the key of that desolate sound.

To grate does not only mean, figuratively, to annoy or disturb, but a grating sound can be produced by moving something sharp and solid over a hard surface. The residuum of the grackles can thus be understood as scraping or rasping on what would be the smooth, evasive surfaces of the "words about the nightingale," reviving the skreaking and skrittering of the beginning. This is not only, in the words of Stevens' later "The Motive for Metaphor" (*CP* 288), to apply "steel against intimation," but to define the euphony and harmony of the words of/about the nightingale, an ever-receding but ever-present bliss, as an impervious rock hard surface. The grating of the grackles is in this way not primarily disturbing or destructive, but is what enables the song of the nightingale be heard at all and take on reality, for 'grating' comes close to being a transitive verb akin to 'producing' or 'speaking,' suggesting that the grackles somehow make "those evasions of the nightingale" real. Possibly, the speaker's need to repeat the declaration that he has never heard, nor shall ever hear the nightingale indicates, in conjunction with the poem's insistent repetitions of words and sounds attached to it, that he may in fact have a deep experience of it.

The initially disturbing grackles unexpectedly partake in the "key"— suggesting a particular range of tonal harmony—of the solemn stillness of the ending, which is positively unclear about which bird is indicated by "that desolate sound." This ambiguity suggests that the sounds are not to be heard except in relation to each other; that the desolate sound, then, is the song of the nightingale grated by the grackles or, which is almost the same, the grackles residing after their repression or evasion by the moonlit night of the nightingale. Their mutual negation—the grackles are *not* heard after dusk and the nightingale has *never* been heard—is in this way turned into an affirmation in which both participate by questioning, ex-cluding each other. Thus, while the sound of grackles in "Autumn Refrain" and "The Man on the Dump" is rendered as a disagreeable, deafening noise, a sort of sonic 'pressure of reality,' it is also a positive force. As a raw principle of empiri-cal reality not muted by the hierarchical 'silencing' of orderly harmony, its import is similar to the "barbaric yawp," Whitman's anti-domestic American sound image for poetic language. Yet having been acknowledged as the truly real, this sound needs itself to be evaded in order to be heard as separate, as not yet part of 'poetic language.'

This relation of strangeness between the poet, whose real ambience—reality—is a world of grackles, and the nightingale, can be formulated as a vital, necessary strangeness at the beginning as well as at the end of poetic creativity. The idea that "Poetry," as one of the *Adagia* claims, "should resist the intelligence almost successfully" (*OP* 197) is not only a frustration, or lack of self-realization on behalf of the reader, but an ethically determined refusal to claim, perhaps unjustly, a familiarity.[53] The problematic 'intelligibility' of the nightingale is a strange example of this. It is familiar, perhaps too familiar, paradoxically intelligible without being heard, but insistently defined as alien. The sound of the nightingale is, using Stevens' pun, both "close" and "closed."[54]

AT THE END OF THE MIND:
PECULIAR BIRDS IN LATER STEVENS

In Stevens' poetry, bird song, like animal sound in general, is used both as what Rosu has called a "sound image"—an image accessible to our mind's ear—and as a metaphor for both cognition and expression. In this sense, as Hollander has argued, "the passionately niggling nightingale" of "The Comedian as the Letter C," as the very "hymn and flight of the vulgar . . . heads a catalogue of problematic songbirds throughout Stevens' poetry."[55] Bird song, as part of what Hollander calls Stevens' "complex," and "bewildering" "master trope" of music, implies a set of oppositions which do not simply correspond to each other: noise vs. harmony, cry vs. song, disorder vs. order, alienation vs. solace. In *Harmonium,* we find both the unpleasant cry of the peacocks in the sinister repetitiousness of "Domination of Black" (*CP* 8–9), and the agreeable warblings of the Romantic "wakened birds" of "Sunday Morning," who "before they fly, / Test the fields by their sweet questionings" (*CP* 68). In *Ideas of Order*'s "Meditation Celestial and Terrestrial" (*CP* 123–4) the very word "warbling," which normally denotes the rather sweet, domesticated sound of sky-larks or nightingales, is turned into a metonym for the primitive, disgusting, inexorability of spring. Thus, bird song is a sign of an primal force that overpowers human attempts at ordering: "What are radiant reason and radiant will / To warblings early in the hilarious trees / Of summer, the drunken mother?" Here, birds are "wild warblers" "warbling in the jungle."

After the troubled thirties, other bird sounds appear in crucial places. In "It Must Change," the middle section of "Notes," the "be thou" of Shelley's attempt to identify with the West Wind reappears as a twitter emitted by a modest sparrow. This phrase, denoting poetic diction both in terms of euphony and its implication of desire for identification and inclusion, is confronted with the destructive, anti-poetic, sounds of the wren, jay and robin. The phonic contrast between discordant, obstructive noise and euphony had already been defined as an aesthetic strategy by Stevens. The play of the sounds of the letter C in *Harmonium*'s "The Comedian as the Letter C" was, Stevens told Latimer[56] (L 293–5), the very point of the poem, whose blank verse is pervaded by eccentric and parodic verbiage and the "hissing and screeching" sounds of this letter. As Stevens had explained, the plosive /k/ was one of the provocative, and comic sounds of the letter C.[57] Even considered on its own, however, the High Romantic "bethou" is repeated to an extent that makes it like any other sound (like dew and the flowers on the dump) and eventually merge with the others into indistinctness.

> Bethou me, said the sparrow to the crackled blade,
> And you, and you, bethou me as you blow,
> When in my coppice you behold me be.
>
> Ah, ké! The bloody wren, the felon jay,
> Ké, ké, the jug-throated robin pouring out,
> Bethou, bethou, bethou me in my glade.
>
> There was such an idiot minstrelsy in rain,
> So many clappers going without bells,
> That these bethous compose a heavenly gong.
>
> One voice repeating, one tireless chorister,
> The phrases of one single phrase, ké-ké,
> A single text, granite monotony,
>
> One sole face, like a photograph of fate,
> Glass-blower's destiny, bloodless episcopous,
> Eye without lid, mind without any dream—
>
> These are of minstrels lacking minstrelsy,
> Of an earth in which the first leaf is the tale
> Of leaves, in which the sparrow is a bird
>
> Of stone, that never changes. Bethou him, you
> And you, bethou him and bethou. It is
> A sound like any other. It will end.

The aura of bird song, and with it, Romantic poetry, is gone here, both as nature and as image; in fact, it is nature that has become mere image, a "photograph of fate" reproduced in a machinery of endless repetition. Monotony—the lack of tonal and/or rhythmic variation—is the other face of pictorial one-dimensionality, suggesting that the air, as "It Must Be Abstract" formulated it, is "is not a mirror but bare board" (*CP* 384). The relation between the two sounds does not, as in "Autumn Refrain," signify a relation between sound as such and silence, light and darkness, before and after, but are only the very physical sounds and their relations; as in the abstract surfaces of modern pictorial art. The result, like the white eyes of *Harmonium*'s "Bird with the Coppery, Keen Claws" a possible forerunner, is an "eye without lid," sight without shadow, an impossibility of evasion or distinction. The nightingale has simply become the grackle and vice versa, whereas in "Autumn Refrain" and "The Man on the Dump" the noise of grackles was both desired and rejected. It was desired in order to be repudiated or rejected because it is a break not only with the smoothness, but with the very interiority and unreality of the nightingale.

"Notes" could well be seen as a continuation of the project implied in the title of *Ideas of Order*, in the sense that it still defines itself as a social project. However, the ethico-politically loaded 'realist' oppositions between interior and exterior, between the ivory tower and social reality, poetic language and the extra-poetic, American grackle and European nightingale, are not foregrounded in the same way. In the context of "Notes" as a whole, "It Must Change" in particular is programmatically obsessed with difference and sameness in repetition, debating the question of how one can begin, say or perceive anything new if the forms for the new, the forms of newness and freshness as such, have themselves "been fresh a long time." This problem is closely related to the acute sense of a conflict between interiority and exteriority, which is part of the problem of how poetry can indeed truly be an "alternative view of being," enabling the poet to "live *in* the world but *outside* of existing conceptions of it," as one of Stevens' adagia formulates it (*NA* 190) (or, echoing Whitman's words, be "in and out of the game at the same time"). Stevens' poems of the thirties are deeply worried about the price paid for artistic autonomy, in terms of the dilemma of closed, self-going poetic language and its unethical closure to the outside. In this sense, these poems express this problem with greater intensity than Stevens' later longer rhythmic sequences—whether the "most radical experience in temporal effect linked to surface movement" which Maeder sees in "The Man with the Blue Guitar," the anecdotal improvisation with allegorical figures in the long sequences of "Notes," "An Ordinary Evening in New Haven" or

"The Auroras of Autumn," or, simply, his refinement of the rhetoric of ever "qualified assertions" which define the capacity of his late poems to transcend their own dilemmas.

In "Credences of Summer," a long sequence in loose pentameter included in *Transport to Summer*, a bird is admonished to sit down and have a close look at the essential decay of things.

> Fly low, cock bright, and stop on a bean pole. Let
> Your brown breast redden, while you wait for warmth.
> With one eye watch the willow, motionless.
> The gardener's cat is dead, the gardener gone
> And last year's garden grows salacious weeds.
>
> A complex of emotions falls apart,
> In an abandoned spot. Soft, civil bird,
> The decay that you regard: of the arranged
> And of the spirit of the arranged, *douceurs,*
> *Tristesses,* the fund of life and death, suave bush
>
> And polished beast, this complex falls apart.
> And, on your bean pole, it may be, you detect
> Another complex of emotions, not
> So soft, so civil, and you make a sound,
> Which is not part of the listener's own sense. (*CP* 377)

One of Stevens' *Adagia* proposes that just as "Whether is a sense of nature. Poetry is a sense" (*OP* 187). In the passage from "Credences," "the listener's own sense" may carry several different, but related meanings; sense as 'meaning,' as the result of signification or expression; the sensory 'input' of exterior physical or linguistic phenomena which impress or affect perception while remaining, in principle, independent of them; and the Kantian idea of *a priori* cognitive forms or structures that permit us to perceive what we do and how we do it, but arguably impede us to go beyond what is permitted by their boundaries or horizons. This notion can be transferred to the ideas of the 'linguistic' and 'cultural' turns in humanistic scholarship and critical theory, in view of which our experience is always culturally and ideologically determined. In this passage, "the listener's own sense," primarily in the third, cognitive, aspect is assumed to be all too favorable to the "arranged," the orderly and harmonious, related to the poetically sounding French diction of *douceurs* and *tristesses;* 'foreign' words that are familiar insofar as they signify that which sounds poetic, an all too familiar kind of strangeness. The sounds of the spirit of the arranged, or the arranged spirit, are not only "soft," harmless and harmonious, but also "civil," suggesting civilized, official, and common (it is a 'common,' collective 'sense') as well as gentle, accommodating, non-violent. The sound of a bird proper to this atmosphere would, we could say, be a "bethou" (even if Shelley's apostrophe carries a radically anti-social implication). But the bird has perceived, or should perceive, a different, more savage, and arguably truer reality—in which there is neither an Order'd Garden (the gardener is gone) nor a wind in the (motionless) willows. Whether this is because of the way the bird watches, with one implacably motionless[58] 'eye'—also 'one' 'I,' a 'singular' emotionless 'self'—or because it discovers a reality that is really fundamentally inert is, as I have argued, purposely unclear.

The need for the bird's 'song' to be radically incompatible with the listener's sense indicates a fundamental difficulty. While it must resist any attempts at arrangement, the means of its resistance cannot itself come only from outside the perceiver's cognitive pre-structuring. It must still be able to be perceived by or 'in' it, to be sensed without making the kind of sense we would want or expect it to have: we must not, in Hollander's superb formulation, be "overwhelmed with the music of our own listening."[59]

An important distinguishing mark of Stevens' very late poetry is the increasing importance of approaching death and the stress on personal transcendence rather than public or collective fictions. The formidable concern about solipsism that pervades many later poems can surely be related to a form of religious search, but in a very different sense from the idea that a new fictive order should be shaped by poets: an idea that Lentricchia has argued is "the hugest banality of literary modernism."[60] Even if it is no less difficult to draw the line between his middle and late poetry as to describe where Stevens' poetry is personal and where it carries a collective purpose, it is obvious that in *The Rock,* Stevens' last collection published in 1954, poems such as "The Course of a Particular," "To an Old Philosopher in Rome," "The Rock," "Long and Sluggish Lines," "The Planet on the Table," and "Vacancy in the Park," only to mention a few, in different ways revise Stevens' earlier poetry, and consider whether and how the poet's life has made a difference or not. To suggest how some of his earlier themes and images play a part in this new setting I will briefly discuss a couple of very late poems in which the image of bird song again plays a crucial role.

My first example is "Not Ideas about the Thing But the Thing Itself" (*CP* 534), the poem placed at the end of Stevens' last collection, *The Rock.*[61]

Here, the site for perception, the inside of the listeners "mind," is tacitly understood in terms of a room, in which somebody wakes up in early morning. The room does not only symbolize the listener's mind but constitutes a sphere of dream and illusion from which one could and should awake; it both protects and blocks the listener from the truth 'outside.'

> At the earliest ending of winter,
> In March, a scrawny cry from outside
> Seemed like a sound in his mind.

Though not exactly a 'skreek' or 'skritter' this tenuous and fragile voice gives the impression of a not yet made, still not harmonious utterance: it is, echoing the consonant clusters of the grackles, a "*scrawny cry.*" Its very "desolateness," like the residual sounds of "Autumn Refrain," suggests it is deeply vulnerable to ignorance and forgetfulness. In the course of the poem, however, this frailty is transformed into a sign of immense power. The simultaneous vulnerability and centrality of this sound—the poem powerfully asserts both its magnitude and its threatening evanescence—makes the poem's insistent assertion on its existence appear as a form of auto-conviction.

> He knew that he had heard it,
> A bird's cry, at daylight or before,
> In the early March wind
>
> The sun was rising at six,
> No longer a battered panache above snow . . .
> It would have been outside.
>
> It was not from the vast ventriloquism
> Of sleep's faded papier-mâché . . .
> The sun was coming from outside.
>
> That scrawny cry—it was
> A chorister whose c preceded the choir.
> It was part of the colossal sun,
>
> Surrounded by its choral rings,
> Still far away. It was like
> A new knowledge of reality.

The listener's epistemological desire, that the bird voice be a thing in itself and not merely an idea of it can be formulated as a need for contact with an otherness that is not simply imagined, not only a thing of the mind. So much depends on the scrawny cry, whose being authentic, actual, would change everything. The sun is no longer a "battered panache," a worn out cliché or decoration, a material, but the sun, as it were, itself, like the moon majestically rising above the dump in spite of the understanding that *all* of its images are on it. Contrary to the despondent notion of "The Rock" that "it is an illusion that we were ever alive" (*CP* 525), the feeling here must be that one has indeed lived, but not so much in terms of having made a measurable difference in the order of things, as in having been affected by them at all. The silence broken by the bird is an overwhelming sense of interiority, of sameness, and the 'epistemological' capacity to hear the "thing itself," the scrawny cry, is a capacity for transcendence.

The poem's play on the letter c (culminating in the pentametrical middle line of the penultimate stanza) is, as Hollander points out, both a question of the alliterative repetition of its /k/ phoneme in 'scrawny,' 'cry,' 'chorister,' 'choir,' 'colossal' and 'choral' but also the sibilant sound of the letter itself which is punningly part of "pre*ce*ded" as well. C as the 'dominant' musical note to which all other notes return, to which all variations refer, the tenor to which all its metaphorical vehicles is meant to lead back, was the natural sublime, punning on "sea," that Crispin had to escape in the first part of "The Comedian as the Letter C" since it was likely to subjugate him: it now returns as that which the speaker himself is too likely to forget or repress, in a very slight but powerful way. The plosives and sibilants of the letter C are now less obviously part of an irony or obtrusive comedy of sound, but function as deepening a very sincere attempt at presenting a sense of otherness. In comparison with how the earlier poems analyzed here foregrounded the fact of their linguistic construction, "Not Ideas" downplays it. This is not only in the sense that language is not thematized as a poetic problem, but also in its own linguistic texture. Even though it contains stylistically elevated diction, its repetitions of phrases and sounds are less obtrusive in relation to syntax, and the rhythm is less conspicuously regular.

The paradoxical sense of passivity in "Not Ideas," of being at the mercy of something other than oneself while the existence of this other depends on one's own agency, recalls an essential point in Emmanuel Levinas' ethical philosophy, which has been central to the way contemporary literary theory has dealt with the ideas of poetic autonomy inherited from modernism: the ethical capacity of an ego to exceed itself by containing an idea of another being that, while letting itself be known, also "over-flows" its sensible manifestation, its own idea, refusing to be reduced to this containment.[62] The relation with the bird is, in this way of seeing it, anything but neutral, but "invests" the listener with an ethical imperative to hearken to and care for its call. Thus, the relation is defined by both submission and care: the bird is both 'below' and 'above' the listener: the weakness and essential fragility of the voice is turned into an overpower-ing presence overflowing one's conception of it—as part of the colossal sun—and then back again into a minimal presence, vulnerable to silence and oblivion.

Insofar as Levinas defines 'desire,' the wish to reach the other, as 'essentially goodness,'[63] his ideas move against Stevens' epistemological conception of poetry as a way to structure or control a chaotic exterior, and thus, as Ziarek has observed, against some of Stevens' own central terms. Ziarek's reading (attempting to rehabilitate Heidegger's ontology in view of Levinas' ethical critique of it) indicates an interesting aspect of the way that the alleged linguistic and ontological closure of Stevens' poetry has attracted positive evaluations from ethical viewpoints. The endless struggle, or failure, of his poetry's epistemological concern to represent the outside of his mind or language can be interpreted positively: "The failure of Stevens' rhetoric, its almost constant relapse into the metaphysical language of self and other (as self), brings home precisely the problems that language expe-riences in noting otherness."[64] Thus, the power of otherness in "Not Ideas" is closely related to its insistence on the closure of the speaker's mind/room, and to the fact that the epiphany of the bird's voice is mediated by linguis-tic analogy, in the sense that it already 'has a form'—the cry was "*like* a new knowledge of reality." If, as Filreis' formulates it, we neglect the poem's reti-cence and caution, and understand the bird's cry really to be "a new central note distinct from any aesthetic idea, an utterance potentially independent of the imagination,"[65] the poem would somewhat paradoxically be less than ideal for Ziarek's evaluation.

In another of Stevens' last poems, "Of Mere Being" (*OP* 141), written shortly before his death, another, more intimidating, bird appears in a very different setting. As the very opposite of a snow bird, this one, perched in a palm tree, recalls the tropical ambience of Stevens' Florida poems. This tree, however, is located "at the end of the mind," a place of ultimate reality or truth—mere being—and, we may assume, given the retrospective element in Stevens' latest poetry, at the end of a life-long effort to get there. This locus, however, tangentially 'beyond' active thought but still in the mind, is defined in terms of stage artifice, a "décor."

The palm at the end of the mind,
Beyond the last thought, rises
In the bronze decor,

A gold-feathered bird
Sings in the palm, without human meaning,
Without human feeling, a foreign song.

You know then that it is not the reason
That makes us happy or unhappy.
The bird sings. Its feathers shine.

The palm stands on the edge of space.
The wind moves slowly in the branches.
The bird's fire-fangled feathers dangle down.

This disdain for humanity and reason recalls *Harmonium*'s "The Bird with the Coppery, Keen Claws" (*CP* 82), another metallic bird that is symbolic of potent phallocentric natural fictions, "flar[ing], perfect cock, in the sun-pallor of his rock." It is also conspicuously similar to "Miracle, bird, or *golden* handiwork" in William Butler Yeats' "Bysantium," written twenty-five years earlier.[66] Yeats' bird is manmade but the alchemical imagery also suggests that it was born from a 'miraculous' principle beyond and superior to, yet somehow also 'in' man. Likewise, Stevens' bird is both a figure of something superhuman and a *figure* of the superhuman: its 'fire-fangled' feathers are very conspicuously wrought. The glistening solidity of both Yeats' and Stevens' birds is also conspicuously related to the fact that their song is thorny, disagreeable and radically intractable.

At the same time as Stevens' sound image inevitably prompts readers to imagine the bird's song, it also forbids them to do so, since imagining it would mean familiarizing, humanizing, even 'civilizing' it, which would ruin the core meaning of the image, that the bird's song is always distant from and undetermined by human concerns. Stevens thus radicalizes the anthropomorphist dilemma, just as he tried to radicalize Williams' dehumanizing of the moon. The sluggish movement of the wind through the branches of the palm tree (moving its leaves, one imagines, into an undulating motion together with the bird's dangling feathers, echoing the slow motion of the poem's rhythm) appears to dehumanize the metaphor of wind as inspiration, just as in *Harmonium*'s "The Death of a Soldier" the ceasing of human wind (the breath of the soldier) does not affect the wind of nature. When the soldier dies, "the wind stops and, over the heavens, / The clouds go, nevertheless, / In their direction" (*CP* 97).

The image of the metallic bird in "Of Mere Being" can, because of the very solidity of the image and its unpleasant sound, be seen as deceptive, even scornful of reality understood in terms of a pragmatic, communicable, shared reality. Thus, it turns the humanist dilemma of the 'trials of device' in which, as I have argued, poetry is implicitly denounced as rigid and impenetrable, all too material, into a triumphant assertion of creativity. The solidity of the forms of poetic language in "Sailing after Lunch" or "Autumn Refrain," figured as monotonous repetition, was a mimetic and expressive impasse in the form of a gap between poetry's forms and reality ('interior' or 'exterior') that the poems themselves tried to abridge. The 'belatedness' of traditional poetic forms amounted, in such a context, to a lack of receptivity, a closure without a sense of truth. One of the strategies for overcoming this impasse, as in "The Man on the Dump," was to insist that reality is in fact constituted, among other things, by belated and therefore dysfunctional poetic device, as though the real is always hidden by a language perpetually out of date. In "Autumn Refrain" the interiority of the inside, the alleged silence of the nightingale, is not only 'mind' or 'self' or 'house,' but is constituted by poetry itself in the forms of its language. Its conventional images and sounds, the forms of the Romantic lyric of interior vision or epiphany were themselves revealed as exterior and material. Since in the end they are seen as just as noisily torturous as their opposite, the raucous voice of the grackles, they could become part of the speaker's 'real' reality. The "anti-poetry" of 'the bird at the end of the mind,' however, is defined as beyond all possible conceptions and conventional, soft and civil, 'senses' of poetry. As such, it is the purity of poetry intensified, a human creation that has become not only superhuman but a- or in-human, hostile of humanity.

In this sense, this late bird seems to represent what Levinas denounced at an earlier stage of his career, in his anguished post-war critique of modernist aesthetics,[67] "Reality and Its Shadow" of 1948. For Levinas, modern aesthetic ideals involved a disconnection from reality, in the sense that the artistic image merely "substitutes" itself for its object. In doing so, it neutralizes its "real relationship" with the world, which would have to be established in "primary conceiving through action."[68] Levinas links this sense of the image, which "marks a hold on us rather than our initiative, a fundamental passivity," to music:

> Possessed, inspired, an artist, we say, harkens to a muse. An image is musical. Its passivity is directly visible in magic, song, music and poetry.

> The exceptional structure of aesthetic existence invokes this singular term magic, which will enable us to make the somewhat worn-out notion of passivity precise and concrete.[69]

Passivity is here not, as in Levinas' later discussions, a phase of one's encounter with the other that signifies one's lack of dominance, but an effect of the tyrannical authority of the artistic image, which leaves no room for dialogue or interpretation, as all the creative powers after the alleged "death of the gods" have been given to artistic language. To some extent, we have described a different thematics: whereas the bird of "Not Ideas" begs to be taken care of, to be interpreted or co-created, the one in "Of Mere Being" it is described as imposing itself on the reader/listener precisely in its refusal as image, music and rhythm, to be interpreted, or become integrated into the "listener's own sense." The ideal of art *represented* in "Of Mere Being"—the perfect image, a work which is complete in itself, finished, and therefore in need of nothing more, has no future and no past—appears to contradict Stevens' imperatives of movement and change. It also goes against the idea that the main value of art's non-conformism is to rehabilitate human dignity in the face of social and ideological mechanism.

The outcome of this discussion hinges partly upon the ontological status given to the poem itself and partly on what values are put into the concepts of the human vs. the inhuman. As I have argued elsewhere, discussions of the dangers of certain forms of art appear imbued by something like a Platonic 'fear of literature,' of letting oneself, like Ion the rhapsode, become involved in its possibly constraining forces, which is also a fear (which may both mean 'horror' and 'reverence,' as in a 'fear of God') of not being able to separate content from form. An important aspect of Stevens' poem—or of any poem—is that it cannot "merely be" what it represents, but only (to reverse Archibald McLeish's influential formulation) "mean" it: it is merely "*of* mere being." The meta-poetic side of Stevens' poetry is in this sense precisely never a question of actual closure, a sign of "art for art's sake," but an effort to argue for a poem's relation to the real, or for the poem's own reality, which can clearly never be defined by itself alone. This 'meta'-level, exposing the poem as meta-phor, reveals its historical, temporal character, its opening in a reading that cannot but reconnect it to the human world.

In the immediate wake of the Holocaust and the 2nd World War, Levinas naturally saw the perils of modernism in the views on language, interpretation and criticism divulged by its major spokesmen rather than as a possible effect of reading artistic works themselves. There is a paradoxical turn at the end of Levinas' essay when he asserts that the discipline of criticism is that which may be able to salvage art, insofar as it brings it back into relation with the human world and its concerns. This implies that his critique has itself on some level been based on imagining the ideal of an autonomy of art as having a real existence.[70] Even if, for example, Pound's turn to European Fascism can be understood in relation to his poetry,[71] the social effect (if it has any) or historical legacy of his poetry may not be limited to these ideas, as is suggested by its frequent appropriation for democratic ideals.

If we suppose that criticism, understood as interpretation, is always present, the bird—emerging from a few printed signs on a page and visualized, comprehended and introduced within the moral and ideological world of a shared, ideologically saturated language—cannot resist interpretation, and is to some extent in the reader's power, then the meaning and character of its (imagined) resistance is itself what is interpreted here. The bird is an image of the a-human, a-chronic or ab-stract, that cannot *but* be (re)interpreted into human terms, becoming 'real' and temporal, while still striking the reader as having a prior, separate and inaccessible existence. In view of later Levinasian theory, the bird's simultaneous dependence on and re-jection of interpretation may accomplish a strengthened sense of humanity, aware of its cognitive limits and content with desiring that which remains strange while reading it, realizing the impossibility to encompass it in a finalizing understanding. The possibility of placing Stevens' work in relation to paradigms of humanism and anti-humanism can itself be intuited in this discussion. Late in his career, Stevens confessed that he had planned to add a part to "Notes toward a Supreme Fiction" called "It Must Be Human," suggesting that the withdrawal implicit in the imperative of the first part of "Notes"—"It Must Be Abstract"—was an integral phase of a new affirmation of humanity. To put it all too simply, then: the intractable 'spissant' density, the uncivil 'barbaric yawp' of the bird's song is either (not neither) good or evil, or both.

Derrida, whose later thinking was intensely concerned with Levinas' challenge to critical theory, has tried to capture the elusive ethics of the poetic 'object' in an exceptionally 'thorny' and admittedly 'farfetched' metaphor. The essay, whose title asks the question of the essence of poetry, "Che cos'e la poesia?," does not only relate to Levinas' ethical imperatives, but confronts it with several of the most central Romantic and modernist notions of poetry. It defines the poem as both a 'thing' (*cosa*) and 'animal' (in the double sense of being 'mute,' incapable of human speech, and in the sense of a spiritual being, 'anima') which is productive of a series of intense paradoxes that, strictly speaking, brings it beyond definition. The poem, eccentrically imagined as a hedgehog (*istrice* in Italian), is both silent and communicative, densely difficult and rhythmically compelling, being actively withdrawn from interpretation while making a forceful ethical claim on it. Further, it is both technological and intimately personal, applying to human response (one needs to 'learn it by heart' which suggests both intimacy and automatization). It is thus both inhuman and human, beyond morality while constantly, necessarily, being translated into a moral human universe, and both a matter of readerly co-creation or translation. As such, however, it appears already to be a fact, to have come from elsewhere. It is both ahistorical and subject to temporal realization, both modern and anachronistically ill-adapted to its historical time. The withdrawal or abstraction of the poem/hedgehog—its spikes turned outward echo Derrida's earlier image of the style or *stylo*—implies both that it is dangerous and that it paralyzes and blinds itself, exposing itself to danger:

> So: your heart beats, gives the downbeat, the birth of rhythm, beyond oppositions, beyond outside and inside, conscious representation and the abandoned archive. A heart down there, between paths and autostradas, outside of your presence, humble, close to earth, low down. Reiterate(s) in a murmur: never repeat . . . In a single cipher, the poem, (the learning by heart, learn it by heart) seals together the meaning and the letter, like a rhythm spacing out time. It blinds itself. Rolled up in a ball, prickly with spines, vulnerable and dangerous, calculating and ill-adapted (because it makes itself into a ball, sensing the danger on the autoroute, it exposes itself to an accident). No poem without accident, no poem that does not open itself like a wound, but no poem that is not also just as wounding. You will call the poem a silent incantation, the aphonic wound that, of you, from you, I want to learn by heart. It thus takes place, essentially, without one's having to do or make it: it *lets itself* be done, without activity, without work, in the most sober *pathos*, a stranger to all production, especially to creation. The poem falls to me, benediction, coming of (or from) the other. Rhythm but dissymmetry.[72]

Of course, Derrida's definition of the poem's capacity for anti-definition is, in all its complexity, a normative and exclusive definition: a poem which is not rhythmic (to be learnt by heart), or does not appear to provide the reader with a great sense of difficulty would clearly be less of a poem. Also, to the extent that the image, like the recent arguments made in this vein by Derek Attridge, is generalizable as a means to discuss the human experience with otherness as such, this creates new problems of definition, indicating that poetry is not a 'thing' or 'essence.'

This unwieldy and unmanageable quotation of Derrida literally condenses volumes of arguments about poetry. It has not been brought into the discussion at this point only to suggest a compatibility with Stevens' poetics, even if many of Derrida's images, such as his reference to animals, the combination of closure and closeness, the combined experience of weakness and power, recall the tropes for poetry that have been central to this discussion. Nor has it been discussed because his image, like Stevens' often do, contains significant echoes from many of his other texts. What it may do is to propose a certain kind of outlook for reading poetry like Stevens,' accounting for and experiencing its complex suggestion of power and vulnerability and its tendency to evince assertion from insistent negation.

Chapter Four

Toward a New Aesthetics
Farewell to Florida

In a letter to Latimer on November 15, 1935, Stevens apologized for the luscious sound play of "The Comedian as the Letter C," explaining that "subject wasn't quite the same thing" in the 20s as in the 30's (*L* 294). This not only demonstrates his awareness that that the thirties poet should deal poetically with the difficult realities of the present, but also suggests that he felt a need to rethink the possible relations between sound and sense; or between "sense (the signified) and the senses (sensory signifier)," whose "separation" as Derrida has argued, "is enunciated by means of the same root (sensus, Sinn)."[1] In any case, the subject of poetry at the time could not be the 'reality' of poetic language itself or, as in "The Comedian as the Letter C," its sounds,[2] but needed to be reality, as it were, 'outside' the sphere of poetic language. Thus, Stevens' attempt to justify his early Florida poems to Latimer, as having "actual backgrounds" explaining that "[t]he real world seen by an imaginative man may very well seem like an imaginative construction"[3] was likely to fail. The actuality (or 'kind' of actuality) looked for at the time was clearly not that of the colors of the imagination, or of solitary epiphany, but needed to be explicitly to do with the difficult social and political realities of the day.

"Farewell to Florida," the poem placed at the beginning of *Ideas of Order,* has often been taken to announce a deep-going aesthetic change or, at least, a compelling and formative desire for such a change. Like many other poems of this period it can be read as a response to the pressure marking Stevens' poetry, to abandon the sensualist language of *Harmonium,* and its many poems inspired by Florida and other tropic regions, for a closer and more active engagement with the social and political world. Due to the "signpost"[4] position it was given in the expanded version of the collection, published by Knopf in October 1936, and its manifest declaration of expressive renewal, it is somewhat self-evidently symbolic of a collection which many critics, like Ben Bellit in 1936, have found it natural to regard as "wholly transitional."[5]

In Brazeau's collection of interviews, Bernard Heringman recalls having asked Stevens about "Farewell to Florida" and its meaning. Stevens answered, Heringman recalls, "something to the effect that it meant *a farewell to the falseness, sham* of Florida."[6] Without making too much of Heringman's memory and Stevens' sincerity, the comment gives us an interesting clue as to what the poem is about. If the South of Stevens' holidays was a 'false' place (contrary to the assertion that the Florida poems had "actual backgrounds") the North must be truer, or at least more authentic. The implicit location of truth in social reality, rather than as later, in a generalized and timeless existential 'poverty,' suggests that Stevens' dependence on the political rhetoric of his cultural critics was a pressure he needed to work through rather than discard. Furthermore, when the distinction between real and unreal is formulated in terms of truth and falsity, it becomes qualitatively different from his later relativist binary of 'reality and the imagination.' In this sense, the kind of realism demanded of Stevens at this time can be understood as a particularly powerful form of political 'logocentrism.' In *Ideas of Order,* the feeling that the tragicomic poet-hero Crispin "could not be content with counterfeit" (*CP* 39) therefore attains a much more intensely ethical and political significance.

As a poem that "Farewell to Florida," so to speak, 'sails away from' and 'says adieu' to, "Sea-Surface Full of Clouds" (*CP* 98–102) can contribute to our understanding of "Farewell to Florida." Written in 1924 and added to *Harmonium* in 1931 it is a perfect, if ambiguous, example of *Harmonium*'s aesthetics of imaginative coloring. The poem's scene, the sea outside the Gulf of Tehuantepec, Mexico, which Stevens and his wife Elsie sailed by on a holiday cruise in 1924, is admittedly not Florida, but clearly belongs to the holiday ambience of the South that Stevens associated with it. The first stanza figures a tropical winter scene where 'summer,' as the entrance of morning sun from out of night's darkness, brings new color to the sea surface.

> In that November off Tehuantepec,
> The slopping of the sea grew still one night
> And in the morning summer hued the deck
>
> And made one think of rosy chocolate
> And gilt umbrellas. Paradisal green
> Gave suavity to the perplexed machine
>
> Of ocean, which like limpid water lay.

Here, the mirror of the sea reflects in part the sun and in part the associations of the contemplating mind, awakened to creativity by the appearance of new hues on the sea surface, and thus itself partaking in the sun's light-giving. Stevens' indebtedness to contemporary painting's flaunting of its material medium is visible in the bright smears of colors, and eccentrically composed objects (rosy chocolate and gilt umbrellas) which stand out rather than melt into a harmoniously composed whole. The crossing of nature with artifice, *techné*, is indicated in the phrase the 'machine of ocean' which, significantly, lay only *like* limpid water, suggesting that the ocean is itself a semblance of water. The poem moves in syllabically very regular pentameter throughout, and a form of imaginative order is provided by its peculiar rhythmic and syntactic mechanics, in which different verbal material is processed as the poem moves forward. It is divided into five parts, whose rhetorical and rhythmic schemes almost exactly correspond to each other.[7]

But just as the creativity of the contemplating mind appears to be part of the natural radiance of the sun there is still, in this stanza, the appearance of a precarious balance between conspicuous artifice and the natural sounds and images of the sea. The description of the sea surface is interrupted by a question echoing that of Hoon.

Who, then, in that ambrosial latitude
Out of the light evolved the moving blooms,

Who, then evolved the sea-blooms from the clouds
Diffusing balm in that Pacific calm?

But while Hoon answered that the world around him was both created and enjoyed by himself, this poem's answer is that the creation has been set in motion by another being:

C'était mon enfant, mon bijou, mon âme.

Opposing an understanding of "Sea Surface" as "the prime example of a pure poem," Joan Richardson has brought biographical detail to it, proposing that the 'enfant' above refers to the conception of Stevens' daughter Holly, while Stevens and Elsie sailed by The Golf of Tehuantepec; if not exactly in November, in late October 1924, nine months before Holly's birth.[8] In my view, Richardson may make the poem purer than it is by fixing its conception to biographical detail: in the other four sections the answer to the Hoonian question is substituted by "mon *frère* du ciel, ma vie, mon or," "mon *éxtase* et mon amour," "ma *foi*, la nonchalance divine" while in the last one, somehow reversing, even 'perverting' Richardson's idea by darker, even extra-marital suggestions, "mon esprit *bâtard*, l'ignominie."[9] Although Holly's conception may well be related to the poem's creation, the sexual promiscuity of the imagination suggested in this phrase amounts, for 'realists' (even biographical ones) to the purity and self-sufficiency of the poem. The idea of the bastard spirit, and the unnameability ('ignominie') of the imaginative act, will weigh on the last stanza's sexual image of how "the sea / And heaven" in the last stanza "rolled as one" while "from the two / Came fresh transfigurings of freshest blue."

The first stanza ends in a new description of the sea surface, where the mirror of the sea and its images melt into each other when the surface is stirred, perhaps by a light wind. The sea, the last line suggests, sometimes shines through that which it reflects, creating a crevice in reflection itself that affects both the reflected and the reflecting medium.

> The sea-clouds whitened far below the calm
> And moved, as blooms move, in the swimming green
> And in its watery radiance, while the hue
>
> Of heaven in antique reflection rolled
> Round these flotillas. And sometimes the sea
> Poured brilliant iris on the glistening blue.

Several images above are echoed in "Farewell to Florida": the "swimming green" in the "silvers and greens" receding from the viewpoint of the leaving boat, and the bloom-like clouds reflected on the sea surface portend the "vivid blooms" that the later poetic traveler claims to have "hated." Such ambiguous hatred can be glimpsed already in "Sea-Surface," when the imagery of the second stanza begins to lean toward the artificial, naming what Heringman claims Stevens defined as "*the falseness, the sham of Florida.*"

> In that November off Tehuantepec
> The slopping of the sea grew still one night
> At breakfast jelly yellow streaked the deck
>
> And made one think of chop-house chocolate
> And *sham* umbrellas. And a *sham-like* green
> Capped summer-seeming on the tense machine
>
> Of ocean, which in sinister flatness lay. (My italics.)

Like Coleridge's "painted ocean," the pacific calm has become a sinister flatness, a mimetic surface without depth, and there is no longer a visible difference between the mirror of the sea and what is reflected on it. The imagination's colors have started painting on themselves rather than adding to reality. Hence, summer itself now only *seems* to be summer; its sunlight is a "jelly yellow" which "streaks" the deck, somewhat like the "gold of the opulent sun" "smears" the "dirty house in a gutted world" in *Ideas of Order*'s "A Postcard from the Volcano" (*CP* 158–9). The introduction of "sham," in its sense of 'deceit' and 'falsity,' implies a significant substitution, as it replaces the death/life opposition of the first stanza by an opposition between falsity and truth. In the terms defined by this "realist" opposition, the aesthetics of freshness implicit in the first part (as part of the metaphor of life vs. death, movement vs. stasis) is on the verge of breaking down.

The poem's remaining parts, which I will leave without further discussion, continue playing on the sea-surface in exhilarating but ambiguous ways. Whether "Sea-Surface" proposes a hedonistic enjoyment of the flamboyant lushness of its language in a more or less celebratory way, or whether it insinuates disgust with it—like the one we have seen expressed in other poems—will not be decided here. It will suffice to say that it certainly reveals a discomfort both with the aesthetics it employs and the locus to which it is attached that would be realized as the ambiguous desire to leave Florida behind in the symbolic first poem of *Ideas of Order*.

The constitutive metaphor of "Farewell to Florida" (*CP* 117–18), that which Kenneth Burke's 'dramatist' idea could help us understand to be the 'scene' for the poem's metaphorical 'agency,' is a journey by boat from Florida, where Stevens used to go on vacations, back to Hartford, Connecticut, where he lived and worked from 1916 until his death. A biographical understanding is thus inscribed in the context of the poem itself (something that does not make the poem more or less pure). Edward Kessler has suggested that he opposition implied by the two places is between the "elemental feeling and passion" of the South and the "reason" of the North.[10] Referring to Nietszche's duality between Dionysius and Apollo in *The Birth of Tragedy*, Kessler argues that "Stevens' north" resembles "what Nietzsche calls the '*principium individuationis*' while the south is an ambience where man can "forget himself through intoxication with physical life."[11] The epigraph of Kessler's first chapter is the statement from the middle section of "Notes" that "North and South," like Dionysus and Apollo, "are an intrinsic couple" (*CP* 392).

While I agree with Kessler's view, it needs to be stressed that the demand in "Farewell to Florida"—the very motive, or *motor*, for its metaphoric movement—is that the transition to reality should be completed: the poem's entire drama lies in its negotiation of the possibility and 'reality' of concluding this transition. There must be a reality at the other end of the journey which is not just a pole in a never-ending motion back and forth, as Kessler's reference to Dionysus-Apollo suggests, nor a mere figment of the imagination. Obviously, this is itself conditioned on an experience of the two places as very distinct. Thus, while Bloom argues that the poem's "ambivalent response to social disorder and the Marxist challenge" is only its "*overt* theme," while its "true," i.e. deeper, "*topos* is Freedom or Emersonian wildness, the aporia in whose midst lies the possibility of meaning,"[12] my interpretation intentionally tries to relate the 'merely' 'overt' theme to its arguably 'true' one, the struggle for expressive and spiritual freedom. It is, I believe, *in* the tension between the historical and the ahistorical that this poem, and Stevens' oeuvre as a whole, seems to me to become most interesting and meaningful.

It is essential to the history of the poem's reception that critics have taken the completion of its movement somehow for granted, using the poem as a convenient stepping-stone in a narration of Stevens' career, a tendency which Kessler blamed on criticism's "hunger to prove development."[13] To an extent, the 'signpost' function of "Farewell to Florida" has itself made the poem a vehicle for transit, something passed over or used in order to get elsewhere: as a rule to Stevens' poetic maturity. Riddel's claim in 1965 that the poem signifies a "step from individual to a social conscience, from the world of vivid sensuousness to the society of . . . men,"[14] is not only interesting because it fails to explain in what way Stevens ever reached "the society of men" in poetry. Also, the apparently self-evident connection between "vivid sensuousness"—what Winters called Stevens' 'hedonism'[15]—and apolitical aestheticist withdrawal itself reveals the ethico-political potency of the poem's opposition. A further consequence of such an implicit, shorthand linkage of individualism, political escapism and sensuous language is that social responsibility and political action demand a language of reason, transparent referential stability and accuracy: an often unspoken foundation even for the 'realism' of later postmodern critics who, as Schaum has argued, are "frequently self-congratulatory in their avoidance of the lyric 'I's' authority and autonomy" but "may themselves be masking a nostalgia for a pure, unmediated presentation of the discourses of the actual world."[16] Thus, assuming that Stevens' response to realist pressure was a poetry of denotative clarity (drawing on the often overstated distinction between the rhythmic sensuousness and metaphoric extravagance of *Harmonium* and his later poetry) Riddel claimed that the poem "clearly displays Stevens' shift to the rhetorical key of the late 1930's."[17] As far as this study is concerned, "Farewell to Florida" is interesting above all because its language does *not* clearly manifest such a shift, except as statement. It imagines a shift towards reality, and the realism of a rational discourse and social responsibility, only by drawing on the full possibilities of the sensuous language of the poem's 'past.'[18]

The boat, the vehicle for the northbound journey of the poetic persona across the poem's imagined scene is, as a 'vehicle' for the poet's transport the boat, doubly metaphorical. As part of the larger metaphor of the sea voyage at whose end the poet will accomplish an involvement with reality, it is a metaphor of poetic power, one of the functions that Aristotle influentially gave metaphor; that of *metapherein,* meaning 'transfer' or 'transport.' This is not primarily to be understood (although this is self-evident) in the way metaphor enacts communicative transport of meaning from one place, or one individual, to another by means of a signifier, but how it transfers meaning from its 'proper' place into new contexts, while giving old contexts new meaning.[19] Even if Stevens insisted that "There is no such thing as a metaphor of metaphor. One does not progress through metaphors" and that reality is therefore "the indispensable element of each metaphor" (*OP* 204), the vessel of "Farewell to Florida" is, in both the above senses, a metaphor of metaphor.

Viewed in terms of temporal succession, the 'transfer' enacted in metaphor *first* implies a deviation from proper meaning into alien territory: something is, because it needs to be, signified by something other than itself. *After* this necessary 'expropriation' of meaning from the signified—which Derrida has analyzed as a general trait of linguistic signification, the 'necessary supplement'—meaning should return to it. The poem "Farewell to Florida" itself can in this sense itself be understood as a kind of thing, an otherness, created *in order to* signify an actual or desired change in Stevens' aesthetics, which we may then decode and 'bring back,' in order to return it to its proper, original, meaning: 'Stevens now begins (or tries to begin) to write about social reality.' However, if we see the vehicle of the poet's transport, the ship, as to some extent *already part* of his power, which would not exist without it in the first place, it is no longer *simply* a vehicle, but *more* than one: the sailor and the boat, like the poet and his poem, are—as far as their capacity to move is concerned—one. In a later poem, "Prologues to What is Possible," which extends and modifies the metaphor of "Farewell to Florida" (*CP* 515–17) the inventor of the metaphor-boat in which he himself is moving, "he that stood up in the boat leaning and looking before him"

> Did not pass like someone voyaging out of and beyond the familiar.
> He belonged to the far-foreign departure of his vessel and was part
>   of it.
> Part of the speculum of fire on its prow, its symbol, whatever it was . . .

This sense of belonging to, being part of, one's creation brings the creative
subject to an epiphanic sense of completion.

> As at a point of central arrival, an instant moment, much or little,
> Removed from any shore, from any man or woman, and need- ing none.

But this feeling of shoreless arrival, the attainment of a purposive motion without purpose, soon brings a realization of the frightening strangeness implicit in
its removal, not only from men and women in general, but from himself.

> The metaphor stirred his fear. The object with which he was compared
> Was beyond his recognizing.

The passive form here is significant; the man is no longer himself the maker of
the comparison, but feels he 'is compared' with his image, as though imper-
sonally: now, it seems, it has been removed even from his own 'shore' and his
own 'humanity.' From his fear, however, that the metaphor has become alien
to its creator—"beyond recognizing"—a positive implication is evinced. The
extra-vagance of metaphor, the way it takes us out of the normal, making us
'wander outside' the beaten path, or in a 'realist' sense, 'away' from the real
without carrying us back to our starting point, may enable the imaginative
man to go outside its initial premises, altering its scene by creating a new one:

>   By this he knew that likeness of
>   him extended
> Only a little way, and not beyond, unless between himself
> And things beyond resemblance there was this and that intended to be
>   recognized,
> The this and that in the enclosures of hypotheses
> On which men speculated in summer when they were half asleep.
>   (*CP* 516)

As Aristotle argues in *The Rhetoric* (III.10, 1410b14f.) metaphor
implies 'learning,' since the metaphor-maker (and its interpreter) need
to understand the basis of resemblance between words or concepts, and

hence becoming aware of the differences as well. This sense of metaphor as a perception of the relation between its elements and the "total experience" of the transfer of signification between them has, as Maeder notes, been emphasized by Susanne Juhasz.[20]

In "Farewell to Florida" this sense of belonging between poet and metaphor is analogous to the relation between the different parts of Stevens' metaphor itself, between the boat and its scene: the fact that the poet-vessel sails *through* and *on top of* a medium—the sea—is ambiguous, since the sea is both what separates the ship, in the poem's imagery of darkness, from the shore on the other side, and what connects and carries it onward: ships presuppose oceans. As we shall see, it is difficult to tell if the rhythmically pounding waves in "Farewell to Florida" are an obstacle, a violent sea that frustrates any attempt to cross it, or a force that propels the boat forward. This ambiguity had been exploited in *Harmonium*'s "The Paltry Nude Starts on a Spring Voyage" (*CP* 5–6) whose modern Venus figure "scuds the glitters, / Noiselessly, like one more wave," and "The Load of Sugar Cane" (*CP* 12), where "The going of the glade-boat / Is like water flowing." Thus, as canto IV of "It Must Change" has it, the sailor, the boat and the sea "are one." This relation is also formulated at the beginning of "Prologues to What Is Possible":

There was an ease of mind that was like being alone in a boat at sea
A boat carried forward by waves resembling the bright backs of rowers,
Gripping their oars, as if they were sure of the way to their destination,
Bending over and pulling themselves erect on the wooden handles,
Wet with water and sparkling in the one-ness of their motion. (*CP* 515)

The ambivalence toward metaphor in the modernism sprung out of Imagism is clearly connected to the scepticism toward Stevens' poetics of its main spokesmen. Even if, as Juhasz has demonstrated, poets like Pound, Williams and Eliot rely greatly on metaphoric signification, the exact 'image' should in their view be itself only. It should not 'transport' any meaning other than that of its signified, whether an object or a complex emotional state. Ideas like the "*objective* correlative" and "*absolute* rhythm" imply an accurate presentation with what is to be expressed (not measurable, of course, except as impression or persuasion). Even if the image would be other to its referent in an ontological sense, such ontological separation may come to affirm a stronger, more exact correspondence with its object. In such a view, our analysis of the metaphoric movement of "Farewell to Florida" indicates nothing but the capacity of metaphor to create an illusory (false) scene that permits an enactment of a merely fictive (unreal) movement, within a *pays de métaphore* disengaged from reality.

But while metaphor can imply an abstraction of meaning from reality—in the sense of withdrawal—it may also be understood, as Brogan suggests in her reading of "Prologues," in terms of "the frightening potential of the impulse toward unity: an annihilation of individuality in the 'one-ness'" of identification,[21] indicating a totalizing or totalitarian impulse in poetic language. Metaphoric language can in this sense be understood as both dangerously weak and dangerously strong, as its disconnection from reality is seen as either lifeless and futile, or oppressively constraining, reductive and silencing. An attentive reading of the metaphors of "Farewell to Florida," however, may instead suggest that the expressive act and its linguistic or material medium can *neither* become "one" *nor* stand in total separation. They are both difficult *not* to distinguish from each other, and to distinguish in an essential way. Resisting the temptation to fix metaphoric language to the status of either a superior (more real) or inferior (less real) reality, may help us remain open to one of the crucial tensions in Stevens' aesthetic project, and move the discussion of his aesthetics beyond a measurement of its 'failure' and 'success,' which is also a measuring of its 'reality' (examples of which are, at one extreme, Stevens' statement that the 'measure' of the power of the poet is the extent to which he is able to abstract himself and reality, and at the other, Perloff's enumeration of 2nd World War events not explicitly referred to in "Notes toward a Supreme Fiction").[22]

Maeder has discussed Stevens' innovative and deconstructive engagement with 'dead,' but still oppressively hierarchic religious metaphors from before 'the death of the gods,' the use of metaphor as a way to (re)establish or (re)discover a connection between the subject and the world by perceiving resemblance, and its capacity for linguistic renovation.[23] She suggests that Stevens' "basic research in the area of poetic language" experiments "with the process of metaphorical substitutions" and explores "how the language might allow not resolution but escape from the narrow world of the quandary about epistemology, to a further horizon."[24] Altieri's useful discussion of Stevens and metaphor refers to a series of influential contemporary takes on the issue (all extensions of Aristotle's argument in the *Poetics*). Derrida's argument is that metaphor, as Altieri puts it, "promises new knowledge at the cost of inevitable confusions between expressive energies," and causes desperate attempts to prevent the distortive 'demon' of metaphor from sneaking into the realm of philosophy.[25] Davidson suggests the possibility of a non-essentialist pragmatic 'use value' of metaphor, while Wayne Booth argues that metaphors "matter in rhetorical contexts not because of *what they name*, but what they allow the speaker to represent herself as in a concrete situation" and that it is thus "less a matter of logos than of ethos." Finally, Altieri reviews Paul Ricoeur's proposal that metaphors "express potentials of being by abolishing the distance between knower and known without canceling the cognitive structure of thought."[26] Altieri argues that the "brilliance of Stevens on metaphor" resides in his "capacity to integrate and to extend all these models for producing alternatives to the demonics [Derrida's account of epistemological slippage] of metaphor."[27] In this study, Stevens poetic language has been studied in terms of several of the above senses: Davidson's position is similar to the one of "The Man on the Dump" and "Sailing after Lunch," Booth's to the metaphorical drama of "Farewell to Florida," while Ricoeur's and Derrida's different takes on the epistemology of metaphor appear relevant to most of the discussion.

While Stevens' later poetry appears easier to understand in terms of a series of explorations performed by a theorist of language: as Altieri phrases it, "Stevens *on* metaphor" rather than "Stevens *in* metaphor." [28] "Farewell to Florida," as a poem moving toward the forties, reveals not only that metaphor is very much a part of the active work of its poetic language but also that the negative ('demonic') aspects of metaphor appeared more strongly bound up with the positive ones at a time when the ethical, ex-clusive violence of poetic construction was more keenly felt than later. Below, exploring the extent to which the creation of order, understood as a phase of the creation of imaginative form, can be formulated as a capacity for metaphor, my discussion of its 'motive' implication of 'transfer,' or 'deviation,' and its related capacity for change and movement, will imply a focus on its temporal aspects, its capacity for excess. This will, in turn, lead to a consideration of other aspects of Stevens' poem that are more conspicuously involved in poetry's temporal and historical realization: rhythm, meter and sound.

The poem begins, and is propelled throughout, by an admonition—an expression of an as yet unfulfilled desire to leave—which is problematically coterminous with the assertion that the man on board is already liberated from Florida's magnetic enchantments: "I am free."

> Go on, high ship, since now, upon the shore,
> The snake has left its skin upon the floor.
> Key West sank downward under massive clouds
> And silvers and greens spread over the sea. The moon
> Is at the mast-head and the past is dead.
> Her mind will never speak to me again.
> I am free. High above the mast the moon
> Rides clear of her mind and the waves make a refrain
> Of this: that the snake has left its skin upon
> The floor. Go on through the darkness. The waves fly back.

The affirmation of freedom in this stanza is central not only semantically but spatially. It is surrounded on both sides and thus even, in a sense, contained and "carried forward," by the persuasive language of the rest of the stanza—the urging onwards of the vessel with which the stanza begins and ends, the visual image of a receding Key West from the viewpoint of the leaving boat, the augural image of the moon and the snake shedding its skin as a sign of liberation. In a rhetorical sense, the stanza is structured as a (not perfectly symmetrical) *chiasmus*. This spatial relation between center and periphery, as between 'core' and 'shell' of meaning—signified and signifier—can itself be understood in terms of the metaphorical composition of 'tenor' and 'vehicle,' since the literal sense of the statement of freedom is 'born out,' 'transported' by the vehicular language surrounding or containing it.[29] The poem's heroism, then, resides not simply in a triumphant sense of a journey sure to be completed, but in the tension between the assertion of freedom and the need for it to be actively realized in the surrounding images. The motion towards freedom and order depends not only on an act of will (as in a reader's 'willing suspension of disbelief') but on the continuity and iterability of both the act and the will.

So seen, the images that make up the total metaphor actually create the literal sense of the poem's declaration of freedom: the poem's metaphor and the poem as metaphor create their own transcendence. The causal order of the metaphorical process can thus be reversed. Since the moon is at the mast-head, riding clear of her mind, the past is dead and the poet is free, and *since* the snake has shed its skin, it is time to leave. Thus, insofar as the journey's search of the real is also a search of the literal, the possible 'logos' of the real, metaphor is enlisted for the unlikely feat of counteracting its own domination; defying, in the words of "Someone Puts a Pineapple Together," "The metaphor that murders metaphor" (*NA* 84). Thus, metaphor's agency in "Farewell to Florida" does not *simply* mean that the activity of metaphor 'undermines,' 'subverts' or 'cancels out' meaning (as is often claimed in postmodernist reversals of positivism). Rather, it may indicate that freedom is not a pure content, but is bound up with a medium and a con-text. If we do not suppose the 'literal' to signify absolute presence, but as metaphors that have 'died' or petrified into unquestioned reality, the 'movement' of metaphor may bring about what Shklovsky called a 'perceptibility' of language. In the sense that metaphoric language, as Gemma Corradi Fiumara suggests,[30] may enrich our perception of the way language may change, embodying what she calls its "metabolic life," the terms of "concrete" and "abstract" may find themselves reversed, as metaphors in this sense entail physical participation in the concrete movement of language rather than intellectual detachment.

One of the dominant images in the first section, the snake, is ideal for discussing this topic. Riddel's intertextual interpretation is based on the appearance of snakes in "Owl's Clover" as a trope for modern reality's 'incessant change,' and suggests that Stevens' main intent is to capture an elusive, fast-moving reality in a poetic language both flexible and accurate enough to do this: "the swiftly changing landscape of historical reality" towards which the poet is headed *is* "time the 'snake.'"[31] The reality of the North, however, is precisely what the poet has *not yet* reached in the poem, and what motivates its motion. In this sense, the snake plays an important kinesthetic part in its metaphoric movement. Bloom's interpretation of the snake is also determined by a reading of another poem, the later "The Auroras of Autumn," where a 'serpent' appears at the beginning as a figure of what Bloom calls "Ananke, or elusive fate." The goddess Ananke, a representative of Necessity in Greek mythology, making an intimidating appearance in "Like Decorations," would thus stand for a principle of reality that refuses to be captured, a "master of the maze" itself unmastered. As a result, Bloom sees it in relation to the poem's seasonal imagery, as "turning the year into autumn."[32] The interpretation of the snake as part of a cyclic seasonal imagery, as the autumnal transport to winter, however, seems insufficient partly because of the poem's linkage of summer to images of death and decay but also in the light of its dramatic resolve (Bloom's merely 'ostensive' theme) to move decisively, inexorably, toward contemporary social reality. Insofar as the poem is shaped as a response to a sternly antimetaphorical realist pressure it will need to resist, like Crispin the monotony of the 'dominant' C, the tragically rhythmic allure of seasonal change. Understood in this way, the poem is an effort at resisting what Kenneth Burke called Stevens' mode of "vacational" poetry.[33] Its transport to winter is not supposed to be followed by yet another return to the South, following a rhythmic alternation of "holiday" and "reality," where holiday is the temporarily 'free' ambience of a metaphoric landscape. It needs to end in a heroic involvement with a reality from which the poet, as the poem's suggestion of suppressed remorse indicates, will never be able to return.

If we instead consider the snake, in the context of "Farewell to Florida"'s drama, in its figurative relation with the poetic sailor or passenger, it can be seen as an augural symbol justifying the decision to depart. The serpent's skin, representing an exterior restraint that the poet needs to be free from, can be seen as an image of change which justifies, both endorsing and acknowledging, the departure. As a metaphor, however, the snake can itself be perceived as insidiously 'wormy,' (but not only because a snake's motion is similar to that of a worm, or because etymologically worm means snake). The shedding of skin is not a final event, but a seasonal and repetitive one, a stage in a perpetual repetition of sheddings and new departures. While this idea corroborates Bloom's interpretation, challenging the utopian import of the metaphor, it does not cancel out its vital motive and emotive functions. It still participates in pointing to a decisively different future.

I will begin discussing the poem's rhythm from a viewpoint established by the poem's own metaphoric scene, representing a modernist-realist desire to achieve relevance through connecting more profoundly with the realities of modern life. Stevens' verse here is, in more than one sense, not 'free verse.' A metric 'scanning' will quickly indicate the meter governing the rhythm of the first stanza as iambic pentameter. The first two lines consist of ten syllables each, and are scanned as five-beat without doing much violence to its 'natural' pronunciation:

> Go on, high ship, since now, upon the shore,
> x ⌐ / ⌐   x ⌐ x⌐ x ⌐
> The snake has left its skin upon the floor.
> x   ⌐   x ⌐ x ⌐   x⌐ x ⌐

The framing possibility of pentameter in the creative or cognitive realization of this stanza is compelling: syllabically, most lines allow it and some lines are almost unthinkable as anything else.[34] It is, however, shot through by conflicting phrasal units and rhythmic figures to which a 'reader' may feel 'bound' to respond, and which may entirely overshadow pentameter by thrusting themselves onto rhythmic perception. Already in the first couplet above, certain factors encourage us to experience a strong-stress four-beat rhythm, if the stress on "upon" is demoted from taking a beat.[35] This pattern could easily be projected onto the next line by demoting the first syllable of 'under.' In other places, the possibility to perceive integral strong-stress four-beat patterns is encouraged by internal and line-stopped rhymes, alliteration, assonance and anaphora, that give figural unity to four-beat phrases like "The *moon* / Is at the *mast*-head and the *past* is *dead*" and "*High* ab*ove* the *mast* the *moon*" that are distinct enough to affirm themselves as independent syntactic and rhythmic entities across line boundaries and within lines.

The prevalence of such repeated four-beat phrases in the first stanza may be a crucial part of its chiastic form, which is not only spatial but rhythmically effective. The repetitions of statements on both sides of the poem's central assertion ('above' and 'below' are also 'before' and 'after') gives the stanza a repetitive, mantric character, which the poem itself formulates as "refrain"-like. "The waves" through which (meaning, as has been suggested, both 'across' and 'by means of') the metaphorical boat is plunging,

> make a refrain
> Of this: that the snake has left its skin upon
> The floor.

"This" does not only point forward deictically, but also 'backwards,' indicating the symbol of the snake, which refers, in turn, 'back' to the message of the stanza as a whole: "I am free." The pointer, whose prominence is heightened by its separation from the preceding line by enjambment, indicates the 'refrainness' of the following phrase both in the sense that it is an independent unit recalling a similar one above/before, and by defining it as a thing to be experienced, seen and listened to. The form of the deictic reference itself formally disappears in its very pointing, before (or behind) the colon, which not only signals a pause, but indicates a separation of seeing and hearing from what is seen and heard—a 'disappearance' both complicated and intensified by the fact that the refrain itself begins with an indexical meta-linguistic 'that.'

There is a conflict implicit here between the imaginative urge to hear, and in doing so actively *create,* a refrain in the sound of the waves—'reading' and internalizing the phenomenon of the natural world as though it signified that which one wants or needs it to signify—and the notion of a *refrain,* which is marked by a sense of iterability and collectivity.[36] This conflict can be understood as an aspect of what we could call the stanza's *paratactic* structure of juxtaposition, comparison, and interaction of repeated segments that are syntactically independent. The kind of parataxis operative in this stanza, however, is quite different from the idea of Poundian parataxis with which Stevens' 'lyrical' poetry has often been negatively compared,[37] and which Easthope connects to the four-beat ballad rhythms as well as modern forms of popular music and verse. Pound's parataxis should be understood in the context of his desire for 'presentation' by which each image retains a quality of unadulterated integrity: the parts of a poem relate to a whole that is supposedly more fragmented and open (both *open to* and *like* modern reality).[38] In the first stanza of "Farewell to Florida," the independent phrases are both part of an overarching metaphor and spatially distributed in a chiastic pattern. In both senses, they are subordinated to an assertion of subjective autonomy: "I am free." Such a 'subjugation,' however, not only questions the primacy of the literal sense of the metaphor, but also the 'autonomy' of the lyrical "I" who makes the assertion, and with it, the poem's claim to purposive movement.

The poem's three other sections continue to 'bear out' the initial assertion of freedom, but are organized around longer phrases, whose syntactical development in a more syllabically regular pentameter medium shapes the poem's rhythmic impetus. In both the second and third stanzas, the future bond with the North and the nature of the poet's compromise with its inhabitants remain undescribed, and the poet's urge to do away with Florida (although allegedly a thing of the past) is even further contradicted by "her" paradoxical ability to live on and haunt, even constitute, the temporal space of the poem itself. Here, my reading agrees with Adelyn Dougherty's idea that "[t]he journey movement—away from Florida, to a "North of cold"—and the suggestion that the speaker reaches at last a land of new freedom is significantly qualified . . . as much by the poet's disposition of stress and pause as by the repetition of the key words in the second stanza, 'mind,' 'bind,' and 'round,' which qualify the meaning on another level of the structure."[39] Thus, as I will try to show, the assertion of freedom is not only bound up with its metaphorical vehicle, but the poet figure remains bound up with Florida, a strongly erotic binding to a singular "she" opposed to the plurality of the world of "men" in the North.

While the rhetoric of the first stanza struggled to enforce a *present*—"I *am* free"—the second one projects the "content" and "sureness" in the future, but only after having been utterly dominated by the past. The call from the South pervades the poem's semantics as well as its phonic and rhythmic material. The heavily 'iambic' statement at the beginning of the second stanza, that

> Her mind had bound me round
> x ∠ x ∠ x ∠

is followed by a long phrase spanning the first eight lines, describing the nature of this binding.

>   The palms were hot
> As if I lived in ashen ground, as if
> The leaves in which the wind kept up its sound
> From my North of cold whistled in a sepulchral
> South,
> Her South of pine and coral and coraline sea,
> Her home, not mine, in the ever-freshened Keys,
> Her days, her oceanic nights, calling
> For music, for whisperings from the reefs.

The siren-like attraction of Florida, which the poem remembers at the same time as it distances itself from it, is accomplished in the sound-play of lines 1–8 and a subtle, contrapuntal manipulation of the five-beat rhythm. The North is implicit only as a brittle affirmation of assuredness of the speaker who is bent, for reasons that the description of the South tries to account for, to go North. Strikingly, the vision of the future constitutes the stanza's most drastic rhythmic alteration:

How content I shall be in the North to which I sail
x   x / x x / x x /   x   x x /

And to feel sure and to forget the bleaching sand . . .
x   x \ /   x x x / x / x   /

These two lines, of thirteen and twelve syllables, perform a contextually 'arhythmical' attempt at declaring the speaker's future freedom. Two strong promotions are needed to keep the established five-beat rhythm ('which' in 9 and, possibly, the second 'to' in 10).[40] The rising triple rhythm of the beginning of line 9 ('anapestic' in foot prosody), sets the pace for strenuous repetition of infinitive phrases in the next one, "And to feel sure and to forget." This intensifies the strain on the five-beat rhythm by lengthening the syllabic distance between beats, making this passage appear anxious and stuttering in relation to the steady rhythmic regularity of the rest of the stanza. As a deviation or hesitation in a dominant rhythmic pattern, however, this tension is not only 'resolved' but, in view of the poem's particular effort, 'submerged' or 'drawn back' into the 'iambic' rhythm of

the bleaching sand . . .
x / x /

Dougherty observes that the 'return' to this rhythm, and to the presence of Florida is realized on the level of sound patterning as well. The ee-sound of "bleaching" harks back to the assonance on ee—in leaves, coraline sea, Keys, reefs, and the -ing of the adjective refers back to the repeated present continuous of 'calling' and the nominalized verb 'whispering,' by which 'her' presence has even manifested itself grammatically.[41] But even as a form of what Herrnstein Smith has called 'rhythmic closure' or, in Kermode's phrasing, a metrical 'sense of an ending,' this phrase also functions as an anti-ending. The three suspensive dots at the end can be taken to indicate that "there is no end to the droning of this surf," as in *Harmonium's* "Fabliau of Florida" (*CP* 23), nor a forgetting of it.

The lines imagining a future 'free' from the bind to Florida in the North, appear as a sudden irruption of a personal voice which, avoiding the poem's dominant rhythmic compulsion and conspicuous play of signifiers, signifies an effort to wake up from a state of dreaminess or half-sleep. Thus, the relationship between the poet and the South could be defined as *hypnotic;* a state of mind linked to Florida in *Harmonium*'s "Hibiscus on the Sleeping Shores" (*CP* 22–3) where the mind, reduced to an animal state, "roamed as a moth roams, / Among the blooms beyond the open sand," a vagary interrupted only by a sexual reaction to the red of the hibiscus, which makes the moth/mind rise up "besprent" seeking "the flaming red / Dabbled with yellow pollen," roaming there "all the stupid afternoon," 'stupid' meaning both 'dumb' and 'in a state of stupor.'

In this sense, a poetic fore-runner to "Farewell to Florida" is Tennyson's "The Lotus Eaters," where the pleasurable drowsiness experienced by stranded sailors is described in terms of a submission to hypnotic rhythm: "and deep asleep he seemed, yet all awake, / And music in his ears his beating heart did make."[42] Although Tennyson's poem partly conceived of this state as a well-deserved escape from perennial human woes, there is a moral unease implicit in the poem: the lotus-leaf's narcotic effect is not only pacifying, drawing the sailors away from a bootless life of action, but also leaves them "careless of mankind."[43] This implicit element of moral critique is made possible by the fact that hypnosis does not simply 'befall' or 'happen to' a defenceless individual, but is partly self-induced and sought for. On some level, it requires a willing renunciation of one's own will to an exterior force, implying a measure of co-creation. Like hypnosis, rhythm can be experienced as a compulsion, or as Amittai Aviram has defined it, a "sublime power," but this power also depends on a capacity and willingness for interaction and participation, and is shared between reader and poetic text.

Robert Hass has argued that since "rhythm has direct access to the unconscious, because it can hypnotize us, enter our bodies and make us move, it is a power." Power, he adds, "is political." [44] Hass' focus is also on the poet as a hypnotizer and the reader as a passive and subjugated receptor of an act of violent intrusion: the power of rhythm is something out of one's control, something alien that enters one's body. In "Reality and Its Shadow," his fearful post-war essay on modernism, Levinas gave rhythm a very sinister meaning, associating it with the disconnected yet powerful artistic image.

> The idea of rhythm, which art criticism so frequently invokes but leaves in a state of a vague suggestive notion and catch-all, designates not so much an inner law of the poetic order as the way the poetic order affects us, closed wholes whose elements call for one another like the syllables of a verse, but do so insofar as they impose themselves on us, disengaging themselves from reality. But they impose themselves on us without our assuming them. (. . .) Rhythm represents a unique situation where

we cannot speak of consent, assumption, initiative or freedom, because the subject is caught up and carried away by it. [45]

Levinas' idea appears to be fearful in the extreme, as it could be argued that rhythm has no such power in itself, especially not printed poems of very elusive significance. His argument, however, does hearken to an instrumentalist idea among modern poets of understanding the function of rhythm as subliminal persuasion. Yeats defined rhythm as a means by which the "will," that which moves a person to impose her mind on exterior being, is tranquilized, compelling the reader more readily to accept the meanings conveyed in the poem's particular language world.

> The purpose of rhythm, it has always seemed to me, is to prolong the moment of contemplation, the moment when we are both asleep and awake, which is the moment of creation, by hushing us with an alluring monotony, while it holds us waking by variety, to keep us in a state of perhaps real trance, in which the mind liberated from the presence of the will is unfolded in symbols. [46]

In this instrumentalist notion, rhythm creates a willing—or, in the worst of cases, unwilling—suspension of disbelief, as it legitimizes a particular 'symbolic' poetic language at the *expense* of shared reality: here we see the link between the idea of the *sham* of Florida and the hedonist compulsion for pleasure implicit in the poem's language. Yeats' idea, that the state of trance effected in rhythmic experience is nevertheless *"perhaps real"* gives rhythm the capacity to cast doubt on the reality of the world outside the poem, in favor of the one constructed inside it. Paul Valéry's idea of the kinesthetic physicality of the poetic experience contains a similar ambiguity. While affirming the performative, active quality of reading—"A poem . . . is action, because a poem exists only at the moment of being spoken; it is in *actu*"—he also emphasizes the compulsive feel of rhythmic experience, in a formulation which may well have been the one Levinas refers to: "This act, like the dance, has no other purpose than to create a state of mind; it *imposes its own laws;* it, too, creates a time and a measurement of time which are appropriate and essential to it: we cannot distinguish it from its form of time. To recite poetry is to enter into a verbal dance."[47] Clearly, even though it appears crucial that one to some extent 'dances' by free will when reading poetry, and that one may interrupt the mental dance when necessary, there are few fields as open to debate in modern critical theory as the relations between a sense of freedom, rhythmic compulsion and aesthetic pleasure. The achievement of Aviram's argument lies in the way he maintains this dilemma unsolved and in the way his concept of sublime rhythm questions oversimplifying ideas of activity and passivity.

"Farewell to Florida" is anything but comfortable with its own sense of rhythmic hypnosis: it needs to break with the sensuous, sexual spell of the South, and wake up permanently. While the poem's implicit 'modernism' recalls Pound's statement in the 81st of the *Cantos,* that "to break with the pentameter was the first *heave*" of poetic modernism, the 'heave' of "Farewell to Florida" is not produced by a break with its hypnotic rhythms but by using them to exert a form of counter-hypnosis. In the third stanza, the poetic persona's repudiation of the South takes the form of claiming that he has always hated it, a hatred which, Bloom suggests, means "loved too much."[48]

> I hated the weathery yawl from which the pools
> Disclosed the sea floor and the wilderness
> Of waving weeds. I hated the vivid blooms
> Curled over the shadowless hut, the rust and bones,
> The trees like bones and the leaves half sand, half sun.

Part II figured the speaker's erotic dependence on Florida as a connection with death, making the poem signify an endeavor to escape a death-like ambience—"the *ashen* ground" of a "*sepulchral* South"—to life. Here the '*vivid* blooms,' which ought to serve as an image of life, are merely 'life-like,' lying 'curled' (like ivy, or a snake) over a 'shadowless' hut, surrounded by images of death and decay, 'rust and bones.'[49] In the last line, this inseparability of life and death becomes a question of intimidating simile: the trees in the South are *like* bones, and their leaves are half sand (death) and half sun (life).

Stuck with hating the thing it loves, the poem needs to move forward: the ship is already supposed to have broken free from Florida and what she represents. This movement from the fixation with the past, transforming the future into presence, is effected by a verbal strategy that we have found in several other poems: the replacement of conjugated verbs with a depersonalized and liberating infinitive.

> To stand here on the deck in the dark and say
> Farewell and to know that that land is forever gone
> And that she will not follow in any word
> Or look, nor ever again in thought, except
> That I loved her once . . .

The lack of a complement to this long infinitive phrase not only accomplishes a vagueness of reference—does the adjective phrase it refers to express regret or satisfaction, joy or pain?—but a potential to be intensely inclusive, condensing a semantic energy of great complexity in an apparently gratuitous way. It is able to refer, it appears, to anything that the poem would be able to mean. The phrase, however, ends in another drifting off, an 'and yet' which qualifies the hatred asserted at the beginning of the stanza: "except, I loved her once." Like the inconclusive ending of the preceding part, this new drift of thought is signaled by three points which indicate a drifting into mute remembrance. The compulsive drift 'back' toward Florida's allures, however, is interrupted as the speaker resumes the farewell, repeating the iambic mantra commanding the vessel to move on:

Farewell. Go on, high ship.

The phrases "the bleaching sand . . ." of the third stanza and "go on, high ship" in this one scan almost identically (the stress on 'high' needs to be demoted) and perform similar functions in the rhythmic structures of both stanzas: both constitute a return from local deviation from the dominant rhythm. In semantic terms, however, their rhythmic 'returns' fulfill diametrically opposed purposes. The return to an iambic rhythm in section II suggested a mental return to the hypnosis of the South, as a result of the way these sounds and rhythms were implicated in the description of Florida. The ending of part III, however, reverses this event, as the iambic injunction here signifies a return to the propulsion onwards which began and ended the first section, indicating the necessity to wake up from hypnotic reverie and continue moving north. This effort appears more efficient than the stuttering vision at the end of part II, since it makes use of a rhythmic language similar to, and equally powerful as, that which the poem has identified as Florida's.

In the last section, the North is finally described as it will be encountered by the speaker: the future is finally 'here,' present in the poem's imagery and rhythms. Very conspicuously, however, its description includes the language of Florida (subjective and objective genitive), as well as the journey away from 'her' and its destination:

My North is leafless and lies in a wintry slime
Both of men and clouds, a slime of men in crowds.
The men are moving as the water moves,
This darkened water cloven by sullen swells
Against your sides, then shoving and slithering,

The darkness shattered, turbulent with foam.
To be free again, to return to the violent mind
That is their mind, these men, and that will bind me
Me round, carry me, misty deck, carry me
To the cold, go on, high ship, go on, plunge on.

The North's 'leaflessness' may at first sight appear to be different from the opulence of the South, had the leaves of Florida not already been associated with a compelling imagery of death, being "half sand, half sun." The "wintry slime" of the North, the poet's home milieu and personal destiny—"*my north of cold*"—is composed of both the social and the natural world, it is "*both* of men and clouds." The added modifier "a slime of men in crowds," a syntactic and rhythmic repetition, describes social reality in terms of people likened to clusters of unsavory substance.

The continuity of this image with the "wilderness of waving weeds" which the poet claims to have hated is confirmed in the third line's "the men are moving as the water moves," which refers back both sonically and visually to the water imagery of the poem's preceding parts. In the next line, "*this darkened water*" makes the analogy reverberate not only with the past (of the poet's figured memory *and* the past of the poem) but with the 'presentness' of the metaphorical transport going on within it. This catachrestic confrontation of metaphors is intensified when "This darkened water," the medium through which the boat moves, is "cloven by sudden swells / Against your sides" (meaning the boat's: the poem is an apostrophe). By metaphorical reverberation, the violence of the ship's movement, passing not only through or on top of the water but 'cleaving' or 'plowing' it, "shoving and slithering, the darkness shattered, turbulent with foam" also involves the society of men who, we remember, "move like the water moves."

The final injunction for the ship to go onward, beginning in mid-sentence, is a repetition of the phrase beginning the poem and, as such, functions both as a kind of closure, a rounding off, and a continuation of the non-final, but determined, northbound motion. Rhythmically, this imploration is separated into two phrases: first the rhythmically strained "carry me, misty deck, carry me / to the cold" whose alliteration on /k/ reinforces its integrity across the boundary between lines 9–10, followed by the final "go on, high ship, go on, plunge on" which is a repetition of former refrains and so an already familiar four-beat unit. Here, the poem's dominant duple rising ('iambic') rhythm, which, as I have argued, has become *involved* in both staying and moving at once, itself features an internal strain, or 'heave' in the difference between "go on" and its rhythmic and syntactic repetition "plunge on" in which the obstruction of the plosive cluster may suggest the painfulness and effort of the heave toward liberation.

The freedom of the poet's persona in "Farewell to Florida" is thus not a radical breaking of chains: the poet is merely "free again." Rather than imagining a journey to a new place, the poem describes a return in which freedom is minimally defined as the possibility of choosing another commitment for oneself, letting oneself be bound by other forces, another "mind" as the poem formulates it. Thus, the poem's assertion that "I am bound to be free" can well be translated into "I am free to be bound" and the forces toward which one is thus bound—to which one will be bound—are imagined in a metaphorical and rhythmic shape that is not identical, but conspicuously similar to that of the ambience of the past. The bearing on the realist discourses of modernist form is clear: reality, in this state of things, does not have 'its own' form that should be rendered as it is in a poetic discourse appropriate to it, but is only formed in relation to the languages that can appropriate it, which both *are* and *are not yet* 'it,' 'reality' or 'the the.'

In the later "Prologues to What Is Possible," *The Rock*'s chief boat metaphor, the North and South linger on, but now as images of opposed poles of poetic creativity—the imagination and reality—and without underscoring the sense of mutual exclusion of "Farewell to Florida"'s either-or, whose final inclusive motion was forced to be utterly violent. The 'freedom' of "Prologues" can partly be seen as a question of its language; its long lines and locally unified but changeable sound-patterning, and its apparent freedom in altering the poem's metaphoric and ruminative course. While the earlier poem was caught in the same metaphoric motion throughout and therefore had to to realize its incompatibility with otherness in an image of violent inclusion, "Prologues" suggests the possibility of withdrawing from this intimidating metaphorical constraint in order to propose other ways of description, or seeing this act in a new way. Thus, having first realized his frightening one-ness with his metaphor, and its opposite implication, the metaphor's independent or 'abstract' life apart from his self, the speaker proposes the possibility of an expansion or heightening of his self precisely by means of the alienating experience in the metaphoric transfer:

> What self, for example, did he contain that had not yet been
>   Loosed.
> Snarling in him for discovery as his attentions spread.
> As if all his hereditary lights were suddenly increased
> By an access of color, a new and unobserved, slight dithering,
> The smallest lamp, which added its puissant flick, to which he

Gave
A name and privilege over the ordinary of his commonplace—

This flick, recalling the paradoxical almost-true "false flick . . . close to kin" of "Notes" is a modest term for 'the imagination.' The original meaning of 'flick' is 'to fling' or wisp away something with a quick movement, but Stevens uses it to describe the instantaneous 'flicker' of light 'thrown' onto a surface, and activates, I would suggest, both these meanings. In "Prologues," the South is no longer a place or a mindset to be feared—even though the fear of metaphor is only a few lines behind—but an aspect or mode of reality: the imagination.

> A flick which added to what was real and its vocabulary,
> The way some first thing coming into Northern trees
> Adds to them the whole vocabulary of the South,
> The way the earliest single light in the evening sky, in spring,
> Creates a fresh universe out of nothingness by adding itself,
> The way a look or a touch reveals its unexpected magnitudes.

The "first thing" in the Northern trees, possibly a migrant Southern bird, thus adds an eloquence that has been lacking to a place that is (i.e. has been imagined as) devoid of life.

The later contemplative scene appears a long way from the violent striving, plunging, cleaving and expunging that is central to many of the poems studied here. But while the later poem clearly appears to propose a more satisfactory ending, a modestly minimalist yet marvelous assertion, the compulsive, inescapable but non-final motion of "Farewell to Florida" may speak to other sensibilities, more excited about language in its dramatically violent, physical and rhythmical aspects. The writerly/nautical violence of its final assertion—as the ship's prow cleaves the sea surface like the bull-point plows the paper—is due to the fact that "men and women," dehumanized into slimy clusters of sea-weed, were made to play a material part in the semantic and rhythmic texture of the poem's scene.

Conclusion

This study has focused on a limited number of poems which by themselves cannot do justice to Stevens' achievement. For instance, a reader of the Spring issue of *Alcestis* in 1935, which presented "Sailing after Lunch," "Meditation Celestial & Terrestrial," "Waving Adieu, Adieu, Adieu," "The American Sublime" and "Mozart, 1935," would surely get a very different view of Stevens than one familiar with the rest of his poetry. But this obvious limitation in scope has also had the advantage of allowing the discussion to stay close to a set of problems that are not only more plainly perceptible in this particular period, but by no means exclusive to it. It has also enabled a closer focus on individual poems than is often the case, doing justice to my belief that Stevens' poetry is not a set of propositions about the order of things, or a theory of language, but a wide-ranging series of inventive and exhilarating verbal experiments which should ideally be experienced at length and close up. While I have frequently attempted to make use of the instructive but sometimes bewildering intra- and extrapoemic echoes in Stevens' work, this has necessarily been downplayed in favor of a closer study of the rhythmic and linguistic events of singular poems.

I have applied a diverse set of concepts and methical tools in my analyses, derived from traditional metrics, cumulative rhythmics and metaphoric theory which, reflecting the disparity of current theory in these areas, are in no way epistemologically watertight or mutually consistent. They may, however, provide common ground from which to relate to and experience elements of poetry that are not strictly semantic, but are likely to influence a poem's affective and semantic realization. In terms of rhythm, my argument has been limited to features of rhythmic experience that are fairly concrete, insofar as they have suggested a beat pulse or meter perceptible in time, but has not accounted for what could be called, in a more metaphorical sense, Stevens' larger rhythms: the way his longer sequences enact, as *Ideas of Order*'s "Gallant Château" proposes, "a few words tuned and tuned and tuned" (*CP* 161) or provide, in the words of the beginning of "An Ordinary Evening in New Haven," a temporal sequence of new exploratory or improvisational possibilities "an and yet, and yet, and yet" (*CP* 465), the ever-qualified assertiveness of the Stevens who, in the words of "Notes," arguably became "of repetition most master." Instead, my study has frequently suggested ways in which his prosodic patterning appears to indicate or reinforce a sense of emptiness, stasis and repetitiousness, which has made for a rather different emphasis than that of Natalie Gerber who has recently suggested that, for Stevens,

> . . . words of the world are the life of the world only to the extent that they circulate, since their reverberations can suspend monumental status or fixed meaning. Far from any Horatian or classical drive to erect poems as monuments, he elects to make poems that are part of the occasion, not a monument to it. They are themselves a system of exchange, a circuit of rhythm, in which the mobility of words resembles the mobility of thought.[1]

In Gerber's discussion, the assumption that Stevens' language approximates the fluency of an act of the mind, coexists with the notion that his use of meter (whose element of abstraction has made it the target of modernist epistemological and ethical critique) exerts a mobilizing and renewing force on perception by drawing attention to language. Thus, meter makes the English language, in the words of the Slavic Formalists, 'perceptible':

> In order to emphasize this aspect of words, their rhythmic mobility, and not their referential monumentality, Stevens uses meter in order to make words return upon themselves and modify their sensibility.[2]

This study has also hopefully conveyed the idea that the 'deforming' force of rhythmic constraint may renew our sense of language, and that an engagement with poetic rhythm may itself bring a creative or co-creative enjoyment to reading by appealing to and challenging our rhythmic and interpretive faculties. But it has also argued that Stevens shared a modernist sense of meter as oppressive and constraining, and that he often used (rather than simply being used by) this intuition of metric figures and rhythmic patterns to imagine a sense of immobility or muteness.

The poems discussed here have not been analyzed in a consistent way throughout, in the sense of applying the same methodical approach to each poem or stanza, but have been discussed in terms of the words, sound patterns and rhythmic events that I have deemed most interesting in relation to each poem's staging of its purpose and agency. In this way, my study indicates—and may be found insufficient in relation to—a much larger area of study which, as Attridge has argued, has been suggested in Richard Cureton's attempt to include phrasing and larger syntactic and semantic structures into a consideration of poetic rhythm.[3] Insofar as each poem's singular attempt to achieve closure indicates elements in Stevens' modernist project as a whole, and renders Stevens himself as exemplary of certain general Romantic and modernist traits, its expressive effort may also acquire a larger meaning.

This indicates that my study, like Gerber's work, has not just been an argument on meter and rhythm, but cannot help being involved in a long-standing cultural debate on modernist art. This can be seen in the way Gerber defines Stevens' metrics in ethical terms:

> The remarkable plasticity Stevens achieves from this seemingly simple decision to treat words in this way as compositional elements is responsible for these metrical poems' versions of freedom that are Stevens' answer not merely to issues of aesthetic form but also to a particular modernist dilemma of what work art can accomplish and what constitutes a defensible mode of heroism.[4]

In a somewhat similar way, Mary Doyle Springer has argued that Stevens' rhythmics is actually more creative, more modernist, more receptive—more open—than that of the "old rhyming poets" from which she tries to dissociate him, arguing that it is based on cumulative rather than abstract principles. This, Doyle Springer suggests, enables it to reflect modern phenomenal or noumenal reality, "the teeming world of the moment."[5] If a reader agrees with most of the discussion in this study, however, it should suggest an alternative to attempts to understand Stevens' poetic language in terms of exemplary openness or mimetic power, while acknowledging that poetic closure is itself an element in or effect of a poem's challenging openness to interpretation.

Strictly speaking, I have treated one of the acknowledged masters of the English language, and perhaps of language as such, as falling prey (or representing himself as falling prey, which is already slightly different) to a sense of language as restrictive and oppressive. This will recall how many of us will occasionally experience that the language we use and, in a sense, inhabit, will at times fail to mould itself to our wishes, or at times appear to create those wishes by its own agency, making us say and do things just for the saying and doing of it, inhabiting us and shaping our identity in ways beyond our control. Thus, I have attempted to emphasize that the reality of Stevens' poetic imagination is to a great extent a matter of its work on a language understood either as having nothing essentially in common with human meaning or, as we have seen, too much in common with it. Clearly, the idea that what "underlies" the "trials of device" is a "blank" suggests a version of poetic epistemology that there is little reason to 'defend': the idea that language signifies a void or uncreated chaos clearly implies a strategic downplaying of its social sense of involvement with other beings. Whether the epistemological and expressive demands put on language by Stevens and other modernists is ethically defensible, or indeed relevant, today is an open question, and this study has not tried to give an impression that his project is ethically or politically exemplary or edifying. It will hopefully have suggested, however, why it was important to Stevens that poetry should resist 'instrumentalist' interpretation or wholesale political appropriation. It may also have indicated ways in which his poetry may actually have a capacity to do this: a capacity which by itself may explain the frequency of the attempts to interpret its resistance to interpretation as meaningful to different critical or political agendas.

Melita Schaum has argued that discussions in Stevens criticism have often implied "a redefinition of the concept of literary modernism itself."[6] The most polarizing and therefore most textually productively statements on Stevens—like Marjorie Perloff's and Helen Vendler's opposed but practically very similar assessments of Stevens' aesthetic closure—appear to be founded on an inclination to attach certain essential qualities and capacities to the text 'itself,' in abstraction from its realization in reading, along with a tendency to downplay the fundamental kinship of different varieties of modernist poetics. While distinguishing between different tendencies in modernism is important, it may also be crucial to retain a sense of their similarities, not only in terms of their cultural outlooks but because different kinds of written modern poetry share, across cultural divides, certain general qualities that appeal to certain general qualities in the way people read. Barbara Herrnstein-Smith has argued that although "free verse, imagism, symbolism and other stylistic developments have made their mark, none of them has created a break between modern and traditional poetry as radical as the break between nonobjective and representational painting, or between atonal or classical music."[7] Letting the peculiar 'fictions of form' proposed or implied by poets in theoretical statements or metaphoric stagings, which often link expressive capacities to larger cultural, political and ethical imperatives, be regulated by the 'fictions' of certain cognitive fundamentals of reading and understanding poetry, may make it possible to resist rehearsing the most moralistic platitudes of poetic evaluation, while not assuming that poetry is devoid of ethical responsibility or alien to social language. Stevens' poetry may make this necessity visible in an exemplary way.

Notes

NOTES TO THE INTRODUCTION

1. Harold Bloom, *Wallace Stevens: The Poems of Our Climate.* (Ithaca: Cornell University Press, 1977).
2. Beverly Maeder *Wallace Stevens' Experimental Language: The Lion in the Lute.* (New York: St. Martin's Press, 1999), 5.
3. Stanley Burnshaw, "Turmoil in the Middle Ground," *Wallace Stevens: The Critical Heritage,* ed. Charles Doyle (London: Routledge, 1985), 139.
4. In the twenties, John Gould Fletcher warned that Stevens would have "either to expand his range and take in more of human experience, or give up writing altogether" (Doyle, 47). The influential critic and anthologist Louis Untermeyer saw Stevens' poetry as an offshoot of the ideology of art-for-arts-sake of European aestheticism, opposed to an American democratic realism (Ibid., 70–1). Gorham B. Munson's definition of Stevens in 1925 as a disaffected aesthete, a 'dandy,' was to be influential for a long time. (Ibid., 78–82). In the thirties, not only Burnshaw but critics like Percy Hutchinson (Ibid., 88–90), Geoffrey Grigson (in "A Stuffed Goldfinch," *New Verse,* no. 19, 1936, 18–19), and Theodore Rhoetke (Doyle, 161) criticized Stevens for his 'escapist' attitude, accusing him of an aestheticist separation from immediate social and political concerns. In the late forties, Yvor Winters criticized Stevens' work for its hedonist abandon of all rational aspirations to truth or, at least, a truth given by a commonly accepted rationality—for Winters, an ethically perilous tendency which also indicated expressive atrophy (Ibid., 224–52).
5. Gerald Bruns has argued that the epistemological urge of Stevens' poetry makes it incompatible with (and ethically insufficient in relation to) later tendencies to regard language in terms of dialogue rather than epistemological instrumentality: See Gerald L. Bruns, "Stevens without Epistemology," *Wallace Stevens: The Poetics of Modernism,* ed. Albert Gelpi (Cambridge: Cambridge UP, 1985), 24–40. Marjorie Perloff argued that Stevens's poetry, and his sympathetic criticism, were part of a reactionary cultural current

whose ideas go against the truly radical implications of modernist formal change. Like Bruns, Perloff applied the theories of Mikhail Bakhtin to argue that Stevens' "lyric" poetry, of Romantic and Symbolist affinities, was essentially "monologic." Marjorie Perloff, "Pound/Stevens: Whose Era?" *New Literary History: A Journal of Theory and Interpretation* 13.3 (1982): 485–10. An extension of this argument can be found in Marjorie Perloff, "Revolving in Crystal: The Supreme Fiction and the Impasse of Modernist Lyric" *Wallace Stevens: The Poetics of Modernism,* ed. Albert Gelpi (Cambridge: Cambridge University Press, 1985), 41–64. While Bruns and Perloff base their argument on formalist assumptions, Mark Halliday understands the lack of the "interpersonal" element of human existence in Stevens' poetry in terms of Stevens' own psychological propensities. See Mark Halliday, *Stevens and the Interpersonal* (Princeton: Princeton University Press, 1991).

6. Helen Vendler, *On Extended Wings: Wallace Stevens' Longer Poems* (Cambridge: Harvard University Press, 1969), 314.

7. This capacity was noted already in 1964 by Joseph Riddel in "The Contours of Stevens' Criticism," *ELH,* Baltimore, MD. (1964): 106–38. Melitta Schaum made the first book-length study of this interesting phenomenon, while formulating a critique of some of the most prominent ethical denunciations of Stevens language. Cf. Melita Schaum, *Wallace Stevens and the Critical Schools* (Tuscaloosa: University of Alabama Press, 1988). John Timberman Newcomb's subsequent study in 1992 includes an evaluation of the historicist trend in Stevens studies: John Newcomb, *Wallace Stevens and Literary Canons* (Jackson: University Press of Mississippi, 1992).

8. Marie Borroff, *Language and the Poet: Verbal Artistry in Frost, Stevens, and Moore* (Chicago: University of Chicago Press, 1979).

9. Anca Rosu, *The Metaphysics of Sound in Wallace Stevens* (Tuscaloosa: University of Alabama Press, 1995).

10. Andrew M. Lakritz, *Modernism and the Other in Stevens, Frost, and Moore* (Gainesville: University Press of Florida, 1996).

11. Charles Altieri, "Wallace Stevens' Metaphors of Metaphor: Poetry as Theory," *American Poetry.* Fall (1983): 27–48. See also his "Why Stevens Must Be Abstract; or, What a Poet Can Learn from Painting," in *Wallace Stevens: The Poetics of Modernism,* ed. Albert Gelpi (Cambridge: Cambridge UP, 1985): 86–118.

12. Brogan deals with Stevens' uses of metaphor and simile in *Stevens and Simile: A Theory of Language* (Princeton: Princeton UP, 1986). In her more recent Stevens study, she argues for a conscious resistance to hegemonic political rhetoric in Stevens' later poetry. See *The Violence Within/the Violence Without: Wallace Stevens and the Emergence of a Revolutionary Poetics* (Athens: The University of Georgia Press, 2003).

13. Angus Cleghorn, *Wallace Stevens' Poetics: The Neglected Rhetoric* (London: Palgrave, 2000).

14. See Perloff's "Pound/Stevens: Whose Era?" and "Revolving in Crystal: The Supreme Fiction and the Impasse of Modernist Lyric." References in footnote 5.

15. Cf. James Longenbach, *Wallace Stevens: The Plain Sense of Things* (New York: Oxford University Press, 1991).

16. Frank Lentricchia, *Modernist Quartet* (Cambridge, Eng.: Cambridge University Press, 1994).

17. Filreis deals with Stevens' poetry in the forties and early fifties in Alan Filreis, *Wallace Stevens and the Actual World* (Princeton: Princeton University Press, 1991). His next book is an extremely detailed study of the way Stevens' poetry was shaped by his relations to contemporary culture and politics, and other writers and intellectuals in the thirties. See *Modernism from Right to Left: Wallace Stevens, the Thirties & Literary Radicalism* (Cambridge: Cambridge University Press, 1994).

18. Joan Richardson, *Wallace Stevens: The Early Years* (New York: Beech Tree Books, 1985). *Wallace Stevens: The Later Years.* (New York: Beech Tree Books, 1988).

19. Milton J. Bates, *Wallace Stevens: A Mythology of Self* (Berkeley: University of California Press, 1986).

20. George S. Lensing, *Wallace Stevens: A Poet's Growth* (Baton Rouge: Louisiana State University Press, 1986).

21. Cf. the introduction "The Five Key Terms to Dramatism" in Kenneth Burke, *A Grammar of Motives* (Berkeley: University of California Press, 1969), xv-xxiii. Burke's fascinating project, to investigate "the basic forms of thought which, in accordance with the nature of the world as all men necessarily experience it, are exemplified in the attributing of motives" is invoked here as a complement to the view of a poem as an epistemological or expressive instrument. The idea of a poem as a strategically formulated response (in the widest sense) to a real situation will be crucial to many of the discussions to come. Even though for Burke the "forms of thought . . . exemplified in the attributing of motives" are "equally present in systematically elaborated metaphysical structures, in legal judgments, in poetry and fiction, in political and scientific works, in news and in bits of gossip offered at random" this study will investigate forms of response that are peculiar to Stevens' poetry, offered by poetry's specialized use of language. As Burke puts it elsewhere: "Critical and imaginative works are answers to questions posed by the situation in which they arose. They are not merely answers, they are *strategic* answers, *stylized* answers." Kenneth Burke, *The Philosophy of Literary Form* (New York: Vintage Books, 1957), 1.

22. T. S. Eliot, *On Poetry and Poets* (New York: Farrar Straus & Cudahy, 1957), 37.

23. For an argument that, while acknowledging its classicist traits, links the modernist formal revolution in poetry explicitly to the Aestheticist aspects

of the Romantic tradition see Timothy Steele, *Missing Measures: Modern Poetry and the Revolt against Meter* (Fayetteville: University of Arkansas Press, 1990). Steele's ultimate purpose, like fellow New Formalists like Dana Gioia, is to mount an argument against the anti-metrical attitude of modern poetry, which he links to the disappearance of collective measures of value that the extreme individualism of free verse modernism has, in his view, brought about. Cf. especially "Free Verse and Aestheticism," 170–222.

24. Stephen Cushman, *Fictions of Form in American Poetry* (Princeton: Princeton University Press, 1993), 8.

25. Ibid., 3.

26. Ibid., 4.

27. Leonard Depieven, *The Difficulties of Modernism* (New York and London: Routledge, 2003). See in particular 104–13.

28. In 1955, a few months before Stevens' death, Randall Jarrell expressed puzzlement about the dominance of Stevens' influence on younger poets: "If someone had predicted to Pound, when he was beginning his war on the iambic foot; to Eliot, when he was first casting a cold eye on post-Jacobean blank verse; to both, when they were first condemning generalization in poetry, that in forty or fifty years the chief—sometimes, I think in despair, the only—influence on younger American poets, would be this generalizing, masterful, scannable verse of Stevens,' wouldn't both have laughed in confident disbelief?" (*Yale Review*, March, 1955) The imagined confident laughter of Pound and Eliot indicates not least Jarrell's sense of the canonical power of their poetics, which must have been acutely felt by Stevens. Jarrell's juxtaposition of the terms "scannable" and "generalizing," associating metrical readability with "generalizing" qualities of which Pound and Eliot would disapprove, is also very suggestive of their authority.

29. In 1955, the British critic Donald Davie complained that Stevens could "never resist" the allure of alliteration, "however banal, however distracting" (in *Shenandoah*, Spring 1955), suggesting that the distracting power of Stevens' rhythmic form cripples the presentational power of poetry which, in Poundian terms, should be the power of all modern poetry. Interestingly, Davie understands Stevens' hedonist predilection for sound repetition in ethical—and realist—terms as a form of decadent meta-poetry "gnawing on its own fat." Doyle, 426–28.

30. The passage is from a letter to Elsie Moll of August 19, 1909.

31. Donald Wesling, *The Chances of Rhyme: Device and Modernity* (Berkeley: University of California Press, 1980), 35.

32. Thus, Wesling argues, "[a]fter the 'June Book,' Stevens tends to avoid end-of-line rhyme because he cannot invariably strike with it the true, unprecedented note." The result, he adds, was that Stevens became "arguably the most skilful technician of blank verse since Milton." Ibid.

33. In response to a letter from Ferdinand Reyher in 1921, complaining about the popularity of free verse, Stevens wrote: "The fact is that not withstanding the large amount of poetry that is written over here at the moment there is practically no aesthetic theory back of it. Why do you scorn free verse? Isn't it the only kind of verse now being written which has any aesthetic impulse back of it? Of course, there are miles and miles of it that do not come off. People don't understand the emotional purpose of measure. I am not exclusively for free verse. But I am for it. However, all this kind of thing I should rather talk about than write about." (May 13, 1921, quoted from Lensing, *A Poet's Growth*, 102) Lensing argues that "Stevens' reference to the emotional purpose of rhythm and measure hints . . . at the theory that meter should be liberated from the form that insisted on numbering syllables and stresses by some predetermined metronome. The musical cadences should be emotional, that is, spontaneous, impulsive, and shrewdly self-effacing. The ideal mode for Stevens was not, finally, free verse, in which even the emotional purpose of rhythm was subverted. At the same time, however, the emancipating effect of free verse was an advance, and he was 'for it.'" (Ibid.)

34. Eliot, *On Poetry and Poets,* 37.

35. Cushman, *Fictions of Form,* 11.

36. T.S. Eliot, "Reflections on Vers Libre," To Criticize the Critic. (New York: Farrar, Straus and Giroux, 1965), 183–89. 187.

37. J. V. Cunningham, "Tradition and Modernity: Wallace Stevens," *Selected Essays* (Chicago: The Swallow Press, 1976), 242.

38. Ibid., 239.

39. Roman Jakobson, "Closing Statement: Linguistics and Poetics," *Style in Language (Papers Presented at the Conference on Style Held at Indiana University, 1958),* ed. Thomas A. Sebeok (New York:: Wiley, 1960), 358.

40. Yuri Tynyanov, *The Problem of Verse Language,* trans. Michael and Brent Harvey Sosa (Ann Arbor, Mich.: Ardis, 1981), 33.

41. Jakobson, "Linguistics and Poetics," 353.

42. Jan Mukarovský, John Burbank and P. Steiner, eds., *On Poetic Language* (Lisse: Peter de Ridder Press, 1976), 14.

43. Ibid., 11.

44. Victor Shklovsky, "Art as Technique," *Critical Theory since Plato,* ed. Hazard Adams (Fort Worth: Harcourt Brace Jovanovich, 1992), 797–805. See also Mukarovsky's *On Poetic Language* on, for example, 17 and 30.

45. Tzvetan Todorov, "Three Conceptions of Poetic Language," *Russian Formalism: A Retrospective Glance. A Festschrift in Honor of Victor Erlich,* ed. Robert Louis and Stephen Rudy Jackson (New Haven: Yale Center for International and Area Studies, 1985), 140.

46. In Stefan Holander, "Between Categories: Modernist and Postmodernist Appropriations of Wallace Stevens," *Rethinking Modernism,* ed. Marianne Thormählen (Basingstoke: Palgrave Macmillan, 2003), 221–38.

47. For a helpful and accessible discussion on these matters, see the introductory interview with Derrida in Jacques Derrida and Derek Attridge, *Acts of Literature* (New York: Routledge, 1992), 1–75.

48. Marie Borroff, *Language and the Poet: Verbal Artistry in Frost, Stevens, and Moore* (Chicago: University of Chicago Press, 1979), 73.

49. Henri Meschonnic, *Critique du rhythme* (Paris: Verdier, 1982).

50. Shklovsky, "Art as Technique," 758. Shklovsky's reference is to Jakubinsky's demonstration of "the principle of phonetic 'roughening' of poetic language in the particular case of the repetition of identical sounds." Shklovsky gives no reference to the text.

51. Tynyanov, "The Concept of Verse Language," 29.

52. For a clarifying discussion of this issue see Brent L. Harvey's "Postface: The Poetics of Verse Language" at the end of Tynyanov's *The Problems of Verse Language,* 157–64.

53. Frank Kjoerup, *Sprog versus sprog* (Copenhagen: Museum Tusculanums Forlag, 2002), 321–25.

54. Barbara Herrnstein Smith, *On the Margins of Discourse: The Relation of Literature and Language* (Chicago: The University of Chicago Press, 1978). Cf. especially "Poetry as Fiction," 14–40.

55. See "Form and Intent in the American New Criticism," 24. In Paul De Man, *Blindness & Insight : Essays in the Rhetoric of Contemporary Criticism* (New York: Oxford University Press, 1971), 20–35.

56. J. Hillis Miller, *The Linguistic Moment: From Wordsworth to Stevens* (Princeton: Princeton University Press, 1985), 283.

57. Wesling, "The Chances of Rhyme," 1–2.

58. Amittai F. Aviram, *Telling Rhythm: Body and Meaning in Poetry* (Ann Arbor: University of Michigan Press, 1994).

59. Julia Kristeva, *Revolution in Poetic Language* (New York: Columbia University Press, 1984).

60. Christopher Collins, *Reading the Written Image: Verbal Play, Interpretation, and the Roots of Iconophobia* (University Park: Penssylvania State University Press, 1991).

61. Susan Sontag, *Against Interpretation* (New York: Farrar Straus and Giroux, 1967).

62. Derek Attridge, *The Singularity of Literature* (London: Routledge, 2004).

63. Bruns' Levinasian idea that the other is in Stevens' poetry never allowed to "answer back" is opposed by Michael Beehler, who argues that Stevens' language teaches an "ethical lesson" by indicating its own limits, refusing to appropriate the other (which could well have taken the form of trying to represent its 'answering back'). Michael Beehler, "Penelope's Experience: Teaching the Ethical Lessons of Wallace Stevens," *Teaching Wallace Stevens: Practical Essays,* eds. Serio, John N. and B. J. Leggett (Knoxville: University of Tennessee Press, 1994), 267–79. A rather similar argument is central to

Krzysztof Ziarek's *Inflected Language: Toward a Hermeneutics of Nearness Heidegger, Levinas, Stevens, Celan* (Albany: State University of New York Press, 1994).

64. "Examples of Wallace Stevens," originally in *Hound and Horn*, Vol. 5 Winter (1932): 223–55. My citation is from Doyle 95–125, 110.

65. Bart Eeckhout, *Wallace Stevens and the Limits of Reading and Writing* (Columbia, Missouri: University of Missouri Press, 2002).

66. Lakritz, *Modernism and the Other*, 41.

67. Eleanor Cook, *Poetry, Word-Play, and Word-War in Wallace Stevens* (Princeton: Princeton University Press, 1988). See also her tour-de-force reading of Stevens' religious and mythical influences in "Wallace Stevens and the King James Bible," *Essays in Criticism: A Quarterly Journal of Literary Criticism* 41.3 (1991): 240–52.

68. This was made most consistently in a mid-sixties book-length study by Frank Doggett, in the eighties by Leggett and Leonard and Wharton, not to mention countless articles tying or comparing Stevens' work to various philosophical discourses. Eeckhout supplies a massive, intimidating, list of philosophical comparisons in Stevens criticism in *The Limits of Reading and Writing*, 45.

69. Todorov, "Three Conceptions of Poetic Language," 142–3.

70. Ibid.

71. Todorov's reference is to Tynyanov's essay "On Literary Evolution." See "Three Conceptions," 143.

72. See for example the chapter titled "The Generic Changeability of Poetic Language, Its Generic Differentiation, Its Perfectability" in Mukarovský, *On Poetic Language*, 17–22.

73. It is important, I would suggest, not to understand these phases only as consecutive, in the sense that the radical "third" conception of poetic language has simply erased or invalidated the other two. The relativist concept of poetic language, one could argue, would quickly lose relevance if it did not describe a culturally compelling and perceptually distinct phenomenon, or respond to an urgent cultural concern: this can be seen, for example, in the fact that literary criticism continues to thrive in spite of the fact that its object has appeared to disintegrate for a very long period of time. One of the most important differences between the Slavic and Anglo-Saxon formalisms as evaluative practices is that, for the former, aesthetic renewal is ultimately strategic and contextual, that the epiphanic moment of poetry is the outcome of an active mobilization of perception rather than structural unity.

74. *On Extended Wings*, 9–10.

75. Annie Finch, "A Review of *Rethinking Meter: A New Approach to the Verse Line* by Alan Holder," *Versification: An Interdisciplinary Journal of Literary Prosody* 2.3 March (1998): 298–302.

76. Derek Attridge, "A Review of Richard Cureton's *Rhythmic Phrasing in English Verse*," *Poetics Today* (1993): 20.

77. Victor Erlich, *Russian Formalism: History—Doctrine* (New Haven: Yale University Press, 1955), 214.

78. Derek Attridge, *Poetic Rhythm: An Introduction* (Cambridge: Cambridge University Press, 1995), 7. Although any stretch of language *could* in principle be counted and named in prosodic or rhythmic description, meter will in this study be reserved for the description of either very regular stress or rhyme patterns and forms of stanzaic structure, or those, like tetrameter and pentameter, which have a significant traditional component. It will also be used when, locally, a metric 'figure' or 'pattern' emerges as part of, or in conflict with (which may be the same) a different, already established, rhythmic principle.

79. Ibid., 3.

80. Ibid., 4.

81. See Kjørup's polemics with Aviram on this issue in *Sprog versus sprog*, 35–41 and 57f.

82. Shklovsky, "Art as Technique," 754.

83. Derek Attridge, *The Rhythms of English Poetry* (London: Longman, 1982), 59. Even if the fact of dialectal, sociolectal and idiolectal differences of course qualify this assumption, prompting rhythmic analysis ever to be wary of over-generalization, it does not, however, take away the relevance of a significantly shared linguistic competence.

84. As Herrnstein Smith argues, however, the most fundamental of such conventions may be operative *before,* and are as such determining of, the artistic operation of the poetic function. The reader, she argues, will approach a poem, on a fundamental level, as a 'fictive' utterance rather than a 'natural' one. She explains the difference as follows: "by 'natural discourse' I mean all utterances that are performed as historical acts and taken as historical events. If one asks what other kind of discourse there is, the answer is simple: there is no other kind; natural discourse *is* discourse. There are, however, verbal structures which constitute, in themselves, neither historical acts nor historical events, but rather *representations* of them and, as such, are understood not to be governed by the same conventions that obtain for natural utterances: and these verbal structures I refer to as *fictive* utterances" (Smith, *On the Margins of Discourse,* 84). While Smith underlines that poems *are* historically motivated utterances in their moment of composition, she stresses the notion that they are not limited to this, and that reading poetry is therefore a *different* kind of interpretive act than decoding a spoken statement, or reading a letter, in the immediate present. Smith's argument is based on the notion that poetry's character as a distinct form of expression with unique possibilities of its own have not disappeared, but that the arguments over poetic language have contributed to expanding its range and subject matter,

transforming its field of concerns as well as the critical terminology designed to address it.

85. Kjørup quotes Manfred Bierwisch's formulation (in "Poetics and Linguistics," published in *Linguistics and Literary Style*, ed. Donald C. Freeman, 1970) that "[t]he actual objects of poetics are the particular regularities that occur in literary texts and that determine the specific effects of poetry: in the final analysis the human ability to produce poetic structures and understand their effect—that is, something which one might call *poetic competence*" (*Sprog Versus Sprog*, 98–99). For Kjørup, this competence does not only cover the recognition of metric patterns, but a fundamental sensitivity to the way poems are organized as verse, as a syntactic discourse taking place in, and modified by, the cognitive intervention of lines and line breaks (101).

86. Ibid., 101, 106, 110 and 129.

87. Attridge, *The Rhythms of English Poetry*, 153.

88. Ibid., 124.

89. See for example Anthony Easthope's chapter on iambic pentameter in *Poetry as Discourse*, New Accents (London: Methuen, 1983), 51–77.

90. Ibid., 126.

91. In cases of syllabic regularity, Attridge suggests it is acceptable to call it by its traditional name, *tetrameter*.

92. In his later *Poetic Rhythm: An Introduction*, Attridge has preferred the term "virtual beat" to the concept of "unrealised beat" used in *The Rhythms of English Poetry*, 86–96.

93. Donald Wesling, *The Scissors of Meter: Grammetrics and Reading* (Ann Arbor: The University of Michigan Press, 1996), 51. While each type of prosody, Wesling argues, "implicitly sees its own preferred poetry as exercising all the powers of language," neither of them "admits the existence of the other, or of intermediate forms between the types" (Ibid.). It may even be, he admits, "that a unified theory of metrics is a logical impossibility" or "that such a theory is inappropriate to the kind and quality of precision necessary just now in literary study" (Ibid., 52.).

94. For an interesting discussion of the relation of four-beat rhythm and free verse see Easthope's chapter "The Modernism of Eliot and Pound," in *Poetry as Discourse*, 134–159; especially the discussion of "intonational metre" on 153–9.

95. Cf. for example Wimsatt's critique of Northrop Frye's idea, in *Anatomy of Criticism*, that "a four-stress line seems to be inherent to the structure of the English language" in W.K. Wimsatt, "The Concept of Meter: An Exercise in Abstraction," *Hateful Contraries: Studies in Literature and Criticism* (Lexington: University of Kentucky Press, 1965), 112–3. Frye's theory is discussed in chapter III.

96. In his reading of a poem such as "To the One of Fictive Music," a syllabically very regular iambic pentameter poem, Stevens often chooses not to

underline its meter, declining to promote normally unstressed words (such as prepositions, conjunctions and other form-words).

97. The concluding line of "Ideas of Order at Key West," for example, "of ghostlier demarcations, keener sounds," is pronounced by Stevens with a rising, question-like intonation of the last word. Cf. Wallace Stevens, *The Voice of the Poet: Wallace Stevens,* ed. J. D. McClatchy (New York: Random House Audio, 2004).

98. (Most rare, or ever of more kindred air
    /   / ¦ x / ¦x x¦ /   /¦ x   /
    In the laborious weavings that you wear.
    x   x¦ x / ¦x   / ¦ x   x ¦x   /)
    William Judd's doctoral dissertation on Stevens' metrics suffers greatly, as he himself recognizes, from the inadequacy and clumsiness of foot scansion to account for the rhythmic variation of his poetry. Cf. William Edward Judd, "The Metrics of Wallace Stevens," (PhD Diss., Columbia University, 1975).

99. See John Hollander, *Vision and Resonance: Two Senses of Poetic Form* (New Haven: Yale University Press, 1985), 135–64 and 187–211.

100. Annie Finch, *The Ghost of Meter: Culture and Prosody in American Free Verse* (Ann Arbor: University of Michigan Press, 1993).

101. Aviram, *Telling Rhythm,* 111.

102. Cf. "The Functions of Poetic Rhythm" in *Rhythms of English Poetry,* 285–315.

103. "Both these poetic features," Eeckhout writes, "—tone and voice—sound notoriously suspect in critical prose, partly because they lend themselves so uneasily to academic protocols of falsification and partly because they invite a language that all too readily restores the metaphysics of phonocentrism. Yet in Stevens' case they are of the essence. If there is one field in which Stevens criticism—for all its undeniably high standards in general—continues to be hard pressed to catch up with its subject and develop the necessary sensibility and analytical tools, it is that of tone and voice. Often it proves much easier to make Stevens' words signify (meanings) than to let them express (feelings)" (Eeckhout, *The Limits of Reading and Writing,* 38–9). These are all estimates, one could add, that people are more or less successfully able to make on a daily basis in what we could call "natural" situations, simply because we are forced to do so in order to get by in the world. The difficulty in doing this is not only a consequence of the serious implications of poetic formalism, where form is not only a possibility of relating to a specific content, but is ideally that content itself. It is also because the interpretation of degrees of sincerity, irony, disaffection, dispair etc. appears to be a largely subjective affair, more subjective, arguably, than simply scanning a line of poetry as pentametrical. This is clearly also to some extent due to the silent and superficial condition of written poetry.

104. Finch's argument, informed by an important feminist attempt at attaining discursive power within a field of 'patriarchal' poetic discourse, is very sensitive to prosodic movement and rhythmic patterning. This makes it quite different to Anthony Easthope's provocative, but contextually heavy-handed *Poetry as Discourse*. From a theoretical viewpoint composed by Marxist theory, structuralist semiotics, and Freudian and Lacanian psychoanalysis, Easthope defines pentameter *as a historical and ideological form*, which for him means that it should be considered as a form of *discourse*. Inspired by the revolutionary impetus of Eliot and Pound's most iconoclastic statements against meter, however, Easthope is inattentive to the possibilities of writing poetry in a metric form which, however 'scannable,' disrupts its own inherited conventions. His conversion of certain events of diachronic change into a synchronic model for aesthetic radicality—essentializing a contingent historical construct, the modern bourgeois sense of pentameter as the adequate form for individual subjectivity, into an abstract (although he claims it is 'material') a-historical form—appears to blind him to the possibility that, aesthetic renewal may hinge on how different modes of poetry adapt to different cultural contingencies and historical moments. Contrary to his alleged purpose to contextualize and de-essentialize iambic pentameter—a particular "metre can be seen not as a neutral form of poetic necessity but as a specific *historical* form producing certain meanings and acting to exclude others"—Easthope therefore appears to rule out the possibility that pentameter's historicity may reside in its being used in new contexts in which it may come to fulfil very different functions from its past ones. Easthope, *Poetry as Discourse*, 64.

105. Finch's review of Alan Holder's *Rethinking Meter: A New Approach to the Verse Line* (Lewisburg, Bucknell University Press, 1995) is significant: "In the final analysis," Finch argues, "Holder embodies a much larger problem in contemporary poetics [than what Finch argues to be a mindless abandonment of foot-prosody for phrasal analysis]. His malaise reflects a widespread confusion between prosodic tools. After extensive thinking about free verse, Holder has decided that prosody's job is exhaustively to describe individual lines of poems, with no outside point of common reference between them. This is a valuable approach—indeed, arguably the most appropriate approach—for free verse. To read metered verse in these terms, however, is like looking at a perspective drawing without any consciousness of the conventions of perspective. It does no justice to the art, and while it may provide interesting insights on a case-by-case basis, as a widespread practice it becomes willfully ignorant." Finch, "A Review of Rethinking Meter," 302.

106. For Taylor, the "paradox" or "mystery" of what he calls Stevens' "apparitional meters" is produced as a discrepancy between "conservative" *appearance* and "speculative" (Taylor's antonym instead of "radical") implications, which lie somewhere "below surface level." See "The Apparitional Meters of Wallace

Stevens," *The Wallace Stevens Journal: A Publication of the Wallace Stevens Society* 15.2 (Fall 1991): 209–28.

NOTES TO CHAPTER ONE

1. Eliot, *On Poetry and Poets,* 31.
2. Robert Buttel, "Wallace Stevens at Harvard: Some Origins of His Theme and Style," *The Act of the Mind: Essays on the Poetry of Wallace Stevens,* ed. Roy Harvey Miller Pearce, J.Hillis (Baltimore: The Johns Hopkins Press, 1965), 29.
3. See Joan Richardson, *The Early Years,* 436.
4. The letter, of February 8, 1955, was to Joseph Bennet. In the same letter, Stevens writes that he "can well believe" that Whitman "remains highly vital for many people. The poems in which he collects large numbers of concrete things, particularly things each of which is poetic in itself or as part of the collection, have a validity which, for many people, must be enough and must seem to them all opulence and élan . . . For others, I imagine that what was once opulent begins to look a little threadbare and the collections seem substitutes for opulence even though they remain gatherings-together of precious Americana, certain to remain precious but not certain to remain poetry. The typical élan survives in many things . . . The élan of the essential Whitman is still deeply moving in the things in which he was himself deeply moved. These would have to be picked out from compilations like *Song of the Broad-Axe, Song of the Exposition* . . . It is useless to treat everything in Whitman as of equal merit. A great deal of it exhibits little or none of his specific power. He seems often to have driven himself to write like himself. The good things, the superbly beautiful and moving things, are those that he wrote naturally, with an extemporaneous and irrepressible vehemence of emotion" (*L* 870–1). In a letter of June 29, 1942, to Harvey Breit, Stevens had politely, but with some malice, denied a request for an interview, apparently because it appeared that Breit might be interested in his 'double life' as insurance lawyer and a poet. Stevens argued that "people of sound logic" (i.e. by implication not Breit) would understand that the modern poet was not "an idler, a man without clothes, a drunk, etc." suggesting that although Joaquin Miller and Whitman had once been seen as archetypal artists, had they also not "been recognized, by people of any sense at all as, personally, poseurs?" (*L* 414).
5. See for example Bloom's Introduction to *The Poems of Our Climate,* "American Poetic Stances: Emerson to Stevens," 1–26.
6. Cushman argues that "Bloom's own work, so often admirable and incisive, is especially guilty" of ignoring the specificity of poetry "as his tracking of figurative patterns leads from the prose of Emerson or Freud to the verse of Whitman or Stevens as though these were interchangeable forms of discourse." *Fictions of Form,* 5.

7. Walt Whitman, *Leaves of Grass* (New York: Modern Library, 1993), 35.
8. Whitman, Walt. *Complete Poetry and Collected Prose.* (New York: Library of America, 1982), 5.
9. Whitman, *Leaves of Grass,* 35.
10. Ibid., 34.
11. Ibid., 64.
12. Ibid., 34.
13. Emily Dickinson, *The Collected Poems of Emily Dickinson* (London: Faber & Faber, 1975), 143.
14. Cf. Fred Miller Robinson, "Strategies of Smallness: Wallace Stevens and Emily Dickinson," *The Wallace Stevens Journal: A Publication of the Wallace Stevens Society* 10.1 (Spring 1986): 27–35.
15. Whitman, *Leaves of Grass,* 34.
16. Ibid., 43.
17. Cf. Marshall Berman's discussion of the big city's crucial importance to the poetics of Pushkin and Baudelaire in *All That Is Solid Melts into Air: The Experience of Modernity* (New York: Simon and Schuster, 1982).
18. Whitman, *Leaves of Grass,* 43.
19. Ibid., 114.
20. See "The Sound of the Music of Music and Sound," 241–2.
21. As Annie Finch has pointed out, there is a powerful presence of the "ghost of meter" even in Whitman, which brings striking artistic possibilities to his apparently free poetic medium. See "Iambic and Dactylic Associations in *Leaves of Grass*" in *The Ghost of Meter,* 31–35
22. See Robert Buttel's discussion of this period in "Wallace Stevens at Harvard."
23. See Richardon's detailed account in *The Early Years,* 399–441.
24. Glen MacLeod, *Wallace Stevens and Modern Art: From the Armory Show to Abstract Expressionism* (New Haven: Yale University Press, 1993).
25. Bonnie Costello, "Effects of an Analogy: Wallace Stevens and Painting," *Wallace Stevens: The Poetics of Modernism,* ed. Albert Gelpi (Cambridge: Cambridge UP, 1985).
26. Michel Benamou, *Wallace Stevens and the Symbolist Imagination* (Princeton: Princeton University Press, 1972). See. for example Lisa Goldfarb's recent article "'The Figure Concealed': Valéryan Echoes in Stevens' Ideas of Music," *The Wallace Stevens Journal* 28.1 (Spring 2004): 38–58.
27. Lentricchia, *Modernist Quartet,* 129–30.
28. Frank Kermode, *Wallace Stevens* (Edinburgh: Oliver and Boyd, 1960), 81.
29. Cf. "The Poetry of Barbarism," where Santayana criticizes Whitman and Robert Browning, in *Interpretations of Poetry and Religion,* ed. William G Holzberger and Herman J. Saatkamp Jr. (Cambridge, Mass.: MIT Press, 1990), 103–30. In "The Elements and Functions of Poetry," in the same collection (151–72), he defines "the great function" of poetry as repairing "to the material of experience, seizing hold of the reality of sensation and

fancy beneath the surface of conventional ideas, and then out of that living but indefinite material . . . build new structures, richer, finer, fitter to the primary tendencies of our nature, truer to the ultimate possibilities of the soul" (161). The function of "the moulds of metre and rhyme" is to give "as yet undetermined" human speech a "heightened power apart from its significance" (153).

30. Santayana's own poetic production, it should be remembered, largely consists of sonnets.

31. Eliot, *On Poetry and Poets*, 25.

32. Santayana's sonnet was published in *A Hermit of Carmel and Other Poems* (New York: Scribner's, 1901).

33. In a journal entry omitted from the *Letters*, but included in Holly Stevens' commented selection, Stevens writes that he spent an evening with Santayana and Pierre La Rose, a close friend of Santayana's: "After dinner the three of us went to S.'s room. I tried to answer his 'Answer to A Sonnet . . . I said that the first suggestion of the organ-pipes came from the wind. He said that the wind was then a stimulus—the organ-pipe—a result etc. We both held our grounds." Holly Bright Stevens, *Souvenirs and Prophecies: The Young Wallace Stevens* (New York: Knopf, 1977), 68.

34. His subjects also included Political Science, History, and an introductory course in Economics. Stevens, however, appears to have excelled in his study of English Composition and Literature, as well as in the other languages, whereas his grades in History and Economics were mediocre (*L* 17, 23). Joan Richardson suggests that "this free choice of courses" catered for "both the wishes of the young man who wanted to be a writer and the wishes of the young man's father, who was sending him to Harvard 'to make something of himself'" (*The Early Years*, 59).

35. Lentricchia, *Modernist Quartet*, 125.

36. In the same Journal entry, we understand that the "we" excludes Stevens himself having this insight. Instead, a very unfavorably described fellow passenger gets to stand as an example of such habits: "There was a girl on the train with a face like the under-side of a moonfish. Her talk was of dances + men. For her, Sahara had no sand; Brazil, no mud" (*L* 73). Stevens' fascination with natural mystery can also be seen in an extraordinary narration about an encounter with the spirit of Nature during a nocturnal walk in Central Park, in February, 1901. On hearing an owl hoot, Stevens experiences a short but intense epiphanic moment: "I stopped and suddenly felt the mysterious spirit of nature—a very mysterious spirit, one I thought never to have to meet again. I breathed in the air and shook off the lethargy that has controlled me for so long a time. But my Ariel-owl stopped hooting + the spirit slipped away and left me looking with amusement at the extremely unmysterious and not at all spiritual hotels and apartment houses that were lined up like elegant factories on the West side of the Park" (*L* 50).

37. In a Journal entry of August 3, 1900, Stevens claims that he is beginning to "like New York + do like it hard," a fascination which begins to manifest itself in Whitmanian representations of New York streets, and a fascination with the city's enormity: in his Journal from October 26, 1900, he observes that "New York is so big that a battle might go on at one end, and poets meditate sonnets on another" (*L* 47). On March 11, 1901, after a visit to Reading, which looked "the acme of dullness," he claims to be glad, "therefore, to get back to this electric town which I adore" (42). On the day after, however, he explains that his New York Days have changed him into a harder human being, having blunted his sensibility in worrying ways: "To illustrate the change that has come over me I may mention that last night I saw from an elevated train a group of girls making flowers in a dirty factory near Bleecker-st. I hardly gave it a thought. Last summer it would have bathed me in tears" (53). In 1902, experiencing considerable economic difficulties, Stevens defines his situation in New York as "a terrible imprisonment," stating that he "*must* find a home in the country—a place to live in, not only to *be* in" (58).

38. Lentricchia, *Modernist Quartet*, 133.

39. The poem begins "A late lark twitters from the quiet skies / And from the west, / Where the sun, his day's work ended, / Lingers as in content, / There falls on the old, grey city / An influence luminous and serene, A shining peace," and goes on to describe how the city is magically illuminated by bird song and the lights of dusk, finally comparing the setting of the sun to the speaker's sense of imminent mortality. See William Ernest Henley, *Poems* (Oxford: Woodstock Books, 1993), 161–2.

40. Lentricchia, *Modernist Quartet*, 133.

41. Buttel, "Wallace Stevens at Harvard," 32.

42. Buttel suggests that this image derives from Stevens' reading of Dante Gabriel Rossetti's "House of Life" sonnet sequence. Ibid.

43. Lentricchia argues that American modernists (he deals with Stevens, Frost, Eliot and Pound) were sensitive to economic pressure to a greater degree than European ones, and discusses Stevens' early statement that earning money, providing, was a masculine activity, whereas poetry seemed a "perfectly lady-like" pursuit. *Modernist Quartet*, 125. Lentricchia's argument examines Stevens' sense of gender in relation to his poetry, contrasting his poetry's gestures toward masculinity with a sense of domestic and feminized existence which, Lentricchia argues, defines much of his later imagery.

44. In 1901, after a period of writing for *The New York Tribune*, Stevens entertained plans to quit working and dedicate himself fully to literature. He was sternly rebuked by his ponderous father, and persuaded to opt for a more solid occupation. After resolving to give up journalism, Stevens took his father's advice and attended New York Law School until the Summer of 1903, practicing as a clerk in the offices of attorney W.G. Peckham until

1904, when he started a career of his own as a practicing lawyer. Stevens would stay in New York, often living quite rough: in a Journal entry of October 23, 1904 (*L* 78), Stevens claims to have been "so desparately poor at times as not to be able to buy sufficient food—and sometimes not any," and in one of his first letters to Elsie Moll, of April 10, 1905, he gives an impression of a hard-working but not very lucrative existence: "I have money in pocket but not in bank + I pay most of my bills promptly and all of them eventually. Still my hands are empty—+ that much idolized source of pathetic martyrdom, mon pauvre coeur!" (*L* 81). In July, 1916, he moved to Hartford to work for the Hartford Insurance and Indemnity Company.

45. "True, it [is] not necessary to start from the soil; but starting with nothing whatever—to make a fortune—is not wholly inspiring after a fellow has spent more or less time lolling about. It is decidedly wrong to start there with one's tastes fully developed + to have to forego all satisfaction of them for a vague number of years. This is quite different from beginning as other men do. It is more like being up already + working down to a certain point" (*L* 63).

46. Lentricchia, *Modernist Quartet,* 130.

47. "Another phase of the thing is that when one has lived for twenty-five years with every reasonable wish granted + among the highest associations—starting at the bottom suddenly reveals millions of fellow men struggling at the same point, of whom one previously had only an extremely vague conception. There was a time when I walked downtown in the morning almost oblivious of the thousands and thousands of people I passed; now I look at them with extraordinary interest as companions in *the same fight* that I am about to join" (*L* 63).

48. Lentricchia, *Modernist Quartet,* 130.

49. In a letter to Ronald Lane Latimer, discussing Stanley Burnshaw's now famous review of *Ideas of Order* in *New Masses,* Stevens writes: "I hope I am headed left, but there are Lefts and Lefts, and certainly I am not headed for the ghastly left of MASSES" (*L* 286).

50. Cf. Joseph Harrington, "The Modernist as Liberal: Wallace Stevens and the Poetics of Private Insurance," *Poetry and the Public: The Social Form of Modern U.S. Poetics* (Middletown, Conn.: Wesleyan, 2002).

51. Filreis also draws attention to the paradoxical political situation of the time, when liberals and conservatives appeared to have traded ideological positions on practical matters: "Indeed New Deal legislation put many business conservatives in the awkward position of *defending* restrictions on competition and *seeking* government-financed bail-outs. Meantime, many liberals found themselves calling for the *relaxation* of the very antitrust laws their ideological progenitors had put in place to keep big business in check." *Modernism from Right to Left,* 77.

52. Ibid.

53. Ibid., 80.

54. Ibid., 75.

55. Stevens' fearful argument is also an aestheticist one: "under both Fascist and Communist systems the finely-tailored agent, [like Stevens himself] wearing a boutonierre, gives way to the letter carrier" (*OP* 236). There is thus in the contemporary social system, for all its malfunctions, at least a hint of what Stevens would later, in a simultaneously visionary and elegiac way, call "nobility," in the an aura of stylish professionalism attached to the services of insurance agents. However ethically weak his argument seems at this point—certainly, the stylish dress of insurance men could be dispensed with for the sake of social justice—the contradictions of Stevens' rhetoric are illuminating. Toward the end of the essay Stevens reassures the reader that "[w]e shall never live in a world quite *so* mechanical as the one that Mr. Wells has imagined, nor in a world in which insurance has been made perfect, and where we can buy peace and prosperity as readily and as cheaply as we can buy the morning newspaper" (236). The "we" of this sentence is clearly suspect, since there were obviously many people at the time who could not afford the morning newspaper. One could also argue that prosperity is not something that can be bought, but the very capacity to buy things, whether because of hard work or inherited wealth. Stevens' final negation of the very fear instilled by his argument is interesting, since it connects with individualist discourses against cultural homogeneity that are built on a *combination* of the fear of homogeneity and anonymity *and* the reassuring as well as politically performative assumption that human existence *can never be* homogenous in the mechanical sense given to it by Stevens. Why fear social security when the urge toward total safety, one of whose risks would be a totalitarian mechanization of life, is a mere figment of our imagination? Conversely, if the "truth" of Wells' novel was final and we *were* indeed mere mechanisms in our essence—merely acting out a purpose unknown to us, manifested in our (mechanico-biologico-historical) urge toward self-perpetuation—how could it then be wrong that the social system reflected or embodied this truth?

56. Thus, as Lakritz has argued, it can be seen as a both "conservative" and "radical" force. As Lakritz' discussion of Stevens criticism suggests, the oscillations between interpreting his poetry for radical vs. conservative purposes itself say something very important about the often simplistic use of these terms: it is "[n]ot simply that radicals can find in him what they want, and conservatives can do the same, but as well that his very radicalism is part and parcel of his conservatism, inextricably linked as a poetic project." *Modernism and the Other*, 29.

57. Robert Frost, *Selected Poems* (London: Penguin, 1973), 170–1.

58. Taylor, "The Apparitional Meters," 223.

59. Aviram, *Telling Rhythm*, 111.

60. Aviram defines his idea of "sublime rhythm" in relation to Nietzsche's *Birth of Tragedy*, Freudian and Lacanian psychoanalysis and their legacy in Kristeva, Nicolas Abraham and Philippe Lacoue-Labarthe.

61. The political discourse of Stevens' time was full of real estate imagery. In his inaugural address of March 4, 1934, Franklin D. Roosevelt had proposed to "restore" the "temple" of Ameican civilization, a collectively owned space for democratic worship, "to its ancient truths," by expelling its profane destroyers, the self-interested capitalists of big business. Roosevelt had also suggested that "plenty is at [the] doorstep" of the American 'house,' in order to legitimize his drafting of the American people to surrender part of their individual privileges for the 'disciplined,' army-like, collective operation that was required to overcome the great economic crisis. Roosevelt's rhetorical downplaying of economics, the claim that the present crisis was, "luckily," "*only* of material things," (italics mine) did not hide the fact that the most important part of his address dealt with the necessity to make political warfare on precisely these economical problems, understood as a threat to American democracy as such. The temple-like Hartford building itself, described by Stevens as "a solemn affair of granite, with a portico resting on five of the grimmest possible columns" (*L* 283), was turned into a publicity asset for the Hartford in the Depression years, whose image was that of a fortress of permanent security and achievement in the midst of violent instability. While it thus safeguarded the "ancient values" of life, liberty and the pursuit of happiness, its own permanency was simultaneously, as Filreis points out, guaranteed by its adaptability to change. See *Modernism from Right to Left*, 85.

62. Latimer, a mysterious presence in the publishing business of the 30s, had several different pseudonyms, and Stevens never met him personally. As an up-and-coming representative of the Left-wing literary establishment, however, Stevens exchanged letters with him between 1934 and 1938, before Latimer disappeared in the Orient. Latimer's *Alcestis Press* was to publish both *Ideas of Order* and *Owl's Clover*, and Stevens exchanged ideas with Latimer on the social function of poetry, apparently because he felt these issues were central to his present concerns. For a detailed description of their correspondence, see Filreis' *Modernism from Right to Left*, especially the chapter "What Superb Mechanics" on 113–36.

63. Filreis, *Modernism from Right to Left*, 84.

64. John Hollander, for example, appears to suggest otherwise: see "The Sound of Music of Music of Sound," 253.

65. John Serio has compared Stevens to Charles Ives in *Bucknell Reiew* 24.2 (1978): 120–31, as has Lawrence Kramer in *The Wallace Stevens Journal* 2.3–4 (Fall 1978): 3–15. David M. Linebarger has discussed Stevens in relation to Edgar Varèse in *The Wallace Stevens Journal* 22.1 (Spring 1998): 57–71. See also Michael Faherty's comparative article on Stevens

and Kandinsky's musical theory in *The Wallace Stevens Journal* 16.2 (Fall 1992): 151–60.

66. Brazeau, *Parts of a World*, 104.

67. "Stevens uses foreign words," Gerber argues, "because their stress pattern is distinct from that of English words. In early poems, Stevens turns to the variant stress pattern of foreign words not so much to satisfy the metrical pattern of his iambic pentameter verse, as to achieve self-conscious, often comic ends. By his mature poetry, the co-presence of words with competing stress patterns serves more philosophical ends, drawing attention to a pervasive concern in Stevens: the variable nature of description, both in our articulation of language and in our articulation of experience." Natalie Gerber, "'A Funny Foreigner of Meek Address': Stevens and English as a Foreign Language," *The Wallace Stevens Journal: A Publication of the Wallace Stevens Society* 25:2 (Fall 2001): 211.

68. In the thirties, Filreis writes, it was possible "to be thunderously denounced for using French, regardless of the speaker's background or revolutionary credentials." *Modernism from Right to Left*, 56.

69. I take "chucuotements" to be a misspelling of "chuchotement," derived from "chuchoter" (to whisper), and "ricaments" to mean "ricanements" (derisive laughter).

70. *The New Oxford Dictionary of English* defines the meaning of cachinnate as "laughing loudly," ascribing its origin to the early 19th century as a coinage on Latin "*cachinnat*, 'laughed loudly,' of imitative origin."

71. Joseph Riddel, *The Clairvoyant Eye: The Poetry and Poetics of Wallace Stevens* (Baton Rouge: Louisiana State University Press, 1965), 114. Possibly, Riddel is interpreting the sound of "shoo-shoo-shoo" in terms of the jazz-like "shoo-shoo-shoo of secret cymbals round" (*CP* 401) in "Notes toward a Supreme Fiction."

72. J. Hillis Miller, "Wallace Stevens' Poetry of Being," *The Act of the Mind: Essays on the Poetry of Wallace Stevens,* ed. Roy Harvey and J. Hillis Miller Pierce (Baltimore: The Johns Hopkins Press, 1965), 146–7.

73. Mutlu Konuk Blasing, *American Poetry: The Rhetoric of Its Forms* (New Haven: Yale University Press, 1987), 84–100.

74. See the chapter "Dickinson and Patriarchal Meter," in Annie Finch, *The Ghost of Meter: Culture and Prosody in American Free Verse* (Ann Arbor: University of Michigan Press, 1993), 13–20.

75. An interesting discussion of the Formalist idea of this perceptual change is to be found in Fredric Jameson's *The Prison-House of Language: A Critical Account of Structuralism and Russian Formalism* (Princeton: Princeton University Press, 1972), 33–6.

76. Even though I agree with the most important critiques of foot-prosody as a possible distortion of rhythmic description, I will at times use the term iambic: both because it is often more economical than, for example "duple rising

rhythm" and because I will often be talking about rhythmic patterns that could be described as metrical, i.e. that they are, or suggest, a kind of rhythmic pattern that, as Attridge formulates it, "can be counted and named."

77. For an example of how, once begun, an analysis of the total semantic event of a poem can be nearly endless, see Richard Cureton's reading of Blake's "The Sick Rose" in the introduction to Richard D. Cureton, *Rhythmic Phrasing in English Verse* (London: Longman, 1992), 1–8.

78. Samuel R. Morse was able to inspect Stevens' record collection while visiting his home in 1951. He tells Brazeau that Stevens "did not like Mozart very much." Brazeau, *Parts of a World,* 154.

79. A compelling argument in defense of the ideal of 'absolute' music, responding to modern arguments against its implicit sense of aestheticist self-sufficiency, can be found in Andrew Bowie, *From Romanticism to Critical Theory: The Philosophy of German Literary Theory* (New York: Routledge, 1997).

80. See Jacques Derrida, *Specters of Marx: The State of the Debt, the Work of Mourning, and the New International* (New York: Routledge, 1994), 110–14.

81. Abrams, somewhat surprisingly given his contemporary context, ascribes less importance to these theories, for the reason that "[t]his point of view has been relatively rare in literary criticism." M. H. Abrams, *The Mirror and the Lamp: Romantic Theory and the Critical Tradition* (London: Oxford University Press, 1971), 26.

82. This point is made emphatically in Emerson Marks, *Taming the Chaos: English Poetic Diction Theory since the Renaissance* (Detroit: Wayne State University Press, 1998), 291.

83. J. Hillis Miller, *The Linguistic Moment: From Wordsworth to Stevens* (Princeton: Princeton University Press, 1985), 6.

84. Ibid., 9.

85. Ibid., 11.

86. Lentricchia, *Modernist Quartet,* 133.

87. Fredric Jameson, *The Ideologies of Theory: Essays 1971–1986* (Minneapolis: University of Minnesota Press, 1988), 199–200.

88. Walter Benjamin, "On Some Motifs in Baudelaire," in *Illuminations* (London: Fontana Press, 1992), 152–96.

89. Lennart Nyberg, "'THE IMAGINATION': A Twentieth Century Itinerary," on 40–54 in Thormählen, (ed.) *Rethinking Modernism,* 50–1. Nyberg raises the question "whether this sense of external pressure of the world is to be seen as primarily a modern [i.e. modernist] predicament, or if it is, like the modern concept of the self as unstable and decentred, ultimately to be derived from versions of the self and world constructed by the Romantics." Ibid., 51.

90. Blasing, *American Poetry: The Rhetoric of Its Forms,* 97. I will return to this topic in the next chapter's discussion of "Sailing after Lunch."

91. Theodor W. Adorno, *Aesthetic Theory* (Minneapolis: University of Minnesota Press, 1997), 21.

92. Concerning "Esthétique du Mal," Riddel argues—in fluent Derridean—that the "ex-centric, displaced, homeless . . . modern writer signifies the exile of all writing," as "the end of the book of the sublime, the order of displacements, the hierarchy of signifieds, is radically disrupted," and "the writer's 'pain' marks an unbridgeable abyss between himself and the 'supremacy' of the 'moon,' between self and figural source." Joseph Riddel, "Metaphoric Staging: Stevens' Beginning Again of the 'End of the Book,'" *Wallace Stevens: A Celebration,* ed. Frank Doggett and Robert Buttell (Princeton: Princeton University Press, 1980), 310.

93. Lentricchia, *Modernist Quartet,* 144–7.

94. Bloom, *Poems of Our Climate,* 189.

95. Ibid., 185.

96. Melita Schaum, "Lyric Resistance: Views of the Political in the Poetics of Wallace Stevens and H. D.," *The Wallace Stevens Journal: A Publication of the Wallace Stevens Society* 13.2 (Fall 1989): 194.

97. Stephen Cushman remarks, in the same vein, that "a more sympathetic reader might explain Stevens's evasion in another way, arguing that, far from operating in a vacuum, his formalism springs directly from his vision of 'the nature and fate of actual society' in America." *Fictions of Form,* 14–15.

98. B. J. Leggett, *Wallace Stevens and Poetic Theory: Conceiving the Supreme Fiction* (Chapel Hill: University of North Carolina Press, 1987), 17.

99. Ibid., 18.

100. Fredric Jameson, "Wallace Stevens," *New Orleans Review* 11.1 (1984): 179.

101. See Altieri, "Why Stevens Must Be Abstract, " in *Wallace Stevens: The Poetics of Modernism,* 86–118.

102. J. Hillis Miller, *Poets of Reality: Six Twentieth-Century Writers* (Cambridge: Harvard University Press, 1965), 247.

103. Leggett, *Stevens and Poetic Theory,* 20.

104. Ibid., 31. My italics.

105. Just as Stevens appears to have recognized Richards' problems in *critical* epistemology as central to his own poetry, Leggett's argument suggests that embracing Richards'—and Stevens'—insight, would enable critics to inquire more freely, and ultimately do more justice to, Stevens' investigations into "modes of mythology."

106. Kent Johnson, "Prosody and the Outside: Some Notes on Rakosi and Stevens." *Carl Rakosi: Man and Poet,* ed. Michael Heller (Orono: National Poetry Foundation; University of Maine at Orono, 1993), 202.

107. Marie Borroff, *Language and the Poet: Verbal Artistry in Frost, Stevens, and Moore* (Chicago: University of Chicago Press, 1979), 72–3.

108. Anca Rosu, "The Theoretical Afterlife of Wallace Stevens." *The Wallace Stevens Journal: A Publication of the Wallace Stevens Society* 24.2 (Fall 2000): 214.

109. Maeder, *Stevens' Experimental Language,* 3.

110. Ibid., 5. Italics mine.

111. Ibid., 4.
112. Ibid.
113. Bakhtin and Medvedev: "The Formal Method in Literary Scholarship," in Pam Morris, ed., *The Bakhtin Reader: Selected Writings of Bakhtin, Medvedev and Voloshinov* (London: Arnold, 2001), 137.

NOTES TO CHAPTER TWO

1. Richardson, *The Later Years,* 88.
2. In his introduction of Stevens to a British readership, Kermode argued that each of Stevens' poems "stands to the others as every poem stands to an inaccessible central poem in which the 'incessant conjunctionings' of imagination and reality are brought to a full close." Thus, he argues, citing Stevens' "A Primitive Like an Orb" (*CP* 441): "'One poem proves another and the whole.'" Frank Kermode, *Wallace Stevens* (Edinburgh: Oliver and Boyd, 1960), 95. James A. Baird has understood Stevens' concept of 'order' in terms of the "structure" of Stevens' oeuvre as a whole, which he submits to a structural analysis in *The Dome and the Rock: Structure in the Poetry of Wallace Stevens* (Baltimore: Johns Hopkins, 1968). Helen Vendler was prompted by the notion of "The Whole of Harmonium," which Stevens claims originally to have planned to call his *Collected Poems,* (*L* 834) to prove the unity and integrity of his oeuvre in *On Extended Wings.*
3. Knight understands the collection both as a "radical aesthetic reorientation of the poet's aesthetic stance after his years of silence" and as a sustained, unitary meditation on poetry's social purpose, arguing that its "poems are not mere fragments [as *Harmonium*'s poems allegedly were] but integrated parts of an aesthetic unit." Steven T. Knight, "The Craft of Contradiction: Poetic Arrangement in Ideas of Order," *The Wallace Stevens Journal: A Publication of the Wallace Stevens Society* 6.1–2 (Spring 1982): 32.
4. *Aristotle: The Poetics, "Longinus": On the Sublime, Demetrius: On Style,* trans. W. Hamilton Fyfe (Cambridge: Harvard University Press, 1960), 81.
5. Jean-Jacques Lecercle, *The Philosophy of Nonsense* (London: Routledge, 1994), 117.
6. T. S. Eliot, *Collected Poems 1909–1935* (London: Faber & Faber, 1954), 87–90.
7. For an argument on the way Stevens' poetry 'hollows out' the discourses it employs see Fred Hoerner, "Gratification and Its Discontents: The Politics of Stevens' Chastening Aesthetics," *The Wallace Stevens Journal: A Publication of the Wallace Stevens Society* 18.1 (Spring 1994): 81–105.
8. Cf. also Samuel J. Kayser's interesting lingustic analysis of the prevalence of non-finite and agentless verbs in "The Death of a Soldier," in Samuel Jay Keyser, "Wallace Stevens: Form and Meaning in Four Poems," in *Linguistic*

Perspectives on Literature, eds. K. L. Ching Marvin, C. Haley Michael and F. Lunsford Ronald (London: Routledge, 1980).

9. P. Michael Campbell and John Dolan, "Teaching Stevens's Poetry through Rhetorical Structure," *Teaching Wallace Stevens: Practical Essays,* eds. N. Serio John and B. J. Leggett (Knoxville: U of Tennessee P, 1994), 119–28.

10. Quoted from John Hollander's "The Sound of the Music of Music and Sound," *Wallace Stevens: A Celebration,* ed. Frank Dogget and Robert Buttell (Princeton: Princeton University Press, 1980), 250. Maeder quotes Stevens' paraphrase of part IX of "The Man with the Blue Guitar", in which he writes that "[T]he chord destroys its elements by uniting them in the chord" (L 363), which is strikingly similar to Levinas' idea that a "wrong note is a sound that refuses to die." See Emmanuel Levinas, *Existence and Existents,* trans. Alphonso Lingis (The Hague: Nijhoff, 1978), 33. See also Walter J. Ong's argument—directed against American New Criticism—that references to poetry as sound, especially as pure sound without semantic meaning, often equal a notion of poetry as an incommunicative, solid, even spatial objectivity. Walter J. Ong, "A Dialectic of Aural and Objective Correlatives," *20th Century Literary Criticism,* ed. David Lodge (London: Longman, 1972), 498–508.

11. As I have suggested in chapter I, attempting to derive a normative answer to this by listening to Stevens reading his poetry may not be very helpful, as he occasionally underlines line breaks by pausing, whereas in other instances he does not.

12. "To behold is to gaze at or look upon, but with a touch of expressed amazement. The beholder possesses the object; his scrutiny is active, going back to the root *kel,* meaning to drive or to set in swift motion." Bloom, *Poems of Our Climate,* 57. My italics.

13. See Maeder's *Stevens' Experimental Language,* 77–123, for the most thorough discussion of Stevens' use of 'to be.'

14. Filreis, *Modernism from Right to Left,* 170.

15. Vendler, *On Extended Wings,* 5.

16. Louis A. Renza, *Edgar Allan Poe, Wallace Stevens and the Poetics of American Privacy* (Baton Rouge: Lousiana State University Press, 2002). Especially relevant to my discussion is the chapter "Private Man, Public Stage" on 122–51.

17. Cf. Frank Kermode, *The Sense of an Ending: Studies in the Theory of Fiction* (New York: Oxford University Press, 1967), 44–64.

18. Ibid. In a letter to T.C. Wilson of March 25, 1935, having been asked by Wilson, then associate editor of the *Westminster Magazine,* to write a review of Marianne Moore's poetry, Stevens writes that "it seems to me that Miss Moore is endeavoring to create a new romantic; that the way she breaks up older forms is merely an attempt to free herself for the pursuit of the thing in which she is interested; and that the thing in which she is interested in

all the strange collocations of her work is that which is essential in poetry, always; the romantic. But a fresh romantic" (*L* 279).

19. Jacques Derrida, *Spurs: Nietzsche's Styles* (Chicago: University of Chicago Press, 1979), 39.

20. Ibid.

21. Filreis, *Modernism from Right to Left*, 166.

22. Ibid., 166–7.

23. Kenneth Burke suggests that in Stevens' definition of poetry in *The Figure of Youth as the Virile Poet* "the key term 'imagination' . . . figures in a theory of poetry that is basically 'scientist.' For poetry is here approached in terms of its search for 'truth,' as a 'view' of reality, as a kind of 'knowledge.' Stevens, Burke points out, does not only quote Descartes "with approval" but also Shelley, among whose terms Stevens "ended on the most scientist term of all: 'sensation.'" *A Grammar of Motives*, 224–6.

24. Jacques Derrida, *Margins of Philosophy* (Chicago: University of Chicago Press, 1982), 250–5.

25. Barbara Herrnstein Smith, *Poetic Closure: A Study of How Poems End* (Chicago: University of Chicago Press, 1968), 152.

26. Cf. M. Keith Booker, "'A War between the Mind and Sky': Bakhtin and Poetry, Stevens and Politics," *The Wallace Stevens Journal: A Publication of the Wallace Stevens Society* 14.1 (Spring 1990): 71–85.

27. See 209–219 of "White Mythology" in Jacques Derrida, *Margins of Philosophy* (Chicago: University of Chicago Press, 1982), 207–271. For a reading of Stevens' metaphor in Derridean terms see Patricia Parker, "The Motive for Metaphor: Stevens and Derrida," *The Wallace Stevens Journal*. 7.3/4 (Fall 1983): 76–88.

28. Distinguishing Stevens' poetry from that of Eliot and Pound, and grouping it together with that of Robert Frost and Marianne Moore, Lakritz argues that what "this tradition, this branch of literary modernism struggles with is not the obstacles in the way of the literary master to control his or her materials in a world where the social or human center no longer holds; this is not a poetry about a lost *social* order, a nostalgia for the past before the huddled masses fled Europe a third and fourth time to make ever new demands on the American principles of pluralism and tolerance. Without giving up the face of humanity, without turning away from the city and its complex life, the poetry of these writers (and in different ways) examines what is left of our place in and relation to nature." Lakritz, *Modernism and the Other*, 8. Several of my readings here, I would point out, has suggested that Stevens often thematizes precisely a "giving up the face of humanity."

29. Lensing, *A Poet's Growth*, 109.

30. Ibid., 110.

31. Bloom, *Poems of Our Climate*, 112.

32. Cf. Paul Endo's discussion of Stevens' poetry in relation to Kant's mathematical and dynamic sublimes: Paul Endo, "Stevens and the Two Sublimes," *The Wallace Stevens Journal: A Publication of the Wallace Stevens Society* 19.1 (Spring 1995), 35–50.

33. Samuel Taylor Coleridge, *Samuel Taylor Coleridge,* The Oxford Authors (Oxford: Oxford University Press, 1985), 313.

34. "The horse in the center of the picture, painted yellow, has two riders, one a man, dressed in a carnival costume, who is seated well up the horse's neck. The man has his arms under the girl's arms. He holds himself stiffly in order to keep his cigar out of the girl's hair. Her feet are in a second and shorter set of stirrups. She has the legs of a hammer thrower . . . A little behind them is a younger girl riding alone. She has a strong body and streaming hair. She wears a short-sleeved, red waist, a white skirt and an emphatic bracelet of pink coral. She has her eyes on the man's arms. Still farther behind there is another girl. One does not see much more of her than her head. Her lips are painted bright red. It seems that it would be better if someone were to hold her on her horse" (*NA* 12).

35. Northrop Frye, "The Realistic Oriole: A Study of Wallace Stevens," *Wallace Stevens: A Collection of Critical Essays,* ed. Marie Borroff (Eaglewood Cliffs, N.J: Prentice Hall, 1963), 162.

36. See Attridge, *The Rhythms of English Poetry,* 114–21.

37. Alan Filreis' detailed historicist reading, along with Harvey Teres' and Angus Cleghorn's discussions, would make a comprehensive reading superfluous.

38. Alan Filreis and Harvey Teres, "An Interview with Stanley Burnshaw," *The Wallace Stevens Journal: A Publication of the Wallace Stevens Society* 13.2 (Fall 1989): 113.

39. In the first book-length introduction of Stevens to a British audience, Kermode describes Burnshaw's review as a "hostile notice," and suggests that Stevens was "sure" that Burnshaw's approach to reality was "inferior." *Wallace Stevens,* 62. This stance has been the object of critical revision, resulting, among other things, in a special issue in *The Wallace Stevens Journal* on "Stevens and Politics" in 1989, with contributions from, among others, Burnshaw himself, Teres, Filreis, Brogan and Longenbach. Burnshaw's account of this episode, and Kermode's eventual excuse, are highly interesting: See Stanley Burnshaw's "Reflections on Wallace Stevens," 22–26 and Alan Filreis' and Harvey Teres' "An Interview with Stanley Burnshaw," 109–21.

40. "Turmoil in the Middle Ground," Doyle, 137.

41. The book is Long's *Pittsburgh Memoranda,* published in 1935, and reprinted in 1990 by The University of Pittsburgh Press.

42. Two months after Burnshaw's *New Masses* review Harriet Monroe provided an aestheticist defense of Stevens, having feared "that his delight in all the beauty and oddity may be shaken by the clamor and confusion of

the modern scene" but finally reassured readers that his "epic will always be one of serene acceptance, and will present values that are immediate yet timeless. Even a revolution, even communism or fascism, will never disturb the firm foundations of his philosophy, or blind him to the delicate perfections of beauty in a miracle-breeding world." Doyle, 141.

43. Cleghorn, *The Neglected Rhetoric*, 65.

44. Ibid.

45. Holly Stevens has remarked that Elizabeth Park in Hartford was "an extension" of his real home, a pastoral sphere for recollection, creativity and meeting friends. *Wallace Stevens: A Celebration*, 113. In his discussion of "Owl's Clover," Filreis discusses Elizabeth Park as a place in which Stevens came face to face with ethnic diversity and social hardship, but in a less intimidating way than during his first New York years. *Modernism from Right to Left*, 234–40.

46. For a discussion of the metaphor of dance in Stevens and Williams see Barbara M. Fisher, "'The Mind Dances with Itself': Choreographic Idiom in Williams and Stevens." *William Carlos Williams Review* 18.2 (1992): 13–23.

47. The play, for which Stevens received a prize of $100 by the Player's Producing Company, was published in Harriet Monroe's *Poetry*, VIII (July 1916): 163–79. It was staged for the first time in February 13, 1920, at the Provincetown Playhouse in New York City. See *L* 216.

48. *CPP*, 603.

49. Filreis, "Turmoil in the Middle Ground," 139.

50. In a fascinating argument, Michael Hamburger has suggested that one of the reasons why the past was attractive to the modernists was because it appeared more tangible than the future, which is more likely to be experienced as abstract: "However elusive as a whole, the past is a repository of fragments that are palpable to the imagination and can therefore be 'shored against one's ruins.'" Michael Hamburger, "Absolute Poetry and Absolute Politics." *Poetry and Politics*, ed. Richard Jones (New York: William Morrow and Co., 1985), 111.

51. Vendler, *On Extended Wings*, 85.

52. Kermode, *Wallace Stevens*, 64. Marjorie Perloff criticizes Stevens for the same reasons that make critics like Vendler and Kermode praise him, claiming that he is at his most assured when he his at his most "lyrical," which for Perloff equals escapist, monologic and aestheticist. Even if the intense concern of "Owl's Clover" is with the relations between poetry and the real, Perloff thus suggests (somewhat like Vendler) that "Owl's Clover" was not Stevens' real, finished 'voice.' "Stevens is at his most assured, I would argue, when he makes no gesture toward the world of 'prose reality'—the world of 'what is direct and immediate and real,' which he finds so distasteful—but rather explores, like his own 'Rabbit as King of the

Ghosts,' the ways of becoming 'A self that touches all edges.'" "Revolving in Crystal," 51.

53. Burnshaw, "Turmoil in the Middle Ground," in Doyle, 140.

54. Maeder, *Stevens' Experimental Language,* 129.

55. Ibid., 146.

56. Ibid., 79.

57. Timothy Clark has suggested that Derrida's ideas, which are implied in most occurrences of the term 'deconstruction,' could well be seen as "a form of dialectics indebted to Hegel, but refusing to subsume the work of negativity into the universal." Timothy Clark, *Derrida, Heidegger, Blanchot: Sources of Derrida's Notion and Practice of Literature* (Cambridge: Cambridge University Press, 1992), 109.

58. Wesling, *Scissors of Meter,* 42.

NOTES TO CHAPTER THREE

1. Albert Gelpi, "Stevens and Williams: The Epistemology of Modernism." *Wallace Stevens: The Poetics of Modernism,* ed. Albert Gelpi (Cambridge: Cambridge University Press, 1985), 10.

2. "Stevens must have known," Gelpi argues, that the word romantic "was a red flag to a *soi-disant* anti-romantic like Williams." Ibid., 10.

3. Notably, Bruns suggests in the same collection that the "polyphonic" American poetry (in which he includes Williams) is opposed to Stevens' lyrical monologism in that it is "beyond epistemology."

4. Johnson, "Prosody and the Outside," 193.

5. Gelpi, "Stevens and Williams," 10–11.

6. Cf. Walter Benjamin, "The Work of Art in the Age of Mechanical Reproduction." *Illuminations* (London: Fontana Press, 1992), 211–44.

7. Parker, "The Motive for Metaphor," 76–88.

8. Pound, *Literary Essays,* 4.

9. Ibid.

10. One of the *Adagia* states that "[t]o a large extent, the problems of poets are the problems of painters and poets must often turn to the literature of painting for a discussion of their own problems" (OP 187) and another one that ethics "are no more part of poetry than it is of painting" (OP 190). See also Stevens' full argument on these matters in "The Relations between Poetry and Painting" (NA 157–76).

11. Costello, "Effects of an Analogy," 66. Costello discusses earlier studies of Stevens and painting, above all Benamou's "Poetry and Painting" from 1959, (included in *Wallace Stevens and the Symbolist Imagination*), which suggests that Stevens tried to imitate painterly effects to make poetic language more 'direct.' Costello, however, argues that it is easy to "say clearly what approaches Stevens did not take. He seldom used painting as a focusing

device (as did Auden), an image of the still moment (as did Keats and Eliot), or a source of emblemata (as Moore so often did). Stevens' poems do not, for the most part, visualize their subjects, making the reader a beholder of an imagined pictorial space. In fact, Stevens' poetry hardly resembles painting at all." (Costello, "Effects of an Analogy," 65) The most important aspect of Stevens' use of painting, she argues, is that "[T]he elements and techniques of painting—light, color, shape, line, plane, space, grisaille, chiaroscuro, etching—are *not approximated in language* but *brought to mind.*" (ibid. 66, my italics) Thus, Costello sees the influence of painterly theory as a kind of formative 'contagion' which, she clarifies, is "the contagion of analogy, not of imitation." (ibid. 68)

12. This clearly recalls the Heideggerian vocabulary applied to Stevens' language in Krzysztof Ziarek's *Inflected Language: Toward a Hermeneutics of Nearness Heidegger, Levinas, Stevens, Celan* (Albany: State University of New York Press, 1994). For a Heideggerian reading of Stevens, focussed on his and Heidegger's ideas about "dwelling," see Frank Kermode's "Dwelling Poetically in Connecticut," *Wallace Stevens: A Celebration,* ed. Frank and Robert Buttel Doggett (Princeton: Princeton UniversityPress, 1980), 256–73. A Heideggerian vocabulary is central in Paul A. Bové's deconstructionist study *Destructive Poetics: Heidegger and Modern American Poetry* (New York: Columbia UP, 1980).

13. See Bloom, *The Poems of Our Climate,* 144.

14. Pound, *Literary Essays,* 6.

15. Insofar as Stevens may be referring to Williams here, this sense is certainly already there in the lazy colloquialism of the title of Williams' *Spring and All,* published in 1923. This collection by itself, it appears to me, is almost impossible to read as anything but intensely romantic in the sense given to it by Stevens: "At any rate, now at last spring is here . . . The imagination, freed from the handcuffs of 'art,' takes the lead." William Carlos Williams, *Collected Poems,* vol. I (London: Paladin, 1987), 184–5.

16. Bloom suggests the necessity of a similar interpretive, extra-textual, intonational choice in his reading of "Notes toward a Supreme Fiction." In canto VI of "It Must Be Abstract," another stanza about the possible inauthenticity of the "only imagined but imagined well" Stevens "proceeds," Bloom argues, "to demonstrate that truly he is no ephebe in the extraordinarily haunting lines beginning 'My house has changed a little in the sun,' where the emphasis falls strongly upon 'has.'" Bloom, *Poems of Our Climate,* 187.

17. Taylor, "Stevens' Apparitional Meters," 213.

18. Bloom, *Poems of Our Climate,* 147.

19. Vendler, *On Extended Wings,* 19.

20. See Bruns, "Stevens without Epistemology." 30. It could certainly be argued that the age of the "hermeneutical turn'" has not simply *succeeded* the "epistemological" and "linguistic" turns, in the sense that it has not *freed* humanity

from epistemological and linguistic problems. A facet of this is that it is difficult to imagine a conversation to work at all without some sort of basic grammar, even if such a grammar could be altered be the creative processes that are
central to the idea of language as dialogue.

21. See, above all, "Forms of Time and the Chronotope in the Novel" and "Epic
    and the Novel," in Mikhail Bakhtin, *The Dialogic Imagination: Four Essays,*
    Michael Holquist ed. (Austin: University of Texas Press, 1981).

22. Lecercle, *The Philosophy of Nonsense,* 168. A challenging reading of Bakhtin
    can be found in Meschonnic's *Critique du Rhythme,* in which he critiques
    the 'politics' derived from what he understands as Bakhtin's essentialist, ahis-
    torical distinction between novelistic discourse and epic and lyric poetry. Cf.
    "Critique du monologue" in *Critique du rhythme,* 447–57. Booker argues
    that Bakhtin's distinction is "directed more at certain formal ways of reading
    poetry than at poetry itself" and that "it is fundamental to Bakhtin's thought
    to suggest a dialogic potential in all language." "Stevens and Bakhtin," 72.

23. A similar connection between Stevens' nonsense, sound repetitions and the
    historical plurality suggested by Bakhtin is made in Rosu's *The Metaphysics
    of Sound,* 7–8.

24. Derrida, Jacques, *Of Grammatology,* ed. and transl. Gayatri Chakravorty
    Spivak. (Baltimore: The Johns Hopkins University Press, 1997), 8.

25. Cook, *Poetry, Word-Play and Word-War,* 16–17.

26. In the fourth section of *Anatomy of Criticism,* "Theory of Genres," Frye
    defines the lyric as "the genre in which the poet, like the ironic writer, turns
    his back on the audience" (271) and of poetic creation as an "associative
    rhetorical process, most of it below the threshold of consciousness, a chaos
    of paranomasia, sound-links, ambiguous sense-links, and memory-links
    very like that of the dream." (271–2) The two modes of "subconscious asso-
    ciation which form the basis for lyrical *melos* and *opsis* respectively" Frye
    provisionally names, on the model of children's language learning, "babble"
    and "doodle"—the former designating the associative organization of words
    in conjunction with each other, and the latter the use of "an object of sense
    to stimulate a mental activity in connection with it"—finally settling for the
    names "charm" and "riddle." The charm is defined as "the hypnotic incanta-
    tion that, through its pulsating dance rhythm, appeals to involuntary physi-
    cal response, and is hence not far from the sense of magic, or physically
    compelling power." (278) *Anatomy of Criticism: Four Essays by Northrop Frye*
    (New York: Atheneum, 1968). Cf. chapter IV for a discussion of this per-
    spective.

27. Charms, Rosu argues, "obliges one to perceive totally different qualities of
    language: its formal design in sound-pattern as well as the power resulting
    from it. (. . .) Besides their formal characteristics, charms and incantations
    are distinguished by their purpose, which goes beyond communication.
    Charms are supposed to produce practical results, to heal, to make rain,

or to rid us of evil spirits. Such a purpose implies a reversal of the relation between language and reality as we normally conceive of it. For instead of representing reality, and therefore being subordinated to it, charms create, and therefore master and control, a reality. This kind of reversal appealed to Stevens on different levels." *The Metaphysics of Sound,* 33–4.

28. "We can see," Frye remarks, "from the revisions poets make that the rhythm is usually prior, either in inspiration or in importance or both, to the selection of words to fill it up. This phenomenon is not confined to poetry: in Beethoven's notebooks, too, we often see how he knows that he wants a cadence at a certain bar before he has worked out any melodic sequence to reach it. One can see a similar evolution in children, who start with rhythmical babble and fill in the appropriate words as they go along." *Anatomy of Criticism,* 275–6.

29. Lentricchia, *Modernist Quartet,* 140.

30. Fisher, "Ambiguous Birds," 4.

31. Ibid.

32. Keats, *Poetical Works,* 258–59.

33. Bloom somewhat casually relates this phrase to Stevens' adagium that "the poet is the priest of the invisible." *The Poems of Our Climate,* 148.

34. See Abrams, *The Mirror and the Lamp,* 42–5.

35. Dennis Taylor has attempted to establish Stevens as a formal renovator in view of his practice of "apparitional meters." The argument is based on an Aristotelian idea of the stanza as "the edifice, the visible image of the form and frame drawn from thinking and pushed toward visible realization." Stevens' meters are thus 'apparitional' because they 'appear' traditional as a consequence of their stanzaic and graphic-syllabic form, while it is precisely this illusory appearance which enables surprising, 'modernist,' deviation from automatized expectations. Even though his argument simplifies the kind of expectations modern readers may have when approaching Stevens' poetry, Taylor indicates an important function of the stanza in the aftermath of free verse, as the dynamic condition for concatenation or enjambment between stanzas. "The Apparitional Meters of Wallace Stevens," 226. Meter, which Taylor simplifyingly identifies with the stanza is thus a paradigm that, in Stevens' version, cannot quite be broken but, at best, be manipulated. As "forms of similitude" stanzas are the metaphorical "as" of congealed mimetic forms that are evaded and played with, in a game of deception and destabilization. My reservation against Taylor's approach is that it depends entirely on assuming that readers *first* interpret the referential aspect of Stevens' "apparitional meters" as *signs* of traditionalism, in order for the 'defamiliarizing' break with expectations to occur at a second stage. This is to some extent to interpret the failure of one's analytical tools—traditional foot-scansion—to determine the rhythmic patterns of Stevens' poems as a sign of radical deviousness.

36. Lakritz' study makes a distinction between the thinking of Eliot and Pound on the one hand, and Stevens on the other: "In Aristotle's treatise on poetry, the classical emphasis on human form making and shaping, an emphasis that has a long and deep tradition in the West, no doubt an emphasis that stems in part from a deep if also anxious Western trust in its own ability to give order to a bewildering world that only barely keeps the forces that elicit 'pity and fear' in check by exercising them in a controlled environment, this emphasis expresses the human desire that, in fact, our shaping of plastic materials is identical with our ability to maintain domination of nature—animals, the landscape, the environment. One could argue that in Pound one has a late avatar of this tradition, despite his inability to maintain his own control over his materials: the great figures of The Cantos are great because of the order they brought into the world, in the form of political and cultural order. And Eliot's great poem of social and cultural disintegration, 'The Waste Land,' is surely the most powerful lament we have that the center does not hold, that human imagination in the form of the great cultural legacy of literature has fallen into pieces. . . . Stevens . . . is different." *Modernism and the Other*, 6–7. Lakritz does not suggest, however, that Stevens' project is removed from these concerns: his poetry shares the sense that we live in a 'fallen' world that needs new fictions to become liveable and abounds with figures of order and centrality.

37. Charles Taylor, *Sources of the Self: The Making of the Modern Identity* (Cambridge, Mass.: Harvard University Press, 1989), 573.

38. Ibid., 481.

39. Christopher Prendergast, *The Order of Mimesis: Balzac, Stendhal, Nerval, Flaubert* (Cambridge: Cambridge University Press, 1986), 10.

40. Ibid., 12.

41. Ibid., 13.

42. To my mind, many attempts at arguing for the positive side of Stevens' nonsensical, negative and defamiliarizing investments in rhythm and sound go too far, giving a permanent privilege to the sound of words by ascribing an entirely different cosmology to Stevens' language. Mervin Nicholson has argued that "Stevens' 'sound' expresses a human capacity *unlike* abstract reasoning, one that articulates a kind of meaning that has *its own* terms and forms; it is related to Saussure's 'sound-image' (or even Derrida's 'arche-writing'). 'Sound' in Stevens is a synesthetic force comparable to touch: 'Poetry is a *sense*.'" In "'The Slightest Sound Matters': Stevens' Sound Cosmology." *The Wallace Stevens Journal: A Publication of the Wallace Stevens Society* 18.1 (Spring 1994): 65. (My italics.) This *sense* is, however, wholly disengaged from sense as linguistic meaning. Dickie's similar argument highlights what she calls the 'pre-verbal' aspects of Stevens' sound patterning. See. Margaret Dickie, "Collections of Sound in Stevens, " Ibid. 15.2 (1991):133–43. An interesting way of dealing with this dilemma is found in Aviram's study,

which argues that the extra-linguistic (pre-verbal) element of poetic language is the object of the poem's signification: a poem is, in this sense, an "allegory of its own rhythm": "poetry simultaneously challenges language and calls language forth." *Telling Rhythm*, 134.

43. The speaker of "Ode to a Nightingale," claiming that he will join the bird "Not charioted by Bacchus and his pards, / But on the viewless [i.e. blind] wings of Poesy" exclaims, in momentary triumph: "Already with thee! Tender is the night, / And haply the Queen-Moon is on her throne, / Clustered around by all her starry Fays." This, however, is followed by another negation: "But here there is no light, / Save what from heaven is with the breezes blown / Through verdurous glooms and winding mossy ways." John Keats, *Poetical Works* (Oxford: Oxford University Press, 1958), 258–9.

44. Rosu suggests that the poem is a parody of a sonnet, a thesis she maintains with some difficulty, not the least since the poem originally published in the first *Alcestis* edition of *Ideas of Order* consisted, as she admits, of fifteen lines. Stevens' excision of the line "The stillness that comes to me out of this, beneath" may, Rosu argues, "have been left out because of its sheer clumsiness, but its omission may also indicate that Stevens wanted the poem to be a sonnet." *The Metaphysics of Sound*, 73.

45. Hollander, "The Sound of the Music of Music and Sound," 248–9. See *The Works of John Milton* (Ware: The Wordsworth Poetry Library, 1994), 29.

46. Cook, *Poetry, Word-Play, and Word-War*, 126.

47. Rosu, *The Metaphysics of Sound*, 75.

48. Ibid.

49. Ibid., 74–5.

50. Rosu's dilemma may well be defined by Astradur Eysteinsson's idea that "as soon as we wish to define modernism through its defiance of realist discourse, and ultimately of communicative language, we run the risk of simply reiterating the formalist theory of 'poetic language.'" This, Eysteinsson argues (referring to to the first chapter of Pratt's *Toward a Speech Act Theory of Literary Discourse*, 3–37), can be seen as a fundamental ambivalence in the theory of defamiliarization since it involves both "a purification and specification of the verbal act as *art*" and "holds forth ... the potential to challenge ideological and social norms." Astradur Eysteinsson, *The Concept of Modernism* (Ithaca: Cornell University Press, 1990), 199.

51. Paul De Man, "Lyric and Modernity," *Blindness and Insight: Essays in the Rhetoric of Contemporary Criticism* (Minneapolis: University of Minnesota Press, 1983), 179.

52. A few of the most important modern theories of poetic form relate a linguistic tradition, which describes poetic language in terms of *foregrounding* and *function*, and a psychoanalytic one that relates rhythmic language to the 'unconscious,' whose subversive status as an 'alternative' 'domain' often relies on a form of mysticism. Luce Irigaray's definition of a particular feminine discourse

may exemplify the use of such a domain for political purposes. For her, the language of woman should not be measured according to the standards of the male, discursive, inherently "measuring" norms, since it refuses to participate in the game of power and domination: "She [the woman] just barely separates from herself some chatter, an exclamation, a half-secret, a sentence left in suspense." Thus, one "must listen to her differently in order to hear an 'other meaning' which is constantly in the process of weaving itself, at the same time ceaselessly embracing words and yet casting them off to avoid becoming fixed, immobilized." Luce Irigaray, "The Sex Which Is Not One," *From Modernism to Postmodernism: An Anthology,* ed. Lawrence Cahoone (London: Blackwell, 1996), 465.

53. Derek Attridge, "Innovation, Literature, Ethics: Relating to the Other." *PMLA: Publications of the Modern Language Association of America* 114.January (1999): 20–31. In a footnote to this comment, Attridge adds that "Far from being new, this conception of literary reading has perhaps been the dominant one in the Western tradition; it embraces Aristotle on the appropriate style for poetry, "Longinus" and the many eighteenth-century and later attempts to develop a theory of the sublime, most Romantic criticism, Freud and most of those influenced by him, and a large swath of modernist and postmodernist criticism." Attridge acknowledges that "the contrary position—summed up in the title of Wayne Booth's book on the ethics of fiction, *The Company We Keep,* and in Helen Vendler's idea 'The most important thing is to feel companioned, as you go through life, by a host of poems which speak to your experience'—reflects an important aspect of many readers' feelings; my concern, however, is with what such an account leaves out." Ibid. 31f. This argument has been developed in *The Singularity of Literature* (London: Routledge, 2003).

54. See the prologue to "Notes toward a Supreme Fiction" (*CP* 380) where the "book of the wise man" is "close to me, hidden in me day and night." Here, I would argue, closure and hiddenness do not only designate an exclusivity of closure to, and hiddenness from others, but also from the speaker's own self.

55. Hollander, "The Sound of the Music of Music and Sound," 248.

56. In a letter of November 15, 1935.

57. "[T]he sound of that letter," Stevens explains to Latimer, "has more or less variety, and includes, for instance, K and S . . ." (*L* 294)

58. In her reading of "Thirteen Ways of Looking at a Blackbird," Maeder points out that the idea that "Among twenty snowy mountains /The only *moving* thing / Was the eye of the blackbird" is based on an anatomical impossibility. *Stevens' Experimental Language,* 113. My italics.

59. Hollander, "The Sound of the Music of Music and Sound," 247.

60. Lentricchia, *Modernist Quartet,* 161.

61. The poem was written explicitly for a special issue of the *Trinity Review,* of May 1954, which celebrated Stevens' seventy-fifth birthday. The issue,

which featured contributions from Stevens' friends, different critics and other poets, also included the poem "The Rock." Alan Filreis reads the poem in the context of a poetic debate Stevens maintained with the younger poet Richard Eberhart. *Wallace Stevens and the Actual World*, 256–60.

62. Emmanuel Levinas, *Totality and Infinity: An Essay on Exteriority*, trans. Alphonso Lingis (Pittsburgh: Duquesne University Press, 1969), 194–219.

63. See Levinas, *Totality and Infinity*, 304–7.

64. Ziarek, *Inflected Language*, 130.

65. Filreis, *Wallace Stevens and the Actual World*, 258.

66. William Butler Yeats, *The Variorum Edition of the Poems of W.B. Yeats* (New York: MacMillan, 1957), 497–8.

67. Jewel Spears Brooker argues that while "Levinas does not use the word 'modernism' . . . the date of his paper and the terms in which he frames his argument clearly suggest that he was concerned with the human implications of the reigning orthodoxy regarding high art. Although he avoids naming names, he describes positions associated with such writers as Paul Valéry, James Joyce, T.S. Eliot and Ezra Pound; in philosophy, the positions are those of Martin Heidegger." Jewel Spears Brooker, "To Murder and Create: Ethics and Aesthetics in Levinas, Pound and Eliot," in *Rethinking Modernism*, ed. Marianne Thormählen, 56.

68. Emmanuel Levinas, "Reality and Its Shadow," *The Levinas Reader*, ed. Seán Hand (Oxford: Blackwell, 1989), 132.

69. Ibid.

70. Levinas admits that criticism, "in interpreting, will choose and limit," but "if, *qua* choice, it remains on the hither side of the world which is fixed in art, it reintroduces that world into the intelligible world in which it stands, and which is the true homeland of the mind." Ibid., 142. David P. Haney has argued that "What Levinas' position does not allow . . . is the way in which one's relation to art can partake of Levinas' own account of the ethical relation to another . . . Levinas gives art too little credit and criticism too much." David P. Haney, "Aesthetics and Ethics in Gadamer, Lévinas and Romanticism: Problems of Phronesis and Techné." *PMLA: Publications of the Modern Language Association of America* 114. January (1999): 43.

71. As Vincent Sherry argues, the appeal to visual immediacy by way of the Image can be seen both in terms of a desire for an increased openness of visual accessibility and a yearning for cultural exclusivity. Sherry's study of early modernism is explicitly intended as a counter-statement against "the long-prevailing faith that modernism, despite the antidemocratic politics of its major figures, affirms a poetics of colloquial music, celebrating the very sounds of common speech." The Image, Sherry suggests, was a means of circumscribing the problem of misinterpretation, of language that was at once too sloppy and all too accessible, infusing poetry with new cultural vigor: "the physiology of the eye accounts both for a new literary language—a

vocabulary of ultravisual immediacy—and the faculty (as they saw it) of dictatorial command." Vincent Sherry, *Ezra Pound, Wyndham Lewis, and Radical Modernism* (New York: Oxford University Press, 1993), 6–7.

72. Derrida, Jacques, "Che cos'e la poesia?," *A Derrida Reader: Between the Blinds* (New York: Harvester Weatsheaf, 1991), 233.

NOTES TO CHAPTER FOUR

1. Derrida, *Margins of Philosophy*, 228.
2. In his letter, Stevens somewhat oddly explains that he "deliberately took the sort of life that millions of people live, without embellishing it except by the embellishments in which I was interested at the moment: words and sounds" (*L* 294).
3. *L* 289.
4. Maeder, *Stevens' Experimental Language*, 194.
5. Doyle, 163.
6. Brazeau, *Parts of a World*, 201. The italics are Brazeau's.
7. James Longenbach understands this poem as "the best example in Stevens' poetry of what the work of a claim's man is on a bad day." *The Plain Sense of Things*, 114–16.
8. Joan Richardson, "A Reading of 'Sea Surface Full of Clouds,'" *The Wallace Stevens Journal: A Publication of the Wallace Stevens Society.* 3–4 (Fall 1982), 60–68.
9. I have de-italicized these phrases in order emphasize the contrasting words.
10. Edward Kessler, *Images of Wallace Stevens* (New Brunswick: Rutgers University Press, 1972), 11.
11. Ibid.
12. Bloom, *Poems of Our Climate*, 111–2.
13. Kessler, *Images of Wallace Stevens*, 12.
14. Riddel, *The Clairvoyant Eye*, 115. My italics.
15. See Doyle, 224–52.
16. Melita Schaum, ed., *Wallace Stevens and the Feminine* (Tuscaloosa: University of Alabama Press, 1993), 188.
17. Riddel, *The Clairvoyant Eye*, 115.
18. This dilemma is implied in Harvey Teres' reference (also a *passing* one, a way of moving on to reading other poems): "Having said his farewells to Florida, Stevens sailed his shaky craft north, not merely in order to relocate the solitary artist in closer range for the exemplary power of the transcendent imagination, but to undertake the more formidable and indefinitely more difficult task of intervening in the political struggle and determining how a place within it might be made for autonomous poetry and the unencumbered imagination." "Notes toward the Supreme Soviet," 156.

19. In W. Hamilton Fyfe's translation, Aristotle defines metaphor as "the application of a strange term either transferred from the genus and applied to the species or from the species and applied to the genus, or from one species to another or else by analogy." Aristotle, *The Poetics*, 81.

20. Suzanne H. Juhasz, *Metaphor and the Poetry of Williams, Pound and Stevens* (Lewisburg: Bucknell University Press, 1974), 32.

21. Jacqueline Vaught Brogan, *Stevens and Simile: A Theory of Language* (Princeton: Princeton UP, 1986), 16.

22. Perloff, "Revolving in Crystal," 41–2.

23. See chapters I and II of Maeder's *Stevens' Experimental Language*, 11–74.

24. Ibid., 61.

25. Altieri, "Stevens' Metaphors of Metaphor," 28–9. Derrida's argument is quoted from "White Mythology: Metaphor in the Text of Philosophy," *New Literary History,* 6 (1974): 5–74.

26. Ibid., 30–1. Altieri's quotations are from *Critical Inquiry,* 5 (1978), in the following articles: Donald Davidson's "What Metaphors Mean," 31–48, Wayne Booth's "Metaphor as Rhetoric: the Problem of Evaluation," 49–72, and Paul Ricoeur's "The Metaphorical Process as Cognition, Imagination and Feeling," 143–60.

27. Altieri, "Stevens' Metaphors of Metaphor," 31.

28. Stevens' "brilliance on metaphor," Altieri argues, enables his forties poetry to assume the following undertakings: "the expression of a typology of desire warranting the necessity of major man, the capacity to resolve the demonic aspects of duplicity and 'difference' inherent in human dependencies on language, and the possibility of making metaphor a metaphor for anagogic relations between the mind and the world." Ibid., 35.

29. Stevens may have intuited a similarity in structure between metaphor and chiasmus: the formulation at the end of "The Motive of Metaphor" of "the vital, arrogant, fatal, dominant X" may refer to the 'chiasmus' as the Roman version of the Greek letter for Ξ or 'khi.'

30. Gemma Corradi Fiumara, *The Metaphoric Process: Connections between Language and Life* (London: Routledge, 1995).

31. Riddel, *The Clairvoyant Eye*, 115.

32. Bloom, *The Poems of Our Climate*, 110.

33. Reading Stevens' 1944 essay "The Figure of the Youth as Virile Poet" Burke cites Stevens' statements that "Poetry gives us an unofficial view of being" and that "philosophic truth may be said to be the official view." (*NA* 40) "On the symbolic level," Burke suggests, "philosophy and reason here seem equated with the vocational (with office hours), poetry and imagination seem equated with the vocational (after hours). Accordingly, when Mr. Stevens tries to illustrate what he means by poetic imagination, he begins; 'If we close our eyes and think of a place where it would be pleasant to spend a holiday . . .'" *A Grammar of Motives,* 224.

34. In this sense, my analysis contrasts with the only existing detailed rhythmic analysis of the poem, by Adelyn Dougherty, whose analytical apparatus, derived from the theories of Trager-Smith and La Drière, provides a very sophisticated analysis of 'natural' language properties like stress hierarchies, (weaker or stronger, even primary/secondary/tertiary stress) and internal relations within what she calls rhythmic groups. It does not, however, account for the way stress (rhythmic grouping etc.) may be related to the presence of an artificial metric pattern pervading or framing the poem's rhythm as a whole. Adelyn Dougherty, "Structures of Sound in Wallace Stevens' 'Farewell to Florida,'" *Texas Studies in Literature and Language: A Journal of the Humanities, Austin, TX.* (1975): 755–64. The books referred to in Dougherty's article are La Drière's article "Prosody" in *The Encyclopedia of Poetry and Poetics,* e.d. A. Preminger, (Princeton, Princeton University Press, 1965), 669–77, and George L. Trager and Henry Lee Smith Jr.'s *An Outline of English Structure,* Washington D.C. American Council of Learned Societies, 1957).

35. I use the word 'experience' rather than 'pronounce' to do justice to this idea. Our choice does not only depend on whether we stress this syllable or not, since the perception of rhythmic beats can be different from, and stronger than, actual prosodic realization. Neither version can be seen as more natural in ordinary pronunciation—while the second syllable of 'upon' is normally given some stress, different speech situations may demand greater or lesser emphasis—and Stevens' own readings, vacillating between underlining meter and overriding it, are of little help. The fact, however, that the first six syllables of the first line are divided into bisyllabic groups by commas and thus intonationally "chopped up"—as Pound advised against—"in separate iambs," could encourage a strong-stress interpretation of "upon the shore" as a single intonational unit or 'foot' carrying one beat. A reader's susceptibility to perceive this may be further heightened by the similarity between the two lines in syntactic and prosodic shape, and the strong sense of repetition provided by the end-rhyme, which can make us consider the first two lines as a 'couplet' unit.

36. This is noted by Dougherty: "A refrain, commonly associated with song, replaces the speech that the poet has rejected, the speech of 'her mind' by which the speaker will never again be touched." "Structures of Sound," 760.

37. Cf. Douglas Mao's argument against Patricia Rae on this issue in Douglas Mao, "How to Do Things with Modernism," *The Wallace Stevens Journal: A Publication of the Wallace Stevens Society* 26.2 (Fall 2002): 160–80. A short version of Rae's argument in *Poetry and Pragmatism* can be found in the same issue of the WSJ, dedicated entirely to discussing Perloff's mid-eighties argument about Stevens' lyrical impasse: Patricia Rae, "Bloody Battle-Flags and Cloudy Days: The Experience of Metaphor in Pound and Stevens," *Wallace Stevens Journal: A Publication of the Wallace Stevens Society.* 26.2 (Fall 2002): 143–59.

38. Cf. "The Modernism of Eliot and Pound," in Easthope's *Poetry as Discourse,* 134–59. Although Eliot's poetry (Easthope refers to "Morning at the Window") is evidence that language can no longer be treated as a transparent medium through which the represented speaker knows a supposedly external reality" (137) poetic language's fragmentary character redeems language, as the "objective correlative" describes the way that signifiers "are given licence to 'float' in their own autonomy but only so they can be correlative to an incoherent state of mind," i.e. cultural modernity. (138)

39. Dougherty, "Structures of Sound," 759.

40. If 'how' in the first line and the first 'to' of the last line are promoted, in which case we would need to do some violence to natural pronunciation, the lines may function as hexameter concluding a pentameter sequence. This is by no means impossible, but it seems unlikely, if we are to assume a degree of interplay of 'natural' and 'metrical' constraints in rhythmic reading.

41. Dougherty's observation on "the qualitative structure of syllables in end-position" is that "full rhyme" in stanzas two and three "modulates into slant-rhyme and figures of consonance and assonance in stanzas two and three. The /s/ alliteration is striking in the sequence 'sound/South/sea/sail/sand,' and the progress through related sounds in lines 13 to 20, with each succeeding word picking up a preceding sound, creates an impression of semantic unity that is, in fact, suggested by the reference." "Structures of Sound," 760.

42. Alfred Lord Tennyson, *Selected Poems* (London: Penguin, 1991), 58.

43. Ibid.

44. Robert Hass, *Twentieth Century Pleasures: Prose on Poetry* (New York: Ecco Press, 1984), 108.

45. Levinas, "Reality and Its Shadow," 132.

46. William Butler Yeats, "Symbol as Revelation," *The Modern Tradition: Backgrounds of Modern Literature* (New York: Oxford University Press, 1965), 63.

47. Paul Valéry, *Aesthetics,* trans. Ralph Mannheim (New York: Pantheon, 1964), 208.

48. Bloom, *Poems of Our Climate,* 111.

49. Dougherty here suggests that the snake leaving its skin on the floor is another sign of an ambience of death. I understand her to mean that a house into which snakes are able to crawl would be an abandoned, or dilapidated, one. "Structures of Sound," 759–60.

NOTES TO THE CONCLUSION

1. Natalie Gerber, "Stevens' Prosody: Meaningful Rhythms," *The Wallace Stevens Journal* 29.1 (Spring 2005): 178–87, 185.

2. Ibid.

3. "One of the regions that have been most frequently pointed to [by proso-
   dists] is the higher-level territory above the arrangement of syllables into
   feet, measure or patterns of beats, that is to say, the domain governed by the
   rhythmic organization of syntax and sense, moving in conjunction with or
   counterpoint to the more local effects of strongly or weakly stressed syllables
   arranged in fixed or free configurations." Attridge, "Beyond Metrics," 22.
4. Gerber, "Stevens' Prosody," 186.
5. Mary Doyle Springer, "Repetition and 'Going Round' with Wallace Stevens," Wallace Stevens Journal 15.2 (Fall 1991): 191–208, 206.
6. Schaum, *Wallace Stevens and the Critical Schools*, 129.
7. Herrnstein Smith, *Poetic Closure*, 236.

Bibliography

Abrams, M. H. *The Mirror and the Lamp: Romantic Theory and the Critical Tradition*. London: Oxford University Press, 1971.

Adorno, Theodor W. *Aesthetic Theory*. Minneapolis: University of Minnesota Press, 1997.

Altieri, Charles. "Wallace Stevens' Metaphors of Metaphor: Poetry as Theory." *American Poetry*. (Fall 1983): 27–48.

———. "Why Stevens Must Be Abstract; or, What a Poet Can Learn from Painting." *Wallace Stevens: The Poetics of Modernism*. Ed. Albert Gelpi. Cambridge: Cambridge UP, 1985. 86–118.

Aristotle. *Aristotle: The Poetics, "Longinus": On the Sublime, Demetrius: On Style*. Trans. W. Hamilton Fyfe. Cambridge: Harvard University Press, 1960.

———. *The Art of Rhetoric*. London: Penguin Classics, 1991.

Attridge, Derek. "Innovation, Literature, Ethics: Relating to the Other." *PMLA: Publications of the Modern Language Association of America* 114. January (1999): 20–31.

———. *Poetic Rhythm: An Introduction*. Cambridge: Cambridge University Press, 1995.

———. "A Review of Richard Cureton's *Rhythmic Phrasing in English Verse*." *Poetics Today*. (1993): 9–28.

———. *The Singularity of Literature*. London: Routledge, 2003.

Aviram, Amittai F. *Telling Rhythm: Body and Meaning in Poetry*. Ann Arbor: University of Michigan Press, 1994.

Baird, James. *The Dome and the Rock: Structure in the Poetry of Wallace Stevens*. Baltimore: Johns Hopkins, 1968.

Bakhtin, Michail. *The Dialogic Imagination: Four Essays*. Michael Holquist ed. Austin: University of Texas Press, 1981.

Bates, Milton J. *Wallace Stevens: A Mythology of Self*. Berkeley: University of California Press, 1986.

Beehler, Michael. "Penelope's Experience: Teaching the Ethical Lessons of Wallace Stevens." *Teaching Wallace Stevens: Practical Essays*. Eds. N. Serio John and B. J. Leggett. Knoxville: University of Tennessee Press, 1994. 267–79.

219

Benamou, Michel. *Wallace Stevens and the Symbolist Imagination*. Princeton: Princeton University Press, 1972.

Benjamin, Walter. "The Work of Art in the Age of Mechanical Reproduction." *Illuminations*. London: Fontana Press, 1992. 211–44.

Berman, Marshall. *All That Is Solid Melts into Air: The Experience of Modernity*. New York: Simon and Schuster, 1982.

Blasing, Mutlu Konuk. *American Poetry: The Rhetoric of Its Forms*. New Haven: Yale University Press, 1987.

Bloom, Harold. *Wallace Stevens: The Poems of Our Climate*. Ithaca: Cornell University Press, 1977.

Booker, M. Keith. "'A War between the Mind and Sky': Bakhtin and Poetry, Stevens and Politics." *The Wallace Stevens Journal: A Publication of the Wallace Stevens Society* 14.1 (Spring 1990): 71–85.

Borroff, Marie. *Language and the Poet: Verbal Artistry in Frost, Stevens, and Moore*. Chicago: University of Chicago Press, 1979.

Bové, Paul A. *Destructive Poetics: Heidegger and Modern American Poetry*. New York: Columbia University Press, 1980.

Bowie, Andrew. *From Romanticism to Critical Theory: The Philosophy of German Literary Theory*. New York: Routledge, 1997.

Brogan, Jacqueline Vaught. *Stevens and Simile: A Theory of Language*. Princeton: Princeton UP, 1986.

———. *The Violence Within/the Violence Without: Wallace Stevens and the Emergence of a Revolutionary Poetics*. Athens: The University of Georgia Press, 2003.

Brooker Jewel, Spears. "To Murder and Create: Ethics and Aesthetics in Levinas, Pound and Eliot," *Rethinking Modernism*. Ed. Marianne Thormählen. Basingstoke: Palgrave MacMillan, 2003. 55–76.

Bruns, Gerald L. "Stevens without Epistemology." *Wallace Stevens: The Poetics of Modernism*. Ed. Albert Gelpi. Cambridge: Cambridge UP, 1985. 24–40.

Burke, Kenneth. *A Grammar of Motives*. Berkeley: University of California Press, 1969.

———. *The Philosophy of Literary Form*. New York: Vintage Books, 1957.

Burnshaw, Stanley. "Reflections on Wallace Stevens." *The Wallace Stevens Journal: A Publication of the Wallace Stevens Society* 13.2 (Fall 1989): 122–26.

———. "Turmoil in the Middle Ground." *Wallace Stevens: The Critical Heritage*. New Masses 17, 1 (October 1, 1935). Ed. Charles Doyle. London: Routledge, 1985. 137–40.

Buttel, Robert. "Wallace Stevens at Harvard: Some Origins of His Theme and Style." *The Act of the Mind: Essays on the Poetry of Wallace Stevens*. Ed. Roy Harvey Miller Pearce, J.Hillis. Baltimore: The Johns Hopkins Press, 1965. 29–57.

Campbell, P. Michael, and John Dolan. "Teaching Stevens's Poetry through Rhetorical Structure." *Teaching Wallace Stevens: Practical Essays*. Eds. N. Serio John and B. J. Leggett. Knoxville: University of Tennessee Press, 1994. 119–28.

Clark, Timothy. *Derrida, Heidegger, Blanchot: Sources of Derrida's Notion and Practice of Literature.* Cambridge: Cambridge University Press, 1992.

Cleghorn, Angus. *Wallace Stevens' Poetics: The Neglected Rhetoric.* London: Palgrave, 2000.

Coleridge, Samuel Taylor. *Samuel Taylor Coleridge.* The Oxford Authors. Oxford: Oxford University Press, 1985.

Collins, Christopher. *Reading the Written Image: Verbal Play, Interpretation, and the Roots of Iconophobia.* University Park: Penssylvania State University Press, 1991.

Cook, Eleanor. *Poetry, Word-Play, and Word-War in Wallace Stevens.* Princeton: Princeton University Press, 1988.

———. "Wallace Stevens and the King James Bible." *Essays in Criticism: A Quarterly Journal of Literary Criticism* 41.3 (1991): 240–52.

Corradi Fiumara, Gemma. *The Metaphoric Process: Connections between Language and Life.* London: Routledge, 1995.

Costello, Bonnie. "Effects of Analogy: Wallace Stevens and Painting." *Wallace Stevens: The Poetics of Modernism.* Ed. Albert Gelpi. Cambridge: Cambridge UP, 1985. 65–85.

Cunningham, J. V. "Tradition and Modernity: Wallace Stevens." *Selected Essays.* Chicago: The Swallow Press, 1976. 225–43.

Cureton, Richard D. *Rhythmic Phrasing in English Verse.* London: Longman, 1992.

Cushman, Stephen. *Fictions of Form in American Poetry.* Princeton: Princeton University Press, 1993.

De Man, Paul. *Blindness & Insight : Essays in the Rhetoric of Contemporary Criticism.* New York: Oxford University Press, 1971.

Depieven, Leonard. *The Difficulties of Modernism.* New York and London: Routledge, 2003.

Derrida, Jacques. "Che cos'e la poesia?." *A Derrida Reader: Between the Blinds.* New York: Harvester Weatsheaf, 1991: pp. 221–42.

———. *Margins of Philosophy.* Chicago: University of Chicago Press, 1982.

———. *Of Grammatology.* Ed. and transl. Gayatri Chakravorty Spivak. Baltimore: The Johns Hopkins University Press, 1997.

———. *Specters of Marx: The State of the Debt, the Work of Mourning, and the New International.* New York: Routledge, 1994.

———. *Spurs: Nietzsche's Styles.* Chicago: University of Chicago Press, 1979.

Derrida, Jacques, and Derek Attridge. *Acts of Literature.* New York: Routledge, 1992.

Dickie, Margaret. "Collections of Sound in Stevens." *The Wallace Stevens Journal: A Publication of the Wallace Stevens Society* 15.2 (Fall 1991): 133–43.

Dickinson, Emily. *The Collected Poems of Emily Dickinson.* London: Faber & Faber, 1975.

Dougherty, Adelyn. "Structures of Sound in Wallace Stevens' 'Farewell to Florida.'" *Texas Studies in Literature and Language: A Journal of the Humanities, Austin* (1975): 16, 755–64.

Easthope, Antony. *Poetry as Discourse.* New Accents. London: Methuen, 1983.

Eeckhout, Bart. *Wallace Stevens and the Limits of Reading and Writing.* Columbia, Missouri: University of Missouri Press, 2002.

Eliot, T. S. *Collected Poems 1909–1935.* London: Faber & Faber, 1954.

———. *On Poetry and Poets.* New York: Farrar Straus & Cudahy, 1957.

———. To Criticize the Critic. New York: Farrar Straus & Giroux, 1978.

Endo, Paul. "Stevens and the Two Sublimes." *The Wallace Stevens Journal: A Publication of the Wallace Stevens Society* 19.1 (Spring 1995): 36–50.

Erlich, Victor. *Russian Formalism: History—Doctrine.* New Haven: Yale University Press, 1981.

Eysteinsson, Astradur. *The Concept of Modernism.* Ithaca: Cornell University Press, 1990.

Filreis, Alan. *Modernism from Right to Left: Wallace Stevens, the Thirties & Literary Radicalism.* Cambridge: Cambridge University Press, 1994.

———. *Wallace Stevens and the Actual World.* Princeton: Princeton University Press, 1991.

Filreis, Alan, and Harvey Teres. "An Interview with Stanley Burnshaw." *The Wallace Stevens Journal: A Publication of the Wallace Stevens Society* 13.2 (1989): 109–21.

Finch, Annie. *The Ghost of Meter: Culture and Prosody in American Free Verse.* Ann Arbor: University of Michigan Press, 1993.

———. "A Review of *Rethinking Meter: A New Approach to the Verse Line* by Alan Holder." *Versification: An Interdisciplinary Journal of Literary Prosody* 2.3 March, 1998 (1998): 298–302.

Fisher, Barbara M. "Ambiguous Birds and Quizzical Messengers: Parody as Stevens' Double Agent." *The Wallace Stevens Journal: A Publication of the Wallace Stevens Society* 9.1 (Spring 1985): 3–13.

———. "'The Mind Dances with Itself': Choreographic Idiom in Williams and Stevens." *William Carlos Williams Review* 18.2 (1992): 13–23.

Frost, Robert. *Selected Poems.* London: Penguin, 1973.

Frye, Northrop. *Anatomy of Criticism: Four Essays by Northrop Frye.* New York: Atheneum, 1968.

———. "The Realistic Oriole: A Study of Wallace Stevens." *Wallace Stevens: A Collection of Critical Essays.* Ed. Marie Borroff. Eaglewood Cliffs, N.J: Prentice Hall, 1963. 161–76.

Gelpi, Albert. "Stevens and Williams: The Epistemology of Modernism." *Wallace Stevens: The Poetics of Modernism.* Ed. Albert Gelpi. Cambridge: Cambridge University Press, 1985. 3–23.

Gerber, Natalie. "'A Funny Foreigner of Meek Address': Stevens and English as a Foreign Language." *The Wallace Stevens Journal: A Publication of the Wallace Stevens Society* 25:2. (Fall 2001): 211–19.

———. "Stevens' Prosody: Meaningful Rhythms." *The Wallace Stevens Journal: A Publication of the Wallace Stevens Society* 29.1. (Spring 2005): 178–87.

Halliday, Mark. *Stevens and the Interpersonal.* Princeton: Princeton University Press, 1991.

Hamburger, Michael. "Absolute Poetry and Absolute Politics." *Poetry and Politics.* Ed. Richard Jones. New York: William Morrow and Co., 1985. 85–116.

Haney, David P. "Aesthetics and Ethics in Gadamer, Lévinas and Romanticism: Problems of Phronesis and Techné." *PMLA: Publications of the Modern Language Association of America* 114. January (1999): 31–45.

Harrington, Joseph. "The Modernist as Liberal: Wallace Stevens and the Poetics of Private Insurance." *Poetry and the Public: The Social Form of Modern U.S. Poetics.* Middletown, Conn.: Wesleyan, 2002.

Hass, Robert. *Twentieth Century Pleasures: Prose on Poetry.* New York: Ecco Press, 1984.

Henley, William Ernest. *Poems.* Oxford: Woodstock Books, 1993.

Hoerner, Fred. "Gratification and Its Discontents: The Politics of Stevens' Chastening Aesthetics." *The Wallace Stevens Journal: A Publication of the Wallace Stevens Society* 18.1 (Spring 1994): 81–105.

Holander, Stefan. "Between Categories: Modernist and Postmodernist Appropriations of Wallace Stevens." *Rethinking Modernism.* Ed. Marianne Thormählen. Basingstoke: Palgrave Macmillan, 2003. 221–38.

Hollander, John. "The Sound of the Music of Music and Sound." *Wallace Stevens: A Celebration.* Ed. Frank Dogget and Robert Buttell. Princeton: Princeton University Press, 1980. 235–55.

———. *Vision and Resonance: Two Senses of Poetic. Form.* New Haven: Yale University Press, 1985.

Irigaray, Luce. "The Sex Which Is Not One." *From Modernism to Postmodernism: An Anthology.* Ed. Lawrence Cahoone. London: Blackwell, 1996. 461–8.

Jakobson, Roman. "Closing Statement: Linguistics and Poetics." *Style in Language (Papers Presented at the Conference on Style Held at Indiana University, 1958).* Ed. Thomas A. Sebeok. New York: Wiley, 1960. 350–77.

Jameson, Fredric. *The Ideologies of Theory: Essays 1971–1986.* Minneapolis: University of Minnesota Press, 1988.

———. *The Prison-House of Language: A Critical Account of Structuralism and Russian Formalism.* Princeton: Princeton University Press, 1972.

———. "Wallace Stevens." *New Orleans Review* 11.1 (1984): 10–19.

Johnson, Kent. "Prosody and the Outside: Some Notes on Rakosi and Stevens." *Carl Rakosi: Man and Poet.* Ed. Michael Heller. Orono: National Poetry Foundation; University of Maine at Orono, 1993. 193–207.

Judd, William Edward. "The Metrics of Wallace Stevens." PhD. thesis, Columbia University, 1975.

Juhasz, Suzanne H. *Metaphor and the Poetry of Williams, Pound and Stevens.* Lewisburg: Bucknell University Press, 1974.

Keats, John. *Poetical Works.* Oxford: Oxford University Press, 1958.

Kermode, Frank. "Dwelling Poetically in Connecticut." *Wallace Stevens: A Celebration.* Ed. Frank and Robert Buttel Doggett. Princeton: Princeton University Press, 1980.

————. *The Sense of an Ending: Studies in the Theory of Fiction.* New York: Oxford University Press, 1967.

————. *Wallace Stevens.* Edinburgh: Oliver and Boyd, 1960.

Kessler, Edward. *Images of Wallace Stevens.* New Brunswick: Rutgers University Press, 1972.

Keyser, Samuel Jay. "Wallace Stevens: Form and Meaning in Four Poems." *Linguistic Perspectives on Literature.* Eds. K. L. Ching Marvin, C. Haley Michael and F. Lunsford Ronald. London: Routledge, 1980. 257–81.

Kjoerup, Frank. *Sprog Versus Sprog.* Copenhagen: Museum Tusculanums Forlag, 2002.

Knight, Steven T. "The Craft of Contradiction: Poetic Arrangement in Ideas of Order." *The Wallace Stevens Journal: A Publication of the Wallace Stevens Society* 6.1–2 (Spring 1982): 32–38.

Kristeva, Julia. *Revolution in Poetic Language.* New York: Columbia University Press, 1984.

Lakritz, Andrew M. *Modernism and the Other in Stevens, Frost, and Moore.* Gainesville: University Press of Florida, 1996.

Lecercle, Jean-Jacques. *The Philosophy of Nonsense.* London: Routledge, 1994.

Leggett, B. J. *Wallace Stevens and Poetic Theory: Conceiving the Supreme Fiction.* Chapel Hill: University of North Carolina Press, 1987.

Lensing, George S. *Wallace Stevens: A Poet's Growth.* Baton Rouge: Louisiana State University Press, 1986.

Lentricchia, Frank. *Modernist Quartet.* Cambridge, Eng.: Cambridge University Press, 1994.

Levinas, Emmanuel. *Existence and Existents.* Trans. Alphonso Lingis. The Hague: Nijhoff, 1978.

————. "Reality and Its Shadow." *The Levinas Reader.* Ed. Seán Hand. Oxford: Blackwell, 1989.

————. *Totality and Infinity: An Essay on Exteriority.* Trans. Alphonso Lingis. Pittsburgh: Duquesne University Press, 1969.

Longenbach, James. *Wallace Stevens: The Plain Sense of Things.* New York: Oxford University Press, 1991.

MacLeod, Glen. *Wallace Stevens and Modern Art: From the Armory Show to Abstract Expressionism.* New Haven: Yale University Press, 1993.

Maeder, Beverly. *Wallace Stevens' Experimental Language: The Lion in the Lute.* New York: St. Martin's Press, 1999.

Mao, Douglas. "How to Do Things with Modernism." *The Wallace Stevens Journal: A Publication of the Wallace Stevens Society* 26.2. (Fall 2002): 160–80.

Marks, Emerson. *Taming the Chaos: English Poetic Diction Theory since the Renaissance.* Detroit: Wayne State University Press, 1998.

Meschonnic, Henri. *Critique du rhythme.* Paris: Verdier, 1982.

Miller, J. Hillis. *The Linguistic Moment: From Wordsworth to Stevens.* Princeton: Princeton University Press, 1985.

————. *Poets of Reality: Six Twentieth-Century Writers.* Cambridge: Harvard University Press, 1965.

————. "Wallace Stevens' Poetry of Being." *The Act of the Mind: Essays on the Poetry of Wallace Stevens.* Ed. Roy Harvey and J. Hillis Miller Pierce. Baltimore: The Johns Hopkins Press, 1965. 162.

Morris, Pam, ed. *The Bakhtin Reader: Selected Writings of Bakhtin, Medvedev and Voloshinov.* London: Arnold, 2001.

Mukarovský, Jan, John Burbank, and P. Steiner, eds. *On Poetic Language.* Lisse: Peter de Ridder Press, 1976.

Newcomb, John. *Wallace Stevens and Literary Canons.* Jackson: University Press of Mississippi, 1992.

Nicholson, Mervyn. "'The Slightest Sound Matters': Stevens' Sound Cosmology." *The Wallace Stevens Journal: A Publication of the Wallace Stevens Society* 18.1 (1994): 63–80.

Nyberg, Lennart. "'THE IMAGINATION': A Twentieth-Century Itinerary." *Rethinking Modernism.* Ed. Marianne Thormählen. Basingstoke: Palgrave Macmillan, 2003. 40–54.

Ong, Walter J. "A Dialectic of Aural and Objective Correlatives." *20th Century Literary Criticism.* Ed. David Lodge. London: Longman, 1972. 498–508.

Parker, Patricia. "The Motive for Metaphor: Stevens and Derrida" *The Wallace Stevens Journal: A Publication of the Wallace Stevens Society* 7.3/4 (Fall 1983): 76–88.

Perloff, Marjorie. "Pound/Stevens: Whose Era?" *New Literary History: A Journal of Theory and Interpretation* 13.3 (1982): 485–510.

————. "Revolving in Crystal: The Supreme Fiction and the Impasse of Modernist Lyric." *Wallace Stevens: The Poetics of Modernism.* Ed. Albert Gelpi. Cambridge: Cambridge University Press, 1985. 41–64.

Prendergast, Christopher. *The Order of Mimesis: Balzac, Stendhal, Nerval, Flaubert.* Cambridge: Cambridge University Press, 1986.

Rae, Patricia. "Bloody Battle-Flags and Cloudy Days: The Experience of Metaphor in Pound and Stevens." *Wallace Stevens Journal: A Publication of the Wallace Stevens Society* Special Issue: Wallace Stevens and Ezra Pound. 26.2. (Fall 2002): 143–59.

Renza, Louis A. *Edgar Allan Poe, Wallace Stevens and the Poetics of American Privacy.* Baton Rouge: Lousiana State University Press, 2002.

Richardson, Joan. "A Reading of 'Sea Surface Full of Clouds.'" *The Wallace Stevens Journal: A Publication of the Wallace Stevens Society.* 3–4 (Fall 1982): 60–68.

————. *Wallace Stevens: The Early Years.* New York: Beech Tree Books, 1985.

————. *Wallace Stevens: The Later Years.* New York: Beech Tree Books, 1988.

Riddel, Joseph. *The Clairvoyant Eye: The Poetry and Poetics of Wallace Stevens.* Baton Rouge: Louisiana State University Press, 1965.

————. "Metaphoric Staging: Stevens' Beginning Again of the 'End of the Book.'" *Wallace Stevens: A Celebration.* Ed. Frank Doggett and Robert Buttell. Princeton: Princeton University Press, 1980. 308–38.

————. "The Contours of Stevens' Criticism." *ELH, Baltimore, MD.* (1964): 31, 106–38.

Robinson, Fred Miller. "Strategies of Smallness: Wallace Stevens and Emily Dickinson." *The Wallace Stevens Journal: A Publication of the Wallace Stevens Society* 10.1 (Spring 1986): 27–35.

Rosu, Anca. *The Metaphysics of Sound in Wallace Stevens.* Tuscaloosa: University of Alabama Press, 1995.

————. "The Theoretical Afterlife of Wallace Stevens." *The Wallace Stevens Journal: A Publication of the Wallace Stevens Society* 24.2. (Fall 2000): 208–20.

Santayana, George. *A Hermit of Carmel and Other Poems.* New York: Scribner's, 1901.

————. *Interpretations of Poetry and Religion.* Ed. William G Holzberger and Herman J. Saatkamp Jr. Cambridge, Mass.: MIT Press, 1990.

Schaum, Melita. "Lyric Resistance: Views of the Political in the Poetics of Wallace Stevens and H. D." *The Wallace Stevens Journal: A Publication of the Wallace Stevens Society* 13.2 (Fall 1989): 191–205.

————, ed. *Wallace Stevens and the Feminine.* Tuscaloosa: University of Alabama Press, 1993.

————. *Wallace Stevens and the Critical Schools.* Tuscaloosa: University of Alabama Press, 1988.

Sherry, Vincent. *Ezra Pound, Wyndham Lewis, and Radical Modernism.* New York: Oxford University Press, 1993.

Shklovsky, Victor. "Art as Technique." *Critical Theory since Plato.* 1917. Ed. Hazard Adams. Fort Worth: Harcourt Brace Jovanovich, 1992. 751–59.

Smith, Barbara Herrnstein. *On the Margins of Discourse: The Relation of Literature and Language.* Chicago: The University of Chicago Press, 1978.

————. *Poetic Closure: A Study of How Poems End.* Chicago: University of Chicago Press, 1968.

Sontag, Susan. *Against Interpretation.* New York: Farrar Straus and Giroux, 1967.

Steele, Timothy. *Missing Measures: Modern Poetry and the Revolt against Meter.* Fayetteville: University of Arkansas Press, 1990.

Stevens, Holly Bright. *Souvenirs and Prophecies: The Young Wallace Stevens.* New York: Knopf, 1977.

Stevens, Wallace. *The Voice of the Poet: Wallace Stevens.* Ed. J. D. McClatchy. New York: Random House Audio, 2004.

Taylor, Charles. *Sources of the Self: The Making of the Modern Identity.* Cambridge, Mass.: Harvard University Press, 1989.

Taylor, Dennis. "The Apparitional Meters of Wallace Stevens." *The Wallace Stevens Journal: A Publication of the Wallace Stevens Society* 15.2 (Fall 1991): 209–28.

Tennyson, Alfred Lord. *Selected Poems.* London: Penguin, 1991.

Todorov, Tzvetan. "Three Conceptions of Poetic Language." *Russian Formalism: A Retrospective Glance. A Festschrift in Honor of Victor Erlich.* Ed. Robert Louis and Stephen Rudy Jackson. New Haven: Yale Center for International and Area Studies, 1985.

Tynianov, Yuri. *The Problem of Verse Language.* Trans. Michael and Brent Harvey Sosa. Ann Arbor, Mich.: Ardis, 1981.

Valéry, Paul. *Aesthetics.* Trans. Ralph Mannheim. New York: Pantheon, 1964.

Vendler, Helen. *On Extended Wings: Wallace Stevens' Longer Poems.* Cambridge: Harvard University Press, 1969.

Wesling, Donald. *The Chances of Rhyme: Device and Modernity.* Berkeley: University of California Press, 1980.

———. *The Scissors of Meter: Grammetrics and Reading.* Ann Arbor: The University of Michigan Press, 1996.

Whitman, Walt. *Leaves of Grass.* New York: Modern Library, 1993.

———. *Complete Poetry and Collected Prose.* New York: Library of America, 1982

Williams, William Carlos. *Collected Poems.* Vol. I. London: Paladin, 1987.

Wimsatt, W.K. "The Concept of Meter: An Exercise in Abstraction." *Hateful Contraries: Studies in Literature and Criticism.* Lexington: University of Kentucky Press, 1965.

Yeats, William Butler. "Symbol as Revelation." *The Modern Tradition: Backgrounds of Modern Literature.* New York: Oxford University Press, 1965. 60–65.

———. *The Variorum Edition of the Poems of W.B. Yeats.* New York: MacMillan, 1957.

Ziarek, Krzysztof. *Inflected Language: Toward a Hermeneutics of Nearness Heidegger, Levinas, Stevens, Celan.* Albany: State University of New York Press, 1994.

General Index

Index of Poems and Other Texts by Wallace Stevens